Varieties
of Unbelief

Martin E. Marty

Varieties
of Unbelief

Holt, Rinehart and Winston

New York · Chicago · San Francisco

Library of Congress Catalog Card Number: 64-14362

Designer: Ernst Reichl
85484-0314
Printed in the United States of America

First Edition

Acknowledgments

The plot of this book was first developed for the Rauschenbusch Lectureship. I thank President Gene Bartlett and his faculty, especially Professors William H. Hamilton and Winthrop S. Hudson, for the invitation, the encouragement, the hospitality. Of course, a book is longer than a series of lectures; I took the opportunity to develop original materials on three other occasions, and have revised these materials for inclusion. These occasions were: the Elmore B. Jeffery Lectures at Goucher College, Towson, Maryland; the Hugh Th. Miller Lectures at Christian Theological Seminary, Indianapolis, Indiana; and the Finch Lectures at High Point College, High Point, North Carolina. I thank the faculties of these institutions and the trustees of these lectureships for their contributions to this volume. Some of the subplots were developed for convocations of ministers: of the American Lutheran Church, at St. Paul, Minnesota; of the United Church of Canada, at Edmonton, Alberta; of the Lutheran Church—Missouri Synod, at Oakland, California; and of the Kentucky Council of Churches, at Lexington, Kentucky. All these lectures occurred during 1963. Since most of them involved audience participation, I want to acknowledge my debt to the audiences for constructive suggestions.

MARTIN E. MARTY

Chicago, Illinois
Epiphany 1964

Grateful acknowledgment is also made to the following publishers who have so generously granted permission to include in this book excerpts from the publications listed:

Association Press, New York, from *Grace and Personality,* a "Giant Reflection Book," by John Oman, 1961.

Beacon Press, Boston, *The Uses of Literacy,* by Richard Hoggart, 1957; *The Sociology and Psychology of Communism,* by Jules Monnerot, 1960; and *The Case for Modern Man,* by Charles Frankel, 1959. These are all Beacon Press paperbacks.

Cambridge University Press, New York, *Soundings,* edited by Alec Vidler, 1962.

Concordia Publishing House, St. Louis, *Profiles of Church Youth,* by Merton P. Strommen, 1963.

Doubleday & Company, Inc., Garden City, N.Y., *Man in the Modern Age,* by Karl Jaspers, 1957; *Irrational Man,* by William Barrett, 1962; *The Religious Factor,* by Gerhard Lenski, 1961; *Progress and Religion,* by Christopher Dawson, 1960. All but the Lenski reference are from Doubleday Anchor editions.

Fortress Press, Philadelphia, *The Living Word,* by Gustav Wingren, 1960; *The Nature of Faith,* by Gerhard Ebeling, 1961; *Faith Victorious,* by Lennart Pinomaa, 1963.

The Free Press of Glencoe, a subsidiary of The Macmillan Company, New York, *Religious Behaviour,* by Michael Argyle, 1959; *The Intellectuals,* edited by George B. de Huszar, 1960; *Husbands and Wives,* by Robert O. Blood, Jr. and Donald M. Wolfe, 1960.

Harcourt, Brace & World, New York, *Sex, Culture and Myth,* by Bronislaw Malinowski, 1962.

Harper & Row, Publishers, New York, *The Finality of Faith,* by Nels F. S. Ferré, 1963; *No Absent God,* by Martin D'Arcy, 1962; *The Dynamics of Faith,* by Paul Tillich, 1957; *Christ and the Meaning of Life,* by Helmut Thielicke, 1962; *The Christian Society,* by Stephen Neill, 1952; *Modern Catholic Thinkers,* edited by A. Robert Caponigri, 1960.

Hawthorn Books, New York, *Atheism,* by Étienne Borne, 1961; *Man and Metaphysics,* by Regis Jolivet, 1961.

Henry Regnery Company, Chicago, *Man Against Mass Society,* by Gabriel Marcel, 1962 (Gateway Edition).

Herder and Herder, New York, *Religious History of Modern France,* by Adrien Dansette, 1961.

Hill & Wang, Inc., New York, *Metatheatre,* by Lionel Abel, 1963.

Holt, Rinehart and Winston, Inc., New York, *The Christian Opportunity*, by Denis de Rougemont, 1963.

John Knox Press, Richmond, Virginia, *Gospel and Myth in the Thought of Rudolf Bultmann,* by Giovanni Miegge, 1960.

McGraw-Hill Book Company, New York, for permission to quote from *Mirror for Man,* by Clyde Kluckhohn, 1949.

The Macmillan Company, New York, *The Modern God,* by Gustave Wiegel, 1963; *Sociology Looks at Religion,* by J. Milton Yinger, 1963; *Nationalism: A Religion,* by Carlton J. H. Hayes, 1960.

Moody Press, Chicago, *Let Europe Hear,* by Robert B. Evans, 1955.

Oxford University Press, New York, *The Semantics of Biblical Language,* by James Barr, 1961.

Pantheon Books, New York, *Belief and Faith,* by Josef Pieper, 1963; *The Natural and the Supernatural Jew,* by Arthur A. Cohen, 1962.

Penguin Books Limited, Harmondsworth, Middlesex, *Personal Values in the Modern World,* by M. V. C. Jeffreys, 1962.

Random House, Inc., New York, *The Natural History of Nonsense,* by Bergen Evans (Vintage Books), 1958; *Resistance, Rebellion and Death,* by Albert Camus, 1961; *Rendezvous with Destiny,* by Eric F. Goldman (Vintage Books), 1956; *The Myth of Sisyphus,* by Albert Camus (Vintage Books), 1948.

Charles Scribner's Sons, New York, *Psychotherapy and a Christian View of Man,* by David E. Roberts, 1950.

Sheed and Ward, New York, *The Movement of World Revolution,* by Christopher Dawson, copyright © 1959; *The End of the Modern World,* by Romano Guardini, copyright © 1956.

Student Christian Movement, London, *Myth in the New Testament,* by Ian Henderson, 1952. (Published in the United States by Alec R. Allenson, Naperville, Illinois.)

University of Texas Press, Austin, *Toward a Reasonable Society,* by C. E. Ayres, 1961.

Theological Studies, Baltimore, Maryland, for permission to quote from Volume XXIII, No. 1, March, 1962.

The Viking Press, New York, *Phoenix, the Posthumous Papers of D. H. Lawrence,* edited by Edward D. McDonald.

The Westminster Press, Philadelphia, *Fundamentalism and the Church,* by A. G. Hebert, 1957.

The World Publishing Company, Cleveland, *An Age of Enormity,* by Isaac Rosenfeld, 1962; *The Son of Man,* by François Mauriac, 1958.

The World Publishing Company, Meridian Books, Cleveland, *Encounters in History,* by Pieter Geyl, 1961; *Hornbook for the Double Damned,* by Samuel Milton Elam, 1962.

Yale University Press, New Haven, Connecticut, *Becoming,* by Gordon Allport, 1959.

To Joel, John, Peter, and Micah Marty
and to Frances and Jeffrey Garcia
II TIMOTHY 3:14-15

Foreword

The Rauschenbusch Lectureship Foundation of The Colgate Rochester Divinity School Rochester, New York

The Rauschenbusch Foundation was established in March, 1929, at the Colgate Rochester Divinity School in memory of the late Walter Rauschenbusch, illustrious exponent of social Christianity and, from 1902 to 1918, professor of church history in the Rochester Theological Seminary, to which institution the Colgate Rochester Divinity School is successor.

The movement for the establishment of this foundation was initiated by a gift of ten thousand dollars from Mrs. Edmund Lyon, of Rochester, New York, conditioned upon the raising of twenty-five thousand dollars from other sources. An amount somewhat in excess of that sum was secured through the generous gifts of citizens of Rochester, alumni of the Rochester Theological Seminary, and others.

The general field of the lectureship is that of Christianity in its social expression and application. A series of lectures upon this foundation is to be given annually during the week of the Spring Convocation at the Colgate Rochester Divinity School, these lectures to be published in book form and known as the Rauschenbusch Lectures.

Contents

Yet these men are little to be blamed, for perhaps they go astray while seeking God and desiring to find him.

For as they live among his works they keep searching, and they trust in what they see, because the things that are seen are beautiful.

Yet again, not even they are to be excused; for if they had the power to know so much that they could investigate the world, how did they fail to find sooner the Lord of these things?

THE WISDOM OF SOLOMON
CHAPTER 13, vv. 6–9

Varieties
of Unbelief

1 Introduction: An Age of Belief—An Age of Unbelief

This book attempts to describe two types and a number of forms of modern unbelief. Unbelief can be defined in as many ways as can its opposite, belief. In this book it represents ways in which people of the recent past have expressed themselves apart from belief in the God of Christian revelation. The sources for such a study are many: the words of believing and unbelieving writers, the literature of the day, the results of opinion polls and surveys by students of society. The methods for coming to these sources and then using them are also many: the student must combine the interests of the historian and the reporter, the literary critic and the social scientist and the religious thinker.

A more detailed definition of belief and unbelief will appear in later chapters. Here we need only explain that unbelief is not always used as a term of judgment or condemnation. It is a descriptive word characterizing the attitude of mind and action of people who withhold belief in the God of the Christian faith. In the Buddhist world or on Islamic soil, unbelief of course would mean something much different. There, Christianity would be unbelief. Not only on soil where the world's greatest historic religions flourish would Christianity be considered unbelief. Where a system such as Soviet Communism prevails, although Christianity may be tolerated, it represents disbelief in the view of history and human purpose which holds that society together.

Today, as always, there is considerable curiosity about those who deviate from historic or prevailing faiths. Many students of the theme are ready to claim for it a central place on the stage of history. Conventionally they quote Goethe:

> The deepest, nay the unique, theme of the history of the world, to which all other themes are subordinate, is the conflict of faith and unbelief. All epochs in which faith pre-

vails—whatever its form may be—are noble, soul-elevating,
and fruitful for the present and for after times. All epochs
in which unbelief, be it under what form it may, wins an un-
happy victory . . . vanish and are forgotten by posterity;
because no one willingly wastes his pains on what is barren
and unfruitful.[1]

Today there are those who would be reluctant to assign the
issue of faith such a central place, and many more would
disagree, at least, with all that follows Goethe's first sentence.
Since the majority of the people in America claim to base their
eternal hope and their present way of life on what they call
faith, or belief, and since the minority must define itself over
against this claim, the issue does awaken curiosity. "What
earthly good is faith?" "Give your children a faith to live by."
"Have faith in God." "I cannot believe any longer." These
are typical expressions of the ways belief and unbelief vie with
each other.

The past four decades have seen a revival of religious
thought which has turned more on faith than on the other
Christian virtues of hope and love. Only recently has there
been a widespread new interest in what had been the nineteenth-century issue for Christianity: faith active in love, or
Christian ethics. In this study we hope not to be caught in a
fascination with faith which neglects to regard the forms it
takes in life. "The greatest is still love—and there is no faith
to which it is not greatest, but faith has to do with love as a
purpose on earth and not merely as a sentiment in the Divine
mind." [2]

People have an enduring interest in the question of belief.

---

[1] Quoted in M. V. C. Jeffreys, *Personal Values in the Modern World*
(Baltimore: Penguin, 1962), p. 86. This is only the most recent instance of
a citation which has long appeared in books on this topic.

[2] John Oman, *Grace and Personality* (New York: Association Press, 1961),
p. 118.

But there are many reasons why the question is intense today, especially in Europe and America where the historic faiths are being challenged in new ways. In Europe great masses of people have formally left behind a Christian heritage. The leaders of the intellectual community are often able to express themselves not only apart from, but in opposition to, the faith. In America, matters have taken a somewhat different turn. But believer and unbeliever alike have reasons for showing interest. What shall they make of the familiar view that in America's mid-century years there was a simultaneous revival of religion and a marked increase of secularity? How could the same people at the same time become more interested in both God and non-God?

The "outsider" is involved in any basic change in the religious community's way of defining itself in the United States. Americans are instinctively theistic as opposed to atheistic. We presume that this is not a controversial statement. When they rely on their theism, their belief in God, they find that their belief takes on the memory of the God of a Judaeo-Christian lineage. That, too, is a matter-of-fact statement concerning things as we would expect to find them. (For convenience and clarity, in this book we have chosen not to deal in detail with the question of belief from the viewpoint of the small but influential Jewish minority, but to restrict the topic to Christianity.) If it can be shown that widespread changes in the traditional way of holding belief are coming about, the whole national community can expect long-range changes in its way of life.

For those inside the community of belief, reasons to be curious are even more apparent. Those who number themselves among the believers claim to be staking their destiny on the survival of the Christian faith. As custodians of its repute in their generation, they are concerned with any crisis that comes to it. The presence of unbelief can be a puzzle, a witness, or a threat to them. It is a puzzle because they cannot fully

conceive how others would fail to see in it a clue to the meaning of life. They find it to be a witness, for the biblical record
prophesies that the faith will always be countered by opposition. It remains a threat because it becomes a cultural and
spiritual problem which can affect the believing community.
When they see it as a threat, believers are tempted to react
by withdrawal or by noisy opposition. Not all forms of unbelief are immediately recognized as such; disbelief and unbelief
can masquerade under the forms of apparent belief.

If unbelief takes a variety of forms, both those who do not
care for the future of faith and those who do can be served by
defining the varieties. In a world where new alliances and new
enmities are constantly taking shape, both recognize the importance of understanding alternative systems of value. The
modern world is pluralist; that is, in it many systems compete
and coexist. No one can completely "go it alone." When masks
are removed and illusions are dispelled, when people learn to
know each other both individually and in groups, they are better served. Christians know that more than two-thirds of the
people of the world do not share their particular beliefs. They
know that in many portions of the world, people are formally
discouraged from believing. They know that on historic
Christian soil many are faithless, and distractions appear on all
sides. Young people, desiring to piece together a coherent view
of the universe and of life's meaning, face apparent chaos.
Christianity is one of many voices that judges and promises.
Curiosity over the status of belief and unbelief in such circumstances is quite understandable and to be expected.

Those who seek on these pages an assessment of whether
there is more unbelief than in the past will be disappointed.
No reliable means of measurement are available. We do not
know how to measure the number of believers today, and we
have no records of the past. One believer of long ago who also
happened to be a prophet complained: "I have been very

jealous for the Lord, the God of hosts; for the people of Israel have forsaken thy covenant, thrown down thy altars, and slain thy prophets with the sword; and I, even I only, am left; and they seek my life, to take it away" (I Kings 19:14). However, his adding machine was as unreliable as are those of others who want to count the believers; we are told that his Lord said that he was preserving seven thousand in Israel as believers. When the years of the early church, the Middle Ages, or the Reformation are cited as ages of belief, in contrast to the present day (or vice versa), the patient observer need not concern himself. The margin of error, the ratio of unreliability, may remain 7000:1. The historian of belief and unbelief can move with some sureness only if he concerns himself with the question of the quality, not the quantity, of unbelief—with the differences in kind, not degree. Parts of this book will ask: What is original about unbelief as it presents itself today?

The question of the quality of unbelief cannot be answered to everyone's satisfaction. Observers differ widely, for a variety of reasons. We may note several types of reaction.

First is the reaction of those within the believing community who observe their culture and in its midst join those who announce, "God is dead." "Ours is the first attempt in recorded history to build a culture upon the premise that God is dead" is the initial statement by a Christian thinker in his preface to a book called *The Death of God,* written by another believer.[3]

Such spokesmen have listened to the nineteenth-century announcer of the death of God, Friedrich Nietzsche, and the twentieth-century celebrator of his absence, Albert Camus. They have carefully studied the cultural effects of the announcement. As they observe man in action, man busy closing off his world and his view of himself without necessary refer-

[3] Paul Ramsey, introduction to Gabriel Vahanian, *The Death of God* (New York: Braziller, 1961), p. xiii.

ence to God, they point to the crisis of faith and concur that, in
profound cultural and spiritual senses, "God is dead!" [4] If
this is true, unbelief is the great new spiritual fact of the era.
Vahanian and others like him are patient to distinguish between a post-Christian culture and a post-Christian theological position. Every age is post-Christian theologically; that is,
faith must be born after an event whose outlines and meanings are not clear. Ours, say these analysts, is new in that it is
culturally removed from the living God.

Not everyone in the believing community who preaches
that God is dead makes the distinction so carefully. Sometimes it is possible that one may make too much of the threat;
for dramatic purposes the preacher may magnify his doubts
against a cosmic screen. Then he engages in what Karl Barth
calls "existential screaming." The French Catholic philosopher
Gabriel Marcel gives an illustration of this posing:

> There is a general modern phenomenon of mental mas-
> ochism, whose causes we ought to be able to lay bare; be-
> cause of this masochism, a growing number of individuals
> feel a periodical need to be outraged—not in their convic-
> tions—that would be too strong a word for the type of men-
> tality I am thinking of—but in their habitual attitudes. A
> philosopher who is so very well known that it is unnecessary

---

[4] Vahanian agrees with Ramsey that the emerging atheism of today's
Euro-American experience is not mere nontheism but antitheism, a consciously taken position. In its place there grows a religiosity which may
mask the absence of belief from view. On the other hand, not all have
taken this position or so shrouded it. The culture, as such, retains some
traces of Christianity. Vahanian quotes poet T. S. Eliot: "A culture has
not ceased to be Christian until it has become something positively else."
What happens in culture is the quiet disappearance of belief. "One does
not lose faith; it simply ceases to inform one's life" (Georges Bernanos,
quoted in Vahanian). In such circumstances, today's man "is not hostile
to religion, or even concerned. He simply does not raise the religious question at all, not even in church" (Samuel H. Miller, dean of Harvard Divinity School, quoted in Vahanian). See pp. xx, 6, 80, 110, 148.

to name him here was playing up to this attitude when he
said to the journalists who had gathered to receive him on a
Swiss airfield, as soon as he got out of his plane: "Gentlemen,
God is dead!" That is a very striking example of the kind of
flattery, under the mask of provocation, which I have just
been speaking of.

I should like to linger for a moment over this anecdote.
Let us leave aside the question of what ultimate judgment we
ought to bring to bear on Nietzsche's tragic and prophetic
affirmation. What is clear is that as soon as Nietzsche's affirmation, "God is dead," is blared forth to journalists or is put
forward as a possible sensational headline, it becomes de-
graded, not only in the sense of losing, in this new context,
all real meaning, but in the sense of becoming an absurd
parody of its original self. There is an existential difference
between Nietzsche's sigh or sob and this sort of publicity
handout, obviously intended to make a cheap sensation:
"Gentlemen, I have a piece of news for you. God has been
liquidated. Isn't that something?" [5]

We cannot judge the motivations for the radical announcement within the believing community to the effect that "God
is dead." Some have seen in it not so much a pose as a secret
envy of the freedom which, it is supposed, the unbeliever
possesses. In our context it fails, because as an announcement
it does not bear up under, or has not been subjected to, systematic scrutiny. It prejudges a complex case and confuses an
important subject where there should be clarity. In the end it
seems to lose effect: believers and unbelievers go their own
way as if no announcement had been made.

If some believers gain effect by radical announcement of
the death of God and the occasion for unbelief, they have their

[5] *Man Against Mass Society*, trans. G. S. Fraser (Chicago: Regnery, 1962),
pp. 106 f. Karl Barth is quoted in an excellent passage on "posing" in
Daniel Jenkins, *The Gift of Ministry* (London: Faber & Faber, 1947), p. 67.

counterparts outside the family of Christian faith. There, men
who agree with them about the occasion for unbelief are be-
wildered by its absence. Ours can as well be described as an
age of faiths. Arguing for a reasonable society and defending
unbelievers as being capable of dedication, C. E. Ayres complains:

> The impartiality with which scientific knowledge has
> called in question the inherited beliefs of all communities
> and sects has given rise to a similarly general and impar-
> tial condemnation of unbelief. Many adherents of all sects
> now agree that nothing is worse than unbelief. Purportedly,
> believers can get on very well together, however contrary
> their several dogmas. It is only heretics who are beyond the
> pale.[6]

Bertrand Russell has argued for decades that, defensive
Christians notwithstanding, ours is an age of beliefs. Superstitions and dogmas, magic and myths, clutter up the halls of
religion as seldom before. Professor Bergen Evans makes fun
of the disparity between reason and faiths or pseudo faiths in
our culture.

> Giant planes throb through the stratosphere, but half
> their passengers are wearing magic amulets and are pro-
> tected from harm by voodoo incantations. . . . Earnest sub-
> urbanites in sack suits go in their automobiles to celebrate
> the ancient rites of Attis and Mithra, theophagous in grape
> juice. On the first Sunday after the full moon following the
> vernal equinox we dye eggs, according to immemorial cus-
> tom, and seven days before the end of the year worship the
> pine tree, as did our neolithic forebears. . . .[7]

[6] *Toward a Reasonable Society* (Austin: University of Texas Press, 1961),
p. 141.
[7] *The Natural History of Nonsense* (New York: Vintage Books, 1958),

One of the few self-named heretics to be accepted as such by the American public, Professor Walter Kaufmann, of Princeton University, constantly complains of the numbers of faiths in what is reputed to be a faithless age. "In a syncretistic age, one must fight the comfortable blurring of all contours and the growing inability to say No. One must insist on important differences." Kaufmann notes that there are twenty-five thousand practicing astrologers in the United States; one hundred American newspapers provide daily divinations. Our coins urge us to trust in God and, until recently, children were assembled in public schools to pray. Wherever one turns, churches are being built and beliefs peddled. The "death of God" does not, in his mind, mean the death of religion.[8]

Apparently decoyed by the presence of the "imperfectly irreligious," some Christian strategists counter those who dramatize the crisis of belief and the prevalence of unbelief. Some may minimize it because it enhances their self-image of the nation or the culture. Others may honestly feel unbelief to be relatively impotent. Presenting the faith may seem to be a simpler matter if one can convince a congregation that almost everyone has it. To others, the shelter of life in the church may create illusions which cause them to minimize unbelief. When any of these motives is present, the defender of the faith will attack those who dramatize the power of unbelief. Thus, theologian Nels F. S. Ferré:

> Modern man not only glories but grovels in despair. Nihilism is the style. All of a sudden the happy ending is

---

pp. 5 ff. In America the prevalence of belief and the security of the churches has forced nonbelievers to resort to exaggeration, wit, and stridency to gain a hearing. Evans' book is a delightful illustration of the art.

8 Walter Kaufmann, *Critique of Religion and Philosophy*. (Garden City, N.Y.: Doubleday, 1961), p. xx; *The Faith of a Heretic* (Garden City, N.Y.: Doubleday, 1961), pp. 261 ff., on "Organized Religion."

taboo throughout the whole world of literature. . . . In
religion, too, there is a fad, if not yet a full-scale fashion, to
announce the death of the gods. The post-Christian era is
upon us. Modern man, we hear, has once for all outgrown
Christian ideology.

Concludes the theologian: "The secularists have been stream-
ing back to the churches." [9]

Between believers who maximize or minimize the faith,
and unbelievers who criticize the prevalence of faiths, we must
try to make our way with little concern for dramatic effect.
The unbeliever, while he may misunderstand or resent faith,
rejects the pose of believers who obscure the extent of their involvement in the believing community. The high priest
among today's articulate nonbelievers, Albert Camus, expressed himself vehemently on this subject to some Domini-
cans in 1948:

I shall not try to change anything that I think or anything that you think (insofar as I can judge of it) in order
to reach a reconciliation that would be agreeable to all. On
the contrary, what I feel like telling you today is that the
world needs real dialogue, that falsehood is just as much the
opposite of dialogue as is silence, and that the only possible
dialogue is the kind between people who remain what they
are and speak their minds. This is tantamount to saying
that the world of today needs Christians who remain Christians. The other day at the Sorbonne, speaking to a Marxist
lecturer, a Catholic priest said in public that he too was
anticlerical. Well, I don't like priests who are anticlerical
any more than philosophies that are ashamed of themselves.
Hence I shall not, as far as I am concerned, try to pass my-

[9] *The Finality of Faith.* (New York: Harper & Row, 1963), pp. 6 ff. Despite his dismissal of the "fad" and "fashion," Ferré does take it seriously
himself, and there is much of value in his book.

self off as a Christian in your presence. I share with you the same revulsion from evil. But I do not share your hope, and I continue to struggle against this universe in which children suffer and die.[10]

Similarly, while doubt and agnosticism go into the make-up of faith, those who in the name of Christianity enter into dialogue with the disciples of Camus do clarity a disservice if they feign kinds of agnosticism which are not permanent elements of faith. In the words of Bishop Gustaf Aulén, as he advises Christians not to misdefine either the faith or the "more or less secularized humanity" it confronts: "It is necessary to let everything be what it is." [11] Unbelief to the Christians concerned with definition then becomes neither the scarecrow nor the corpse.

On these pages we shall not be discussing so much whether God is dead or living. The Christian witnesses to a living God, but he is not equipped to speak with authority about "how things are going in the heavenly majesty," to use Martin Luther's phrase. He must content himself with observing the world of men and, if he chooses, what he claims to be the effects of God's movements among, and words to, men. In a fundamental statement on "The Structure of the Problem of God," John Courtney Murray, S.J., provides a context in which an historian can approach the question.

The problem of God has, as its obverse, the problem of the godless man, the *a-theos*. It is better to put the problem thus concretely, rather than to speak of the "problem of atheism." It is not as if atheism were some sort of doctrine or

10 "The Unbeliever and Christians," *Resistance, Rebellion, and Death,* trans. Justin O'Brien (New York: Knopf, 1961), pp. 70 f.

11 *Church, Law and Society* (New York: Scribner, 1948), p. 91. This dictum makes its way frequently into my writings. Its importance for one who reports can be overlooked because of its obvious advice.

intellectual position that, as such, presented a problem,
needed to be made intelligible, and could be understood.
The problem only becomes a problem when it is concretely
stated in terms of the godless man, who is existent and
present in history. The reality of the problem appears in the
fact that, within the religious tradition derivative from the
Bible, the phrase, "the godless man," asserts a contradiction
in adiecto. St. John Chrysostom was simply stating the central truth of this tradition in his famous dictum: "To be a
man is to fear God." The presence of God, says the Scripture, in both Testaments, is integral to the very structure,
as it were, of man's historical existence, just as God, who
is the Author of nature, is integral to the nature of man.
*Therefore the man who does not fear God somehow does
not exist, and his nature is somehow not human. On the
other hand, there he is. That is the problem.*[12]

We can extend this to the parallel problem that runs through
this book, that of a secularized society. We might say in para-
phrase that "a society which does not fear God somehow does
not exist, and its nature is somehow not human and social. On
the other hand, there it is. That is the problem."

The goal of this study is to attempt to set forth the problem
of the godless man and the godless society which, in Christian
terms, were not supposed to exist. But there he is, there it is.
That is the problem. In the scope of the same study it is not
possible to set forth a full-scale theological solution to the
problem. At best, we shall describe some efforts to keep the
matter open, not sealed off. We shall set forth what appear to
us to be some recent descriptions of the classic theological
phrase "justification by faith," descriptions which have a bearing on the problem of unbelief and the prospect of belief.
Even this will be largely confined to a discussion of certain personal and cultural factors in justification.

[12] *Theological Studies*, XXIII, No. 1 (March, 1962), 1 ff. (Italics added.)

Since this is an introductory chapter, it is hoped that the reader will not only indulge us in, but may profit from, a personal word. I came to this study of contemporary life after some years of historical research on the general absence of organized and outspoken unbelief in the American free society, in an era and in a place where such unbelief could have occurred.[13] Today's situation differs from that of the past. One senses that in America's heart, profound changes have occurred, changes which are not reflected in the externals of church life and the continuing good will shown religion. Since studying historic American antireligion, I have concerned myself largely with a study of norms and values in American society and religion. Now it has seemed time to venture into the questions of the beliefs which produced them, were transformed by them, and were then masked by them. Such a study has only begun. It is interesting to speculate on the effects of intensive study of belief systems other than one's own. I can recall from sermons heard as a boy that whenever the unbeliever set out to write a book on the follies of Christianity, he satisfied the illustrative needs of the preacher and "got religion." Does the study of "the problem of the godless man and the secular society" expose one to the converse risk? I should report that the combination of frustration and em-

13 This review was condensed into a book, *The Infidel: Freethought and American Religion* (New York: World, 1961). While I am on this personal note, an anecdote may be illuminating. En route to deliver several lectures on the subject of modern unbelief, I was doing some last-minute study aboard a jet airliner. In order to pre-empt some seats, I spread out research materials. *The Future of Unbelief, The Faith of a Heretic, Why I Am Not a Christian,* and other books light enough for in-flight reading were boldly displayed. My travel agency, no doubt to inhibit me or to expose my incognito, persists in writing "Reverend" before my name on tickets. When the stewardess came by she looked at the book titles and the ticket. Stewardesses, it is well known, are less oracular but just as Delphic as taxi drivers in our society. Asked she: "Just whose side are you on, Reverend?" If, in the course of this book, the reader may wonder from time to time, then an exercise in empathy will have succeeded!

pathy hardly moves one forward: frustration over misstatements of the faith; empathy for those who do not believe but are obviously fellow humans.

I am tempted to resort to the French Catholic student of atheism, Étienne Borne, and his summary statement:

As time goes on the reasons for denying and the reasons for believing both become stronger and more pressing. When civilization and Christendom were the same thing it was socially impossible not to believe: from this, faith both profited and suffered. In a secular, tolerant and free society, belief cannot avoid public argument with unbelief. It is wounded, but more free; disarmed, but purified by the break with some political connections. . . . Any Christian who curses modern times and accuses them of having killed God and brought agony upon man, is much mistaken. . . .

Mankind may disappear altogether; if not, it can slip back towards paganism or can go on forward, but only by ever improving in modernity. The Christian was and must remain the first modern man, because it is Christianity which gives impetus to the movement and renewal of history; because faith in a transcendent and immanent God has desecrated nature, secularized society and set man in his true place again . . . and lastly because the greatest intensity, the most unfathomable depth of holiness is found in that mystery which joins man's state to the divinity. . . .[14]

[14] *Atheism*, trans. S. J. Tester (New York: Hawthorn, 1961), pp. 121 ff.

2 A Christian Definition of Belief

"Unbelief" in its varieties and forms does not appear in a vacuum. It occurs as an event in history, over against "belief" in its varying definitions. This reality forces us to raise the question of the meaning of belief in the Christian tradition. If today there is a crisis of belief, if many are accused of departing from it or opposing it, and if others are pictured as its defenders, we shall need to isolate some elements of the definition of belief.

Christians today would no doubt be more prepared to talk about "unfaith," because in their vocabulary the opposite word, "faith," occurs more frequently than "belief." But "unfaith" is a clumsy and seldom used synonym for "unbelief," and we shall wish to deal with the language as it is inherited. Actually, the word "faith" has some colors which "belief" lacks; it is more frequently described as a comprehensive relationship to God, based on God's movement to man. "Belief" is somewhat more hardened and objectified to mean a doctrine, a fact, a part of the content of faith. For present purposes, however, we must be content to blur some distinctions between the two terms. They are of extreme importance when the fullness of man's relation to God is to be discussed by theologians. Dealing as we wish to with unbelief as an event, the distinctions are less important. We shall talk about belief only in minimal terms, as briefly and broadly as possible, in order to come to the main themes of our argument.

The discussion of belief is entered into warily, of course, because it can be a trap to divert the whole discussion of unbelief. Any sophomore skeptic, as well as every senior citizen of the believing community, well knows that one man's unbelief is another's belief. This book is not intended to help people choose among the religions of men. Our task is to isolate the experience of those who, on soil which was historically Chris-

17

tian, today continue to profess that faith or who hold openly
or quietly to other belief-systems.

The dangers before us are many. There is, first, the temptation to try to define "the essence of Christianity," a concept
which has eluded some of the most profound theologians and
historians Christianity has produced. A second temptation
would lead toward an attempt to produce a "one-man ecumenical movement." That is, in order to proceed to a definition of
unbelief, one may try to impose an artificial consensus on divided Christians, with the suggestion that everyone accept this
version of the faith, and all will be well. Similarly we could be
detained or decoyed by the attempt to define faith in such a
way that it anticipates all possibilities and absorbs all exceptions. Still another pitfall lies in the temptation to rule out the
variants by calling them unbelief, when actually they are attempts at a positive statement of the meaning of faith in a
time when some historic meanings are in question.[1]

1 In our time, many theologians have attempted such projects. The most
familiar of these in recent years has been Rudolf Bultmann, with his project of demythologizing. Bultmann calls into question the "mythical" detail
of the biblical events to which belief is related. He subjects the biblical
documents to radical tests of historical accuracy. The project is undertaken in the interest of faith. From the opposite angle, Paul Tillich has
tried to provide a permanent base for faith in a philosophy of being; for
different reasons he minimizes the importance of biblical events and documents. These projects are related as embarrassments by critics of the church
from without and within. Thus Walter Kaufmann, in the books referred to in Chapter 1, fn. 8, suggests that duplicity, equivocation, and
—to use his term—"gerrymandering" are involved in these efforts. He
argues that the belief of the most noted theologians of today would not
have been recognized as such by the mass of uncritical believers in history,
and is not by such believers today. (See the chapter "Against Theology" in
Faith of a Heretic, pp. 103 ff.) In the interests of a certain kind of Protestantism, William Warren Bartley, III, undertakes similar criticism. (*The
Retreat to Commitment* [New York: Knopf, 1962], pp. 73 ff., on Paul Tillich.) Needless to say, many "fundamentalist" Christians share their concerns. The questions they raise are crucial for an understanding of the
theological task of today, but they have little to do with our discussion of

In a recent work, Josef Pieper has undertaken a philosophical definition of belief and faith which could not have been written apart from the Christian historical experience. Pieper gives the kind of advice that is necessary to take in a work of this type: distrust the perfection of excessively precise definitions of words so historically coated as belief is. Yet some definition is necessary and he is correct in beginning with these words: "To believe is equivalent to taking a position on the truth of a statement and on the actuality of the matter stated. More precisely, belief means that we think a statement true and consider the stated matter real, objectively existent." [2] Such a philosophical definition does seem to begin at the opposite pole from which biblical discussion of faith begins. Faith is, at first, less interested in truth, actuality, reality, objectivity, though it can never avoid these issues.

One uses the word "belief" where other terms do not suffice. Obvious examples of difference present themselves when "knowledge" or "pretending" are introduced. But the assent implied in belief is as strong as in knowledge: it appears without reservation. "It is part of the concept of belief itself that man is certain of that in which he believes." [3] Immediately another element is introduced: one believes on the word or testimony of another. *"Ad fidem pertinet aliquid et alicui credere."* [4] To believe means to believe someone and to believe something.

"Everyone who believes assents to the testimony of someone." "Belief is always addressed to a person." The first of

---

the disparity (or lack of disparity) between the professed inherited belief and the actual motivating beliefs of men's lives today.

2 Josef Pieper, *Belief and Faith,* trans. Richard and Clara Winston (New York: Pantheon, 1963), p. 7.

3 *Ibid.,* p. 15.

4 St. Thomas Aquinas, *Summa theologica* II, II, 129, 6. (Quoted in Pieper, p. 17.)

these two sentences is by Thomas Aquinas; the second by
Martin Luther—evidence that on this score no difference of
opinion existed between the Reformer and the last great
teacher of a still undivided Western Christendom.[5]

Belief has an element of volition. One can believe only if he
wishes to. "I 'must' believe him." "I 'can't' believe him."
"Nemo credit nisi volens." [6] If belief is dependent, there
must be an author of belief, a witness, one whose testimony is
accepted, a knower. The believer participates in the knowledge of the knower. For the Christian, this comes from hearing
the testimony of God in his word and in the words of men dependent on that word. In the end, then, Christian belief re-
sides in God: "Belief in revelation can be supported only on
the ground that God has actually spoken in a manner audible
to man." [7] It is precisely at this point that the problem of modern unbelief is born. Man has often experienced, but perhaps
never so acutely as now, "the silence of God," "the absence
of God," or—even more dramatically—"the death of God."
To that topic, most of these chapters will be devoted.

Now we return to one element which can serve to locate the
question of the "something" of belief. We are far from ex-
hausting the biblical meanings of the faith-relationship to
God. Actually, this relationship begins from the other end—
not with man's listening or knowing or willing, but with the
faithfulness of God who initiates a relation to man. Now we
are only to follow to its end the traditional discussion of
Christian belief, which finally locates the something that is believed. Here the problems of minimums of creeds, essences
of faith, "one-man ecumenical solutions" become hazardous.
Pieper, in his book, resorts to two words:

5 Pieper, *op. cit.,* p. 18.
6 St. Augustine, *In Joannis evangelium, tract.* 26, 3, in J. P. Migne,
Patrologia latina, XXXV, 1607. (Quoted in Pieper, p. 26.)
7 Pieper, *op. cit.,* p. 75.

According to the theologians, the essence of the Christian faith can be summed up in two words. Those two words are Trinity and Incarnation. The "universal teacher" of Christendom has said that the whole content of the truth of Christian faith can be reduced to the dogma of the Trinitarian God and the dogma that man participates in the life of God through Christ. (*Duo nobis credenda proponuntur: scil. occultum Divinitatis . . . et mysterium humanitatis Christi. [Summa Theologica] II, II, 1, 8.—Fides nostra in duobus principaliter consistit: primo quidem in vera Dei cognitione . . . ; secundo in mysterio incarnationis Christi.* II, II, 174, 6.)[8]

These two words do not begin to exhaust the catholic fullness of faith. Many who are but dimly aware of the meaning of either word are certainly to be numbered among Christians. People in every age look for new ways to state their belief in these realities. Therefore, we need not quibble about the words, but they unquestionably point to two central dimensions of the catholic faith. They are at the heart of the ancient ecumenical creeds which are still professed in most churches, including most Protestant churches of the Christian family, to this day. No theologian of the Eastern Orthodox churches would dissent far from "the universal teacher's" location of the foci of belief.

The vast majority of the Orthodox and Protestant churches of the world belong to the World Council of Churches, whose basis states:

The World Council of Churches is a fellowship of churches which confess the Lord Jesus Christ as God and Savior according to the Scriptures and therefore seek to

8 *Ibid.,* p. 88 and Note 3 for Chap. IX, p. 103.

fulfil together their common calling to the glory of the one God, Father, Son, and Holy Spirit.[9]

The man Christ Jesus is confessed as Lord, as God and Savior, so the Incarnation is implicit; the Trinity is explicitly referred to. The Scriptures serve as testimony for the birth of the confessed faith and the common calling. Conservative Christians in the United States who do not belong to the larger ecumenical movement do not reject it because of what is in its basis. Many of them, for instance, belong to the National Association of Evangelicals whose basis is more explicit, and includes:

1. We believe the Bible to be the inspired, the only infallible, authoritative word of God.

2. We believe that there is one God, eternally existent in three persons, Father, Son and Holy Ghost.

3. We believe in the deity of our Lord Jesus Christ, in His virgin birth, in His sinless life, in His miracles, in His vicarious and atoning death. . . .

7. We believe in the spiritual unity of believers in our Lord Jesus Christ.[10]

Clearly, the formal profession of faith of the vast majority of the Christians of the world revolves around the foci mentioned by Pieper and based in Aquinas' summary.

[9] Quoted in Henry P. Van Dusen, *One Great Ground of Hope* (Philadelphia: Westminster, 1961), p. 150.

[10] Quoted in James DeForest Murch, *Cooperation without Compromise* (Grand Rapids, Mich.: Eerdmans, 1956), pp. 65 f. It is interesting to note that a modern denomination with a partly liberal heritage and one that is hesitant to impose a creed finds itself intuitively in the shadow of the ancient creeds and their foci when it produces a united testimony of faith. I refer to the United Church of Christ, formed in the United States in 1957 through a merger of the Congregational Christian and the Evangelical and Reformed churches.

God is and God acts; he is beyond man's experience and he is in it; he is transcendent and he is immanent; he is named among Christians by the symbol "Trinity" and his action is marked in what is referred to as "Incarnation." These are reference points for the content of faith from which to some extent unbelief is measured in churches.

Throughout this brief discussion it will be obvious that one cannot easily separate "belief in" from "belief that." The biblical term for faith in both the Old and the New Testaments greatly stresses the former. The Old Testament, full of reference to God's faithfulness and man's response, does not possess a noun to cover our word "belief":

> There is no word in the Old Testament in Hebrew meaning "faith" or "belief"; that is to say, there is no noun form representing nominally the act indicated by the verb *he emin* "believe"—a fact which is widely known and acknowledged. And just as there is no *nomen actionis* corresponding to *he emin*, there is also no *nomen agentis* meaning "believer." [11]

In the New Testament, belief is a category and the believer is regularly referred to. "Belief in" usually preoccupies the lexicographers. Thus Arndt and Gingrich list two pages of references under *pistis:* "1. that which causes trust and faith" (e.g., faithfulness, reliability, solemn promise, proof, pledge); "2. *trust, confidence, faith.*" Finally, *pistis* refers to "that which is believed, *body of faith* or *belief, doctrine.*" "This

11 James Barr, *The Semantics of Biblical Language* (London: Oxford University Press, 1961), p. 173. The quoted sentence, it is interesting to note, appears in a brilliant and controversial chapter (" 'Faith' and 'Truth'—an Examination of Some Linguistic Arguments," pp. 161-205) in which Barr criticizes those who have emphasized the Hebrew background of the term "faith"—"and in particular on the basis of this Hebrew background [those who] . . . emphasize the moment of the faithfulness of God towards man as well as the faith or believing of man towards God."

objectivizing of the *pistis* concept is found as early as Paul: Romans 1:5; Galatians 1:23 . . . and perhaps Galatians 3:23-25." [12]

But if in recent theological talk the fashion has been to stress the biblical lineage of "belief in" at the expense of "belief that," in practical life the two are not seen to be in great tension. Attempts to rule out one at the expense of the other do violence to the fuller expression of faith throughout Christian history, and we shall minimize the tension in our study. Unbelief will refer, therefore, to neglect or rejection of the "something" of faith and the "someone" as well.

Two young professors, one a philosopher and the other a theologian, both oriented to the discussion of language and logic, agree that "belief in" and "belief that" are inseparable.[13] Frederick Ferré isolates a number of functions for Christian utterance in religious language. Each of them can be implied in our ensuing discussions of unbelief. These are:

1. The ceremonial function (as in calls to worship or responses);
2. The self-committal function (through which one joins and rejoins the community);
3. The liturgical function (the church is now at worship);

[12] William F. Arndt and F. Wilbur Gingrich, *A Greek-English Lexicon of the New Testament and Other Early Christian Literature* (Chicago: University of Chicago Press, 1956), pp. 668-670. This lexicon is based on the work of Walter Bauer. For the most complete lexicographical study of *pistis,* see 'Faith" by Rudolf Bultmann and Artur Weiser in *Bible Key Words,* trans. Dorothea M. Barton, P. R. Ackroyd, and A. E. Harvey (New York: Harper & Row, 1960-61), III, 1-125. This definition is taken from Gerhard Kittel's *Theologisches Wörterbuch zum Neuen Testament.* James Barr's book is a full-length attempt, often quite convincing, to point to the limits of the usefulness of a lexicographical and etymological approach to biblical concepts.

[13] See Kent Bendall and Frederick Ferré, *Exploring the Logic of Faith* (New York: Association Press, 1962), especially Ferré's chapter, " 'Belief That' and the Dimensions of Faith," pp. 43-76.

4. The reassuring function (men build each other up and comfort each other thus);
5. The judging function (by which man's distance from the ideal is measured);
6. The challenging function (to help people rise above their current moral status);
7. The ethical function (by which people determine to will a better way of life);
8. The existential function (in which decision and self-interpretation come about);
9. The convictional function (our convictions define us, so we state them);
10. The scientific function (which permits the judgment concerning the truth or falsity of propositions in the light of some norm);
11. The historical function (the question of historical accuracy behind the "belief that");
12. The attentional function (to point the way of others to pattern in nature and history);
13. The metaphysical function (where possible, to indicate "reality" behind the world man perceives readily).

Certainly, "belief that" is not only an inherited element of faith but a practical item in the living community of believers.

We have not tried to make more or less of the symbols Trinity and Incarnation than these symbols can bear. There has been no interest in incorporating all elements of Christianity under these historic verbal banners or in using them to point to subtleties of heresy. They are to serve here only as reference points in the catholic, or inclusive and historical strand, so that we can begin to discuss unbelief. The unbeliever is not the one who has doubts about the mode of Incarnation or the adequacy of the Trinitarian formula. Rather, he is the one who is inattentive to the stirrings of a living God, witnessed to in the ancient formulas transformed in the life of the churches today. The merit of this provisional "ecumenical definition" is also partly that it enables us to show how the vast majority of people in "Christian America" conceive of the faith in these terms and express an assent to them.

3

A Christian Definition of Unbelief

Unbelief takes many forms. Just as it was necessary at the beginning to define belief as broadly as possible, now it is advisable to prevent the definition of unbelief from becoming prematurely precise. Unfaith, the opposite of the biblical terms for "belief in" the faithful activity of God, is not in common usage. The modern dictionary defines it matter-of-factly as "absence or want of faith; faithlessness; distrust; unbelief." Unbelief is the common form. It is defined as "withholding of belief; incredulity or skepticism, especially in matters of religious faith."

A difficulty of language appears when it is noted that disbelief and unbelief in today's usage convey degrees of intensity somewhat different from that in biblical usage.

Unbelief may suggest a mere withholding of belief; disbelief implies a positive rejection of what is stated or asserted; as, an attitude of general *unbelief*, with reference to a given rumor, may be changed by evidence to one of absolute *disbelief*. In Biblical usage, however, *unbelief* has the stronger sense of disbelief in divine revelation . . . (Mark 16:14; Heb. 3:19).[1]

Some students of the subject are reluctant to employ the term "unbelief" except in the rarest of circumstances. However, their interest is colored by theological concerns in the definition of belief, whereas we are studying the kinds of belief or lack of belief behind the norms and values of everyday life.

Josef Pieper, from whose definition of belief we have profited, defines unbelief in such a way that it virtually disappears.

We all know that we can hardly begin to talk about the "modern spirit" without hearing the term "unbelief" crop up early in the discussion. We should be reminded, however,

1 *Webster's New International Dictionary,* 2nd ed.

that the great tradition of Western theology recommends extreme caution in the use of this word. Above all we should
clarify what precisely is meant by "unbelief" (as sin). It happens very often that a person hears the tidings of the faith
but is not reached by them (which may very well be caused
by the internal style of those tidings). The message is simply
not perceived as something that can really concern the
hearer; and in that case, of course, no belief arises. But such
non-belief cannot be termed "unbelief." In another instance,
the content of the tidings may be well grasped; but for a wide
variety of reasons it does not occur to the hearer that they
can possibly be a supernatural message, divine speech, "revelation" in the strict sense of that word: and therefore no genuine belief comes into being. But once more "unbelief"
would not be the right term for this lack of belief. Nor can
we call unbelievers those who refuse to become involved at
all and will not give their mind to considering the credibility
of the testimony. Such refusal may be indefensible; it may be
wrong; but it is not identical with unbelief. Unbelief in the
precise sense of the term is only that mental act in which
someone deliberately refuses assent to a truth which he has
recognized with sufficient plainness to be God's speech.

One may ask whether unbelief in this sense ever occurs.
To this we must reply that in actuality the usual counterpoise to belief seems to be less sheer unbelief than . . . inveterate inattentiveness. . . . There is no sense in attacking
this inattentiveness as "unbelief." [2]

Pieper is clearly operating on different terrain than does the
dictionary. His understandable interest is in protecting "the
great tradition of Western theology," and in that context his
precise definition of unbelief is in place. The dictionary has—
and we as observers must have—a somewhat different interest.

[2] *Belief and Faith* (New York: Pantheon, 1963), pp. 71-73. (Italics added.)
See also pp. 61-62.

Just as he found it fruitful to keep the definition of belief provisionally broad, we must keep unbelief somewhat ill-defined and undifferentiated. Why? Because we shall be observing social phenomena against a landscape where it is exactly "the great tradition of Western theology" that is being called into question or left behind. We shall be content for now to say that as an historical event on Euro-American soil, unbelief includes Pieper's "non-belief" or "lack of belief" or "refusal to become involved at all" or—best of all—"inveterate inattentiveness."

Writing with a different goal in mind, Arthur A. Cohen is careful to isolate unbelief as something *less* prevalent and less serious than disbelief. Once again, we find that the positive intention of a student commits him to a restriction of the negative. However, Cohen's restrictions make of unbelief something much different from Pieper's. Criticizing Abraham J. Heschel, the Jewish theologian, for making unbelief seem to be "sheer dishonesty," Cohen sees unbelief as something quite casual. In Cohen's phrases, disbelief is the profound modern tragedy. It represents in modern literature (Nietzsche, Dostoevsky's Kirillov or Stavrogin, Sartre)

the response of man to a world no longer inhabited by the living God. . . . Such disbelief issues from belief. The disbeliever affirms that God no longer counts, that He is ineffective, meaningless, trivial. The cruelty and suffering of history, the solitude and despair of individuality, the anguish of the lonely ego cannot be mitigated by this burned-out God. Disbelief is real and tragic.

Unbelief is rather different and far less terrifying. The unbeliever is simply not interested—God is an amusing or grand hypothesis, but little more. The fact of historical belief is a curiosity to unbelief or else a mere possibility among innumerable possibilities. . . . Unbelief is not the doctrine of significant minds, for serious thinkers know the history of belief and the grounds on which it was affirmed sufficiently

well to disbelieve. They do not put away belief with boredom and disinterest. No! For the thinker there is belief or
disbelief. Unbelief—the condition of being unaware—is the
situation of those who do not think deeply at all.[3]

Just as Pieper narrows the definition of unbelief to protect
the seriousness of "the great tradition of Western theology,"
Cohen does so to protect the seriousness of the modern disbeliever against the casual profaner of the historic experience of
faith. Once again, lacking his motivation, we can continue to
mass together a number of phenomena, including disbelief,
under the broad coverage of unbelief, whose varieties we shall
then attempt to discern.

In the New Testament, unbelief is as radical as Pieper makes
it out to be (or as Cohen makes disbelief to be), but it is not at
all infrequent. *Apistia* occurs relatively infrequently (Matt.
13:58; Mark 6:6; 9:24; 16:14; Rom. 3:3; 4:20; 11:20, 23; I Tim.
1:13; Heb. 3:12, 19), but people are named "unbelievers" with
more frequency. There, before "the great tradition of Western
theology" had been formed, unbelievers, disbelievers, nonbelievers, the unserious, the inattentive, were all classified together. Villagers in Palestine, the disciples themselves, one of
Jesus' petitioners, the ancient people of God, the young Saul
(Paul), the Israelites wandering in the wilderness—all were
filled with *apistia;* that is, they "withheld belief" or engaged in
"positive rejection" when confronted with a witness to divine
revelation.

When the term "unbelief" is used, it appears as the final, absolute, and supreme evil; unbelief undercuts or annuls God's
activity in Christ. In the Johannine literature (John 16:9,
I John 5:10), unbelief is explicitly termed the prime fault of
man, for it is an affront to the veracity of the divine. Related to
apistia is its ethical counterpart, *apeitheia* (Rom. 11:30, 32;

[3] *The Natural and the Supernatural Jew* (New York: Pantheon, 1962),
pp. 252 f.

Eph. 2:2; 5:6; Heb. 4:6, 11). *Apeitheia* is the issuance of unbelief into disobedience; the term connotes rebellion and contumacy based on *apistia,* the lack of faith and trust.

Those who, in the Western theological tradition, make faith the basis of the God-man relation in a radical way (as Protestantism does), restore the extensive and radical application of the term "unbelief" to man's inattentiveness or withholding of belief. John Calvin defined faith as "a steady and certain knowledge of the Divine benevolence towards us, which, being founded on the truth of the gratuitous promise in Christ, is both revealed to our minds, and confirmed to our hearts, by the Holy Spirit." For Calvin, unbelief departed from the knowledge of the action of the divine benevolence toward us; it denied the promise in Christ and the revelation of God. As such, it was the prime fault. Martin Luther, who based all on faith, extended unbelief—in the Johannine way—to the moral category. In his explanation of the First Commandment, in the *Large Catechism,* he defined a god as that to which man looks for all good and in whom he finds a refuge in all need. To have a god is nothing else than to trust and believe him with one's whole heart. Failure to trust or to give whole assent is unbelief.

By now three interests are represented: two of them narrow the definitions of unbelief and disbelief, and thus find them rarely represented in pure form. The third enlarges the category and extends it as widely as possible. We have cited these examples to point to the complexity of the problem and to remind ourselves and the reader that we may make of the term "unbelief" pretty much what we desire, depending upon the definitions of belief and the immediate practical intention of the argument. In our context, unbelief is a broad and rather neutral category, within which later distinctions are made.

One other debate over the nature of unbelief must be cited here because of its theological importance, even though *at this point* a solution of the problem would not greatly color the development of our research and thought. In Protestant thought,

particularly under the influence of the twentieth-century theologian Karl Barth, unbelief is depicted as the natural state of
man. When the world is pictured as secularizing itself, moving
"beyond God," maturing or coming of age out of its adolescence, this historical and cultural development is described as a
natural unfolding, as man becoming what he really is and is intended to be. Such a position is based on a radical view of man's
opposition to God and God's radical distance from man. On
this basis, Christian theology finds a natural affinity with secular man and his "natural" unbelief. All the irreligious movements of the time are the immediately recognized kin of Christian faith. The Christian differs, in that he paradoxically adds
to a view of life without faith the positing of x as equal to
God. From the secular or natural realm where all talk about
God is meaningless, man comes to this x via the category of
faith, which Gustav Wingren calls "an exceptional bulge in an
otherwise straight line of human events." Others have recalled
that in Christian teaching, man was originally made for God;
his heart is restless until it finds its rest in God. Unbelief, then,
is not a natural state but an event which enthralls man, a state
which holds domain over him. Thus Wingren observes:

> For Luther, unbelief is *demonic*. It is not "human" to
> doubt and "paradoxical" to believe; on the contrary, where
> doubt arises, it is diabolical powers that strive for mastery in
> human life. So, for Luther doubt is not of the intellect but is
> *despair* about life and redemption. . . . Someone is thus ac-
> tive in opposition to the Creator wherever unbelief is found
> —that is to say, where death is found.[4]

This debate has profound meanings for preachers and ministers to the faithful community, and will be important to recall
later when we point to reconstructive attempts by believers.

[4] *The Living Word*, trans. Victor C. Pogue (Philadelphia: Muhlenberg,
1960), pp. 92 ff.

For our observation of the varieties of unbelief today, to introduce the distinction between "natural" or "unnatural" unbelief would be to introduce a moral dimension that could clutter the development. Just as Pieper was protecting the great tradition of Western theology by finding pure unbelief rare and perhaps nonexistent, so Wingren sets out to protect the great tradition of Western—and particularly Protestant—preaching and pastoral activity. To decide against Wingren and his spiritual kin at this stage would prejudice the case for or against preaching in the recall of faith. To decide for him would be to introduce elements of judgment against the "honest unbeliever" or disbeliever and to imply congratulations to the imperfectly irreligious or relatively religious.

If we now refer to our definition of belief, we find that unbelief implies any kind of serious or permanent departure from belief *in* God (as symbolized by the term "Trinity") and from belief *that* God not only is but acts (as symbolized by the historic reference "Incarnation"). Each such departure represents a failure to be attentive to the witnesses: God speaks audibly; or he speaks in Scripture, preaching, the church's tradition, or the affairs of men. "Failure to be attentive" can imply that man has listened and rejected, or has never listened or really heard, or has ceased listening, or has so surrounded himself with other structures of security or other gods that vital faith is not possible or necessary.

Whenever this occurs, from the viewpoint of the Christian faith we have present and existent the godless man to whom Murray refers (see pp. 13-14) or the secular society which we shall be detailing. The godless man may possibly have moments of attentiveness or half-belief. The secular society may have— and no doubt does have—people who live authentically by faith, but its motivating center (in Euro-America) is no longer necessarily a reliance upon the living God. The theologian may say that godless man and secular society have merely changed allegiances, followed other gods, clung to other promises. The historian is first of all concerned only to see the extent to which man and society have become secularized, or have established themselves apart from their historic faith.

Secularization, which will be defined in detail later, can mean that man has moved beyond God, that he has dropped all attention, that he has pursued other gods. It may also mean that, on the soil of the West with its recall of historic Christian witness, many modes of expressing faith and institutions for perpetuating it may survive, but may be so reinvested with meaning or obscured by other meanings that the historic reference is lost. It will become necessary, therefore, to locate unbelief around and in the churches. Where the professedly believing communities survive, what in the environment suggests that large numbers of people positively disbelieve or do not care? That they have replaced God with the gods or have so surrounded him that he no longer matters? Again, where the professedly believing communities survive, what in their institutional and spiritual life suggests that large numbers of people do not find the activity of God all-important? How do religious organizations reveal that people in them do not see God to be faithful, do not recognize a need for response in living faith, do not recognize God beyond what is apparent to them (Aquinas' *occultum Divinitatis*) or near (in the *mysterium humanitatis Christi*)?

The momentary, casual, daily personal presence of disbelief or inattention in the individual Christian is not our particular concern. That takes as many forms as there are people and varieties of personal responses in faith. The present task is to see how unbelief in its broad sense is institutionalized and present as a more or less permanent cultural phenomenon.

4

The Originality
of Modern Unbelief

What is original about unbelief today? In what ways does the variety of disbeliefs which are culturally present and sustained today differ from that of the past?

To avoid misunderstanding at this point, we shall lay our cards on the table and suggest that in this chapter it is necessary to become methodologically messy, or at least apparently so. The purpose of the chapter is to give an account of a wide spectrum of attempts by witnesses to locate the originality of today's unbelief. Our objective is not to present original material or new findings based on original research, but rather to call upon a prestigious committee of observers and reporters in order to form a composite picture of how unbelief is regarded today. The attempt is not to engage in name-dropping; I am sorry that I cannot think of another way to form the composite, for it may appear that the argument at this point is eclectic and derivative.

There are good reasons for following this method, however, just as there will be good reasons for departing from it later. The authorities cited will be either intuitive people, artists at discerning the signs of the times, or careful researchers, the fruit of whose studies on this point can be briefly summarized. Some of their observations will be tested in what follows; for the present, we shall ask for provisional acceptance of the drift of their conclusions. Most of them see unbelief to be either an accidental or unconscious development (as in secularity) or a purposive, conscious development (as in secularism). In the latter instance, most of them are eager to subject secularism to systematic scrutiny, to see it—as its proponents do not always do—as a speculative hypothesis. I can best explain this chapter, then, as one man's report on a community project which would isolate elements of originality in modern unbelief.

The variety of witnesses will itself serve one function: Within the American churches the view of extensive modern unbelief is often obscured or made to seem remote. The relative institutional security of the churches seems to render nonreligious or antireligious forces less potent and less observable in America than in Europe and elsewhere. In this chapter that security will be called into question and the remoteness in part overcome by the testimony that follows.

What is original in today's unbelief? It is misleading or fruitless to ask this question as if unbelief itself were a new phenomenon. If there are some believers who see all times fulfilled in their own, there are more—and usually the somewhat more informed and reflective ones—who do the opposite: they see examples in history of "ages of faith" when, because it seems culturally and socially impossible *not* to be named a believer, belief came easily to man. On such a premise, the modern age will always compare unfavorably with biblical times, with the millennium of the church's domain in Europe or with some other mythical golden age. The Bible gives no license for its readers to draw the conclusion that belief came without struggle to man or that faithfulness prevailed in its time. Even the most casual reading of medieval history reveals the extent of ignorance, faithlessness, apathy, and rebellion in "the Age of Faith." The Reformers, by their own admission, left the world and the church in many ways as they had found them, and faith did not prevail. As a modern process, secularization is now centuries old. Words like "humanism," "renaissance," "enlightenment," "discovery," "the scientific world view," the period of modern "revolution"—each of these spells cultural complications for faith.

For every Christian who is self-consciously oriented to the Bible, belief seems least complicated in the days of prophets or apostles, when the "audible speaking of God" and the visible action of God are often presumed to have been apparent. Norman Gottwald says of the book of Isaiah: "A close reading of the prophet sweeps away forever the unfounded nostalgia that it was easier to believe in God in Bible times. Faith always involves the possibility of loss." For Roman Catholics the temptation comes with the view of cathedrals and systems in the twelfth and thirteenth centuries. Much of the Catholic literary, artistic, and philosophical revival earlier in this century was a reaction against the modern, secular, and unbelieving world and an escape into neo-medievalism. For example, Alexander Dru says of Charles Péguy: "The atmosphere [for his medieval world in the twentieth century] is all too familiar: the deliberately archaic world of a stylised, mediaeval Catholicism, the refuge of the convert in reaction against the modern world, returning in his poetry to the true fold of the past."

Protestants tend to turn to the sixteenth-century Reformation or to the "great century" (to use historian Kenneth Scott Latourette's widely accepted phrase), the nineteenth. But the poetry of nineteenth-century Christendom, for example in Britain, gives one pause. This poetry, celebrating the problem of belief and the presence of half-belief, met wide acceptance. Thus Matthew Arnold wrote in "The Scholar Gypsy" of:

> Light half-believers of our casual creeds,
> Who never deeply felt, nor clearly willed,
> Whose insight never has borne fruit in deeds,
> Whose vague resolves have never been fulfilled;
> For whom each year we see
> Breeds new beginnings, disappointments new;
> Who hesitate and falter life away,
> And lose tomorrow the ground won today.

Arnold, in the often-quoted "Dover Beach" was bemoaning the passing of the ages of faith:

> . . . The sea of faith
> Was once, too, at the full. . . .

And in "Stanzas from the Grand Chartreuse," he spoke of himself, symbolic of the man of his time,

> Wandering between two worlds, one dead,
> The other powerless to be born,
> With nowhere yet to rest my head. . . .

Tennyson was celebrating the "faith that lived in honest doubt" as being more potent than that in "half the creeds" which were seen to be losing their power. Thomas Hardy wrote of the "Funeral of God." What was true of British poetry and essays was even more true on the Continent, where Hölderlin, more than any poet before him and perhaps more than any since, spoke of the passing of the gods. The rise of sociology led to confident predictions such as that of Guyau in 1897 that the future belonged to nonreligion as the past had belonged to religious faith.

There were theological witnesses in the nineteenth century pointing to the difficulties of believing. Most notable of these was Kierkegaard, who has served a modern dramatic critic in his attempt to suggest that unbelief is not wholly original in our time. Lionel Abel, criticizing Martin Esslin, the celebrator of *The Theatre of the Absurd,* writes:

> Esslin says that our present sense of absurdity springs from the loss of humanly important realities. Of what realities? Well, Esslin thinks we have lost God. I should like to know when this occurred. But Esslin probably means merely that we have lost a belief in God once natural to us. Now I confess to having very little nostalgia for those periods of history when it was "natural" to believe in God. Was such belief ever really natural? Søren Kierkegaard, for one, thought that Christian education, "natural" in the nineteenth century—this kind of education we have lost—was

the main obstacle to Christian belief; for Kierkegaard, true belief was always possible, always miraculous.

In the United States, public expression of unbelief has been the activity of a small minority, but it has been sufficiently noisy that one cannot claim it to be an original problem today. The names of Sinclair Lewis, H. L. Mencken, Clarence Darrow, and William Cowper Brann in the decades of the recent past—and of Mark Twain and Robert Ingersoll in the latter years of the nineteenth century—point to a widespread popular interest in anticlerical or antireligious expression, if not to a profound agony over the problem of belief.[1]

Just as it is dangerous to misread the past with the intention of dramatizing modern unbelief, so it is inaccurate to see all signs of the modern world leading toward the varieties of unbelief. To many scholars, an inevitable tendency, or drift, is apparent. Others see the Christian deposit in culture as residual—there is less now than last year and there will be still less next year. But both those who attack and those who defend belief are often puzzled by the complexity of signs, the ambiguities of life today. In the United States, John C. Bennett (who is not given to dreaming of a golden age of the Christian past) can say that "pervasive Western secularizing influences are strongly felt and yet there is a remarkable revival of religious interest, and religious institutions grow rapidly and show signs of unusual vitality." From outside the Christian community, the unusually astute essayist Isaac Rosenfeld complains of the dual tendencies of culture: "Ours is a de-

[1] The reference to Isaiah is from Norman Gottwald, *A Light to the Nations* (New York: Harper & Row, 1959), p. 319; Alexander Dru comments on Péguy in *Temporal and Eternal* (New York: Harper & Row, 1958), p. 7. Lionel Abel writes on Esslin in *Metatheatre* (New York: Hill & Wang, 1963), p. 140. Guyau's work is available with an introduction by Nahum N. Glatzer, *The Non-Religion of the Future* (New York: Schocken Books, 1962).

generating mixed culture of sacred and secular elements," and argues eloquently for the displacement of sacred elements by the secular in order to unify, purify, and vivify culture.

Modern culture is capable of producing many kinds of religious and spiritual impulses and beliefs. Thus the translator of a book by Nikolai Berdyaev can see, along with the integrating impulse of Christianity "an age only comparable with the Hellenistic for its diversity of opinion, its easy acceptance of pseudo-faiths and its glib rationalistic exposition of the sacred mysteries." In that mixed environment, Westerners may too casually dismiss their own religio-cultural heritage and the beliefs that motivated it. Historian Pieter Geyl complains of those who call his own kind of thinker "chauvinist":

> There is something thoroughly unhealthy in that habit of depreciating our own spiritual heritage. The West has no faith any more, it is asserted, and the accusers vie in offering, one this, the other that, which might serve. As if an ideology could be plucked from the air! No faith? Well, I believe in ourselves, in our own tradition, which with its tireless experimenting and trying out changes, gives evidence that it still has something to offer to the world.

For decades, Karl Jaspers, as capably as anyone, has pointed to the doublesidedness of today's culture: to its belief and unbelief, its secularity and its spirituality. He has been unwilling to let go the cultural lineage of the spiritual and of Christian belief, but he has also been unable to see sufficient vitality in it.

> Religion, indeed, persists, administered by the Churches and the creeds; but in the mass-life it is nothing more than consolation in time of trouble or than an orderly conduct of life, being rarely now persistent as an effective vital energy. Although the Church retains its efficiency as a political

power, religious faith actively held by individuals grows con-
tinually rarer. Nowadays the great traditions of the
Churches have often become nothing more than a futile attempt to restore their irrevocable past, side by side with a
broad-minded adoption of all kinds of modern thought. . . .

[Yet] although there is no freedom in the Church, the
Church, nonetheless, is a necessary condition of such liberty
as is at any time attainable. It preserves the extent of spiritual value, a feeling for the inexorability of transcendental
reality, the urgency of the claims which the transcendental
makes upon man. Great would be the dangers attendant
upon its unnoted decay to become part of the mass-apparatus
in tacit alliance with unfaith and with the consequent loss
of that which it still possesses competent to function once
again as a source of freedom.

Roman Catholic scholars have often criticized Jaspers. Thus
Josef Pieper sees in him a mental type prevalent over much of
the West's secularized territory. It is characterized by "reluctance to abandon the content of traditional religious faith,"
and by "the incapacity to accept that content on the basis of
belief in the revelation—though that belief alone has made
these truths accessible to us and is their ultimate bulwark."
Hans Urs von Balthasar sees Jaspers in the act of finding "even
the fanaticism of unbelief [today to be] still influenced by
its biblical origin." The presence of the term "still" indicates
that even those hopeful of, wistful over, or irritated about, the
continued presence of Christian belief in the modern world
see it as on the defensive. But the signs are not all one-way.[2]

2 See John C. Bennett, *Christians and the State* (New York: Scribner,
1958), p. 3; Isaac Rosenfeld, *An Age of Enormity* (New York: World, 1962),
p. 221; George Reavey in Nikolai Berdyaev, *The Meaning of History* (New
York: Meridian, 1962), p. 7; Pieter Geyl, *Encounters in History* (New York:
Meridian, 1961), pp. 289 f.; Karl Jaspers, *Man in the Modern Age,* trans.
Eden and Cedar Paul (Garden City, N.Y.: Doubleday, 1957), pp. 152, 206;
Josef Pieper, *Belief and Faith* (New York: Pantheon, 1963), p. 71; Baltha-

The mass of comment by those who have assessed the spiritual
and secular forces—the marks of belief and unbelief—points to
the originality of modern unbelief. We are interested in that
which occurs only on once Christian soil and not in seeing
other world-religions or—at least not at all times—their milieu as being the mark of unbelief. Nor will discussion of Christian heresy, heterodoxy, or faithlessness enter in at this stage.
Keeping in mind the cultural dimensions of our definition of
faith, we shall look at the culture which surrounds those who,
in a primitive era, were defined as unbelievers because "they
have not received the God and Father who called them by the
Incarnate Son." [3]

1

The first original feature in the experience of modern unbelief is the Christians' awareness of its extensiveness around
the world.

We resist the temptation, as promised, to place the numbers
of today's believers on a scale and to compare them with those
of the past; far too many elusive factors come into play. Notable among these are the notorious inability (because of the nature of faith) to count the number of those who authentically
live by faith, and the fact that we have no reliable guides to
past statistics for comparison.

Any careful student of the Christian mission today would
have to accept the first sentence of A. M. Henry's book on
missionary theology: "There is [a] prodigious increase of unbelief in the world. . . ." Father Henry is not a hand-wringer
and does not indulge in extended criticism of Christian faithlessness. He speaks, as we must here, of the observable reality that Christianity is a small minority in the world; its era of

---

sar's essay appears in A. Robert Caponigri (ed.), *Modern Catholic Thinkers*
(New York: Harper & Row, 1960), p. 19.

[3] St. Maximus the Confessor, *Quaest. 60 ad Thal.*, in J. P. Migne, *Patrologia graeca*, XC, 637.

dramatic expansion into new territories is past. It meets new resistance among the powers. Its strength remains in parts of the world where secularization is a most striking reality. ". . . 91 per cent of all Catholics are found in Europe and in the new Europe constituted by North and South America. The continents of Asia, Africa, the ocean islands, where the vast majority of people (about 70 per cent) live, have barely 10 per cent of all Catholics." The figures for Protestantism would not differ significantly.

Mission historians regularly note that the 28 per cent of the world that can be called Christian is rapidly shrinking, again not primarily because of Christian faithlessness but because of the open facts of population growth elsewhere and the political resistance to Christian "intrusion" behind the Iron and Bamboo curtains and because of new nationalism and anticolonialism in Africa and Asia. This is not the place to account for the latter factors nor to deplore historical events and mistakes of the missionary period. It is only to record as one would with an adding machine.

From the viewpoint of classic theology, the bulk of the world's population which persists in beliefs other than those associated with Christianity is not "culpable" (to use St. Maximus the Confessor's term) because it has not really been confronted with "the God and Father who called them by the Incarnate Son." To the non-Christian who resents or is uninterested in Christianity as a missionary faith, the question of the extensiveness of unbelief does not seem to be important. He may rejoice in the termination of Christian expansion. At the same time, he can be shown to be involved in the change, for insofar as Christian beliefs have left their stamp and deposit on Euro-America, the decrease of that deposit's strength will, for better or worse, markedly change the relations of the West to the world. Only the believer gives the problem of unbelief that name, but others are affected.

After a century of expansion, much of mankind remains

unbelieving. Parallel to this fact is the heightened awareness by Christians that this is the case. Though never a majority in the world, Christians did not formerly give much thought to the world as a whole, but expansion made them acutely conscious of their minority status on a global scale. The ancient church was a tiny minority which had a built-in rationale for its statistical weakness: it was young. The millennium of Christendom, when Christian beliefs motivated the political life of both Eastern and Western Roman empires to a varying extent, occurred at a time when awareness of Asia or "the Turk" was dim. The nineteenth-century expansion was coupled with some sense of hope that the world might be evangelized. Twentieth-century changes in transportation and communication have brought home to all people who share Christian belief an awareness of Christian limitation. Much of the recent revolution has been in communications, producing a psychic effect based on interaction between believers and once remote nonbelievers. This interaction can produce new motivation for missionary work or even new fanaticism and hatred of "the outsider." Just as often it can be shown to create uncertainty, failure of nerve, hesitation, a relativization of belief. As Henry Sidgwick observes in his *Ethics:* "The denial by another of what I hold true, impairs my confidence in it." The Christian experience of denial by others in the majority of the world's population leads to an impairment of confidence in existing beliefs. Ten men of faith, living in a valley and cut off from awareness of the rest of the world, can have a confidence in their belief-system which is threatened when it is exposed to other powers and motivating beliefs.[4]

The term for the changed reality is, of course, "world revolution." However mapmakers, demographers, population ex-

---

[4] See A. M. Henry, O.P., *A Mission Theology,* trans. Albert J. La Mothe, Jr. (Notre Dame, Ind.: Fides, 1962), Chap. 1, "The Church in the World Today."

perts, social scientists, or journalists view a revolution which limits Christian possibility, the believer, like Father Henry, perceives the change as "increase of unbelief." While Henry is interested in the missionary dimension, Catholic layman Christopher Dawson has for years been the most articulate spokesman for a corollary cultural concern. Even those of us who may not agree with him as to the extent of Christianity's future dependence on its European rootage cannot easily dismiss the fact that the movement of world revolution has severed itself from the spiritual heritage, based in no small part on Christian belief, which motivated Europe and "new Europe." Dawson quotes Nirad Chaudhuri of India: "Are we witnessing a whole society's senile decay of memory?" Dawson takes hope from what he calls "the almost miraculous survival of Christianity in a secularized culture" and the ways the Roman Church has overcome its own decadence in that period. While he thus concedes that belief can be renewed "against the spirit of the age," he is wary of the future:

> We must not forget that the Catholic revival of the nineteenth century was rendered possible by the survival of a living Christian tradition among the masses, whereas today secularism has penetrated deeply into the popular consciousness. The problem that we are facing today is therefore quite unlike that which confronted the Church in the post-Reformation period.

To Dawson's mind the overt persecution of believers in Communist Russia or in Nazi Germany may well be a transitory phenomenon, "but the tendency to the secularization of culture is continuous and universal and there is no sign of any return to the ideal of a positive Christian culture. . . . Everywhere Christians, whether Orthodox, Roman Catholic or Protestant, are tending to be self-conscious minorities set in an alien or hostile world." [5] Today's world struggle between Western democracy and Eastern Soviet Communism is polarized around a Eurasian and a Euro-American secular ideology, with no real religious ideological option available.

Because Dawson is so learned and so informed, we can hardly compare his sense of awareness to that of the vast majority of common people who make up the believing communities of Euro-America and their derivative Christian colonies. Yet such people travel, read, converse, listen to radio and watch television, and in many ways are less able than he to find signs of hope for the future of belief. They may be less confident about the Christian future because they are less adequately oriented to the previous experiences of Christian survival. It may be argued that American religious organizations often serve to screen these world realities from the vision of their members. But over the decades the extensiveness of the unbelieving world community, as Christians perceive and name it, will have a telling effect in the United States.

2

The second original feature in the experience of modern unbelief is the Christians' awareness of the depth of penetration of its character into the many areas of life.

Modern unbelief is seen to be catholic in two ways, just as the Church Catholic has been and is so. There is first the Latin dimension of catholicity, which turns on the word *universalis*. Unbelief is universal, as we have just noted, in the negative sense of encompassing so much of the world, in taking in a whole field of definition while ruling out other fields (e.g.,

[5] Christopher Dawson, *The Movement of World Revolution* (New York: Sheed & Ward, 1959), pp. 1, 65 f., 76. While profiting from Dawson's work and agreeing with much of his historical analysis, I have dissociated myself from his "therapy" in a book-length discussion, *Second Chance for American Protestants* (New York: Harper & Row, 1963).

Christian belief). The Greek dimension of catholicity is less bounded, more positive. (*Katholikos* means "through-the-whole," penetrating in depth.) Instead of fencing-in (as the Church Universal does when it carries on missionary work, confesses or defines itself) it is outgoing, flooding being.[6]

Catholic unbelief differs vastly from individual, personal, negative expressions of disbelief. It represents a worldwide cultural spirit, manifested in the varieties of unbelief which will be depicted in the following chapters. This is not the unbelief of the metaphysical atheist who intellectually rebels against God, or of the moral atheist, the conniver whom the Bible names a "fool" for having said in his heart, "There is no God." The catholic unbeliever may be generous, outgoing, not concerned to kill off the old gods because he is preoccupied with the new ones. In the United States the experience of real atheism is rare because, many argue, the intensity of faith is not such to awaken authentic rebellion. But the unbelief which is positive, or *katholikos*, in character represents an entirely different matter.

Any book—and there are coming to be many—which explores the disbelief of atheism of our time provides a convenient catalogue of the areas of life reached by unbelief. M. Holmes Hartshorne presents these as negative features or criticisms: the psychological, the sociological, the epistemological, and the moral. Each of these criticisms has its positive corollary. Christian faith is criticized *so that* something authentic can replace it. So, too, there is an apparent negative dimension to unbelief in the categories provided by Ignace Lepp, but each of these conceives of itself as a positive, world-embracing vision (with the exception of "neurotic atheism," which interests Lepp particularly as a priest-psychotherapist who once had been an atheist). Marxist atheism has univer-

6 Walter L. Ong, S.J., *American Catholic Crossroads* (New York: Macmillan, 1959), pp. 63 ff., enlarges on this distinction.

salistic pretensions and positive offers for every realm of life. Rationalist atheism extends the fair promises of reason. Existentialist atheism may be full of despair, but it offers authenticity as an embracing vision in an absurd universe. Most of all, there are atheists "in the name of value," from Nietzsche through André Malraux to Camus.[7] Since it will later be our purpose to delineate varieties of unbelief, it is not necessary here to do more than mention the inclusive claims of many forms of unbelief today.

3

The outstanding original feature of thoughtful and radical unbelief in our time is its reluctance to deal with "transcendence."

The great majority of people in Europe or America, when asked, profess to believe in the existence of God or in a higher power of some sort. But at the heart of philosophical, scientific, or literary unbelief (whether as atheism, which knows, or as agnosticism, which does not know), there is a general unwillingness to accept the reality of a transcendent order, one which is beyond our immediate experience. Along with this reluctance, of course, goes a more formal dismissal of the idea of a personal God.

The dramatic way to put this, is to follow the Nietzschean prophetic tragedy and announce, "God is dead!" The prophet has the right to witness to God's death as the preacher witnesses to his life. But the analytic person is more careful. Denis de Rougemont properly scorns those who gave the phrase popularity, repeated it as self-evident, and formed schools of thought around the announcement. Similarly, he is critical of Christians who take the rhetoric of the statement too seriously.

[7] See M. Holmes Hartshorne, *The Faith to Doubt* (Englewood Cliffs, N.J.: Prentice-Hall, 1963) and Ignace Lepp, *Atheism in Our Time*, trans. Bernard Murchland, C.S.C. (New York: Macmillan, 1963).

Have we ever asked any of those who say that God is dead just what they mean by such an assertion? What God is dead? The God they imagine, or the God to whom so many people pray? A convenient caricature, or the First Person of the Trinity? The God about whom philosophers speculate, or the God whom prophets announce? A psychological attitude, or an ontological reality? Or is God only a password in the new conformism? To insist upon a little honest clarity would be a way of pointing out to these modern writers a few of the inextricable difficulties into which their assertions plunge not only their own but all Western thought.

Theirs is not a mere romantic indulgence: "As far as I'm concerned, God no longer exists." They insist on novelty in their message, and in the objectivity of their news. Philosophically, the sentence is nonsensical, says de Rougemont. Historically, similar problems are present. If the Eternal God had lived and then died, he would not have been the Eternal God. If God the Unknowable were dead, we would be saying we know everything, which is also absurd. If the Revealed God were dead, "an unprecedented cosmic event would have occurred in time and space (but where and when?). . . . If the scriptural revelation of the Living God is considered problematical, what are we to say of the upside-down revelation [Nietzsche and Sartre] offer us?"

Of course, de Rougemont's analysis helps us only negatively: it does not produce a living God, either. What can be stated is that the God hidden and revealed in Christian belief "is unbelievable to many contemporary minds." Sartre says: Once he spoke and now he is silent. This means: At least *we* cannot hear him. The silence of God and the deafness of man represent observable phenomena; they make talk of the originality of unbelief possible and help it to rise above the absurd.

What have we gained? We still have to reckon with the fact that today's thoughtful unbeliever is not moved by arguments

over the existence of God. It has often been observed that Paul,
who among the Athenians on Mars Hill was able to deliver a
sermon on God which was greeted as a scandal when he
preached Christ's resurrection, would today not gain a hearing
past the first line.

All these demonstrations may seem sensible and convincing to one who believes in the existence of God. But modern
man, who no longer has faith, will never be convinced of
God's existence through such artificial and complicated ar-
gumentations. Fundamentally, they all presuppose faith; in
fact, they merely transpose the act of faith into the medium
of rational thinking, and this is their true philosophical significance.

Christian faith has never been dependent on proving the existence of God, and many today feel that the faith is less bur-
dened since it is no longer possible to interest people in the
proof. But a situation is novel when people cannot be interested in the attempt.

Étienne Borne puts it well: "There is now an attempt to up-
root and destroy not only God but the very ideas of religion and
salvation." Christian apologists make of this what they can.
Karl Rahner, S.J., sees in the uprooting of the idea of transcendence a liberation of God (in the minds of man), for "God
is not a piece of the world, but its presupposition." The fact
that

the world has become an entity rounded off in itself, which
is neither actually open at certain points where it merges
into God, nor undergoes at certain observable points the
causal impact (*ursächlichen Stoss*) of God (if we disregard
for the moment the supernatural dispensation of salvation);
but it points to God as its presupposition only as a whole,
and even not so obviously. Today man realizes that this is so,

having gradually acquired a scientific concept of the world
that is just as profane as the world itself, which is not God.

We may concur with Rahner that there are benefits in the
view which sees a radical breach between God and the world,
but historically it represents a different problem for Christian
apologists than when the transcendent was seen to break into
the finite order, in the common opinion of the scientific community.

God as an object tends to disappear from concerns in the
community of letters (and in the theological tradition which,
coping with this problem, also stresses the subjective relation
to God). Philosopher C. E. M. Joad refers to modern civilization's "dropping of the object" (by which he means God, abso-
lutes, objective values, located in an order which is not in
time and space). André Malraux consistently speaks of "the end
of the absolute." Gerhard Szczesny, as disturbed over *ersatz*
objective religions as he is over historic faith, distinguishes
between religions which concentrate on the object and those
which focus on the subject or the subjective. Christian objecti-
vism and objective religiosity tend to disappear. "While the
objectivists were discovering that there was simply no more
room in the world for the personal and autonomous God of
Christian representation, the subjectivists were revealing that
the Christian idea of God was nothing more than a sublime
projection of human attributes."

To C. E. Ayres the "dropping of the object" does not yet
appear to have been complete. The result is a half-sacred, half-
secular world which lacks the best of either and produces
moral agnosticism. "As we have learned more and more about
the world we live in, and have learned to do more and more
with it, otherworldly considerations have dropped farther and
farther into the background of our everyday life. But they
have by no means disappeared." The experience of man in
such a time is confusing. William F. Lynch, S.J., has put it

well: "There never was a time when the mind was more affected by the terrible remoteness of God. For many he has
never seemed less immanent." [8]

4

With the general disinterest in a transcendent order, men
experience an aloneness in the cosmos and come to be content
with this experience.

Once again, a number of witnesses suggest that the corollary
of a loss of faith in a transcendent order (and a hidden God)
is a change—some would call it a loss—in the sense of man's
identity and especially in his sense of relation to the world
of nature and history. "Now that the idea of God has dipped
below the horizon," says Martin C. D'Arcy, S.J., "man has
ceased to be able to see himself and what he is or should be."
D'Arcy quotes a parable of man's aloneness in nature which
sets the scene well:

Once upon a time two explorers came upon a clearing in
the jungle. In the clearing were growing many flowers and

[8] For the discussion of the phrase "God is dead!" see Denis de Rougemont, *The Christian Opportunity,* trans. Donald Lehmkuhl (New York:
Holt, Rinehart and Winston, Inc., 1963), pp. 4, 7. On the disinterest in
proofs, see Erich Frank, *Philosophical Understanding and Religious Truth*
(New York: Oxford University Press, 1945), p. 29. Étienne Borne is quoted
from *Atheism,* trans. S. J. Tester (New York: Hawthorn, 1961), p. 71.
Karl Rahner discusses "the world an entity to itself" in "Wissenschaft
als Konfession?" in *Wort und Wahrheit, IX* (November, 1954), 811-813. The
reference to Joad is from his *Decadence: A Philosophical Inquiry* (London:
Faber & Faber, 1948), pp. 248-249. Gerhard Szczesny devotes many pages of
his *The Future of Unbelief,* trans. Edward B. Garside (New York: Braziller,
1961), to the objective-subjective distinction, but see especially pp. 93, 112.
C. E. Ayres, *Toward a Reasonable Society* (Austin: University of Texas
Press, 1961), p. 39, is devoted to the partial loss of the sense of transcendence. Finally, see Lynch, *The Integrating Mind* (New York: Sheed & Ward,
1962), pp. 98 f.

many weeds. One explorer says: "Some gardener must tend this plot." The other disagrees, "There is no gardener." So they pitch their tents and set a watch. No gardener is ever seen. "But perhaps he is an invisible gardener." So they set up a barbed wire fence. They electrify it. They patrol it with bloodhounds. . . . But no shrieks ever suggest that some intruder has received a shock. No movements of the wire ever betray an invisible climber. The bloodhounds never give a cry. Yet still the Believer is not convinced. "But there is a gardener, invisible, intangible, insensible to electric shocks, a gardener who has no scent and makes no sound, a gardener who comes secretly to look after the garden he loves." At last the Sceptic despairs: "But what remains of your original assertion? Just how does what you call an invisible, intangible, eternally elusive gardener differ from an imaginary gardener or even from no gardener at all?"

The common man does not wait around as long as the deliberative philosophers who tell the story and discuss it or as long as the explorers who people it. He needs a catharsis and has provided it in the public realm today. Mircea Eliade, himself a student of the religious impulse and inclined to find such impulses wherever possible, has observed, apparently in a way contradictory to his own vocation: "Modern man's originality, his newness in comparison with traditional societies, lies precisely *in his wish to live* in a basically desacralized cosmos." (Italics added.) The volitional element suggests that man, sensing his aloneness, finds some aid by taking action and choosing to see nothing sacral in his universe.

There is a broad concurrence among observers on this most important point. John Courtney Murray, S.J., in the essay which states our problem, undertakes a pithy but accurate historical summary, and then ventures for the broad brush:

"One would have to say that the modern godless man is characterized by his will to understand and explain the world without God." While this change may only involve "the God of explanation," yet it *does,* in fact, represent change and originality. This "godless man who is typical of the postmodern era is . . . [without] prototype in history; he is a new phenomenon."

So far has he moved from "the God of explanation" that for him the nineteenth-century's "warfare between science and religion" is all over; no reconciling is necessary. Today the issue is the quest for any kind of meaning in life in a secular world. For this reason, not all men will evidence the clear volition that Eliade suggests. Many of them, in the absence of the Incarnation, cope with aloneness by drifting. Thus Federico Fellini, the motion-picture director:

> Like many people, I have no religion and I am just sitting in a small boat drifting with the tide. I live in the doubts of my duty. . . . I think there is dignity in this, just to go on working. . . . This is the way things are, you say, now what are we to do? Today we stand naked, defenceless, and more alone than at any time in history. We are waiting for something, perhaps another miracle, perhaps the Martians. Who knows?

Christian believers, of course, are not exempt from the pervasive tendencies of the time. Whoever has sat under the pulpit of a prophet knows the extent to which the disappearance of "the Christian mind" is bewailed in the churches. British Anglican layman Harry Blamires makes this disappearance the theme of all his writing. The mind of modern man "has been deprived of any orientation toward the supernatural. Tragic as this fact is, it would not be so desperately tragic had the Christian mind held out against the secular drift." The Christian-secular dialogue has broken down because there is no distinctive Christian mind and tongue.[9]

5

In the areas of the world where the church has been established it is being displaced.

On few points in the composite is there more widespread agreement than on this, in the words of Gerhard Szczesny, that while the "events of our century certainly have not led to a renascence of the Christian faith" they have "brought about a revival of the secular currency and authority of Christianity." That is, as institutions the churches hold considerable political power and the allegiance of great numbers of people. But as forces to shape the ideas of the day, they have been losing their place. There is nothing new about Christianity being a minority voice in the world. What is original is that, on a worldwide scale, there is a growing sense that it has been tried and has failed, that it was established and now deserves to be disestablished or merely to be allowed to survive in a harmless way. (We shall discuss this subject later. See "Unbelief within the Christian orbit," pp. 177-186.)

In the United States the popular disinterest in organized religion is not so obvious. Sixty-four per cent of the population is affiliated with a church or a synagogue, and a much larger percentage thinks of itself as related to a religious institution. In

9 Martin C. D'Arcy, *No Absent God* (New York: Harper & Row, 1962), pp. 13, 16. The "gardener" illustration originated with Antony Flew and Alasdair MacIntyre. Eliade is quoted by Thomas Altizer in "Mircea Eliade and the Recovery of the Sacred," *Christian Scholar*, XLV, No. 4 (Winter, 1962), 267. See also Murray, "The Structure of the Problem of God," *Theological Studies*, XXIII, No. 1 (March, 1962), 19, 21. Fellini is quoted in M. V. C. Jeffreys, *Personal Values in the Modern World* (Baltimore: Penguin, 1962), p. 87. Harry Blamires, *The Christian Mind* (New York: Seabury, 1963), is of interest for its whole argument; see especially Chap. 1, "The Surrender to Secularism."

England or Scandinavia, where only a small percentage of the population pays attention to the weekly life of the church, the disaffection is more apparent. Hard-core resistance in Germany or France must be reckoned with in any discussion of unbelief or secularization. The countries under Soviet dominance have not had the opportunity to see a renaissance of church life.

An example of the church's awareness of this problem is the profound pastoral letter of Emmanuel Cardinal Suhard, the Cardinal Archbishop of Paris, in 1947. Suhard, asking, "Who Will Unite the World?" found the church impotent because of its own decline. "Today what she herself calls 'the apostasy of the masses' proves her failure. . . . Through a thousand crevices she is dissolving and she sees whole peoples breaking away from her one after the other. . . . She no longer holds the attention of men." It was precisely for this task that the church was seen to be important in the definition of faith: to be the witness, to gain attention, to summon people to faith. In the church the word of God is professed to be preached, and Christian tradition is guarded and dispensed.

Many outside the church have tried to suggest the root of the problem, though few have done so as persuasively as Cardinal Suhard. We are not interested here in the social faults of the church or its identification with losing political powers, but with the issue of belief as such. A philosopher and a pundit speak for many at this central place. Alfred North Whitehead spoke for Protestantism's problem in 1933, but all Christians could read themselves into it: "Its dogmas no longer dominate; its divisions no longer interest; its institutions no longer direct the patterns of life." As long ago as 1914, Walter Lippmann could say that the church was no longer being valued for incarnating human desires. It was answering questions that were not being asked and refusing to face those that were. Attempts by liberal Christianity to adapt to the modern world were often pathetic in character. At a German lay academy in 1949 a German governor set forth the situation of church people in these terms:

> We should be blind indeed if we did not observe that the overwhelming majority of our [church] people have been inwardly secularized. Only a small minority, an almost insignificant minority, live in faith and by faith.

The variety of examples—a German agnostic, a French cardinal, an American philosopher, an American political commentator, a German provincial governor—all these hardly provide a systematic picture, and exceptions could be found. But the instances do add to the composite picture of a lack of contemporary interest in the church as the summons to belief.[10]

6

Modern unbelief represents originality not in the sense of surprise but as the decisive culmination of a centuries-long process of secularization.

The histories of the church in the modern world, even though they can be given over to the record of the most noted expansion of the believing community in twenty centuries, still find their themes set by potent forces outside the church.

[10] Szczesny, *op. cit.*, p. 11. *The Church Today, Growth or Decline*, trans. James J. Corbett (Notre Dame, Ind.: Fides, 1948), is Cardinal Suhard's statement. He discusses the decline of the church, pp. 17 ff. In the introduction, John Courtney Murray says that it is a "commonplace that the crisis is worldwide. But what is less commonly insisted on is the fact that the crisis is fundamentally the same the world over. This is a unique historical fact" (p. 9). Whitehead is quoted in Winthrop S. Hudson, *American Protestantism* (Chicago: University of Chicago Press, 1961), p. 166. See Walter Lippmann, *A Preface to Politics* (Ann Arbor, Mich.: University of Michigan Press, 1962), p. 174. First published in 1914, this book deserves comparison with the same author's *A Preface to Morals* as early, comprehensive statements of twentieth-century unbelief in America.

James Hastings Nichols' *History of Christianity 1650-1950* is subtitled, "Secularization of the West." Alec R. Vidler titles his work *The Church in an Age of Revolution,* and the usually exuberant Kenneth Scott Latourette also lets world revolution stamp his five volumes, *Christianity in a Revolutionary Age.* Of course, the process has not all been one-way, and Bishop Gustaf Aulén's intentionally imprecise description of the result is perhaps as accurate as one should wish it to be: What has been produced is a "more or less secularized humanity."

The history of secularization could make a separate book, a separate library of books. All the disciplines of life, the academies, the arts and crafts and vocations, the entertainments, the churches themselves, experienced the progressive cutting off of realm after realm from its rootage in the West in a view of divine intervention in the world of men. The initial shock— and still for many the most profound—was the dislocating experience of astronomy. Man was edged out of centrality and his world replaced at an obscure and unstable corner of an expanding universe. Where was God, who had been "up there" or "out there"? The God of explanation began to disappear from realm after realm. The separation of church and state in the political order removed God and church from their formal legal base in society. The disciplines of political and social science, sociology, critical history, biblical criticism, psychology, comparative religion—each of these served, as it developed, to remove from consideration the God who had been the x of human equations. What had been explained, through a veil of mystery or behind a pillar of dogma, now met natural explanation. "We turn toward God only to obtain the impossible," said Shestov. "As for the possible, men suffice." The fields of philosophy, the arts and literature, relied less and less on a view of the transcendent, even though they are assigned the task of piercing the limits of normal experience.

Man himself seemed to be threatened when the processes of history were secularized into messianism by Karl Marx and his successors; when Charles Darwin and his school explained away man's special origins; when Sigmund Freud and his disciples probed the subconscious of man and came up with natural explanations for mysterious behavior.

Exceptions in practical living are permitted in the free world. But the *logic* of modern philosophy, as John Courtney Murray contends, is atheist; so is that of modern politics. "Religious faith and secular faith are mixed in modern man," comments Gustave Weigel, S.J. "He knows that the melange is producing malaise, but he stubbornly refuses to drop either the old or the new." What about America?

> We pay lip service to religion and the churches, but actually our action as a nation rests on naturalistic secularism. No one has given us a systematic expression of this theory but elements of it are clear enough. It is an amalgam of skepticism, empiricism and pragmatism. It despairs of knowing reality in itself and restricts its knowledge to what is experienced. . . . This naturalism will permit no appeal to anything not enmeshed in the order of the experimental.

The religious quest is itself secularized, apart from reference to the religious object. From Benjamin Franklin to William James, this quest was carried on in the United States through a focus of interest "on how whatever people believed or wanted to believe overshadowed whatever might be out there in the 'real' world."

Practical daily living takes on a different cast, even among the religious. Says British psychologist Eugene Rolfe, "Almost all of us nowadays conduct our lives for all practical purposes as if God did not exist." Man is "trebly alienated: a stranger to God, to nature, and to the gigantic social apparatus that supplies his material wants," says William Barrett in his summary of the secularizing process.

Religion, before this phase set in, had been a structure that encompassed man's life, providing him with a system of images and symbols by which he could express his own aspirations toward psychic wholeness. With the loss of this containing framework man became not only a dispossessed but a fragmentary being.

No judgment is herewith passed on the future implications for faith as a result of secularization. Later it will be indicated that secularity may have new promise for faith; now it is noted as another part in the cluster which makes up the originality of modern unbelief.[11]

7

Contemporary secularism is not consistently atheistic. It has produced a remarkable assortment of *ersatz* faiths, ideologies, and philosophies of history.

The virtue of a restricted working definition of unbelief,

[11] For an adequate historical summary of the scientific and literary development toward the secular, see Franklin L. Baumer, *Religion and the Rise of Scepticism* (New York: Harcourt, Brace, 1960). Nichols' book is published by Ronald Press of New York (1956); Vidler's, by Pelican (Baltimore, 1961); Latourette's five volumes by Harper & Row (New York, 1958 ff.). Shestov is quoted in Albert Camus, *The Myth of Sisyphus* (New York: Vintage, 1959), p. 25. C. F. von Weizsäcker, *The History of Nature* (Chicago: University of Chicago Press, 1949), is a full-length discussion of the secularization of nature, the desacralization of the scientific order. Many problems raised by secularization in the literary realm are discussed in Stanley Hopper (ed.), *Spiritual Problems in Contemporary Literature* (New York: Harper & Row, 1957). The statements on the atheistic logic of modern philosophy and politics are from Murray, *op. cit.*, p. 20. Gustave Weigel, *The Modern God* (New York: Macmillan, 1963), is a representation of the problem of society when religion coexists with secularism; see especially pp. 26, 32. On William James, see Daniel J. Boorstin, *The Image* (New York: Atheneum, 1962), p. 212. Eugene Rolfe, *The Intelligent Agnostic's Introduction to Christianity* (London: Skeffington, 1959), p. 19, is the source for comment on daily living; see also William Barrett, *Irrational Man* (Garden City, N.Y.: Doubleday, 1962), p. 35.

such as we proposed, stands out most clearly here. For the people who live in the secularized world are not necessarily beliefless. We are speaking of unbelief as an event, an historic phenomenon especially on Euro-American soil and in reference to the Christian faith. Those who have studied the man of today are not agreed on what is at the root of beliefs in a secularized society. For this reason the word "pluralist" has attained a wide vogue. Many beliefs and no beliefs combine in the contemporary picture.

Paul Tillich, who uses a broad definition of religion, finds almost no unbelievers. After surveying the faith of humanism, he says,

It is almost ridiculous to speak of the loss of faith in the Western secular world. It has a secular faith, and this has pushed the different forms of religion into a defensive position; but it is faith and not "unbelief." It is a state of ultimate concern and total devotion to this concern.

Helmut Thielicke describes the process:

1. Whenever God the Creator is deposed as the absolute and sovereign Lord of the world and our life, the *gods take over.*

2. But whenever the false gods are enthroned, there is always *conflict between the gods. . . .*

3. Whenever God is deposed and the false gods are worshiped, the result is always a *twilight of the gods. . . .*

The late Waldensian professor at Rome, Giovanni Miegge, contends less optimistically that man today has opted not for theism but for pantheism:

On the modern world-view God is everywhere and nowhere. The two expressions may be regarded as synonymous.

They do mean, however, that it is by no means easy to reconcile such a world-view with belief in God; it seems almost inseparably connected with a pantheistic or atheistic understanding of things. It is, however, possible to raise the question whether this pantheistic attitude is in reality the corollary of a purely *scientific* interpretation of the world; or whether it is in fact due simply to the fact that modern man in the depths of his being has made a declaration in favour of pantheism and against theism.

Rosalind Murray insists that "the contemporary world is Pagan in every sense in which the word is used." The options are many, depending upon the contexts of the authors. But most of them agree that the secularization of the West has not left a vacuum but a terrain filled with images and idols and ideologies.[12]

8

In the mixed sacred and secular cultural setting there is a widespread agreement that men need not seek a consensus to form community and be productive.

Most societies have conceived of themselves as being rooted in a single religious or ideological matrix. In a sense this is still true, but the basis becomes so broadened (e.g., pluralism as the agreed-upon ground rule of a free society) that it has little of the element of judgment as regards the workings of the society. It may well be demonstrable that each society has at heart one real religion or belief-system. But men today are more ready

[12] These examples are from Paul Tillich, *The Dynamics of Faith* (New York: Harper & Row, 1957), p. 69; Helmut Thielicke, *Christ and the Meaning of Life* (New York: Harper & Row, 1962), p. 131; Giovanni Miegge, *Gospel and Myth in the Thought of Rudolf Bultmann* (Richmond, Va.: John Knox, 1960), p. 94; Rosalind Murray, *The Good Pagan's Failure* (London: Fontana, 1962), p. 16.

than in the past to live in contentment without finding a consensus.

Some of this was implied in the sentence of Professor Paul
Ramsey to which we referred earlier: "Ours is the first attempt
in recorded history to build a culture upon the premise that
God is dead." If the criticisms of the rhetorical statement "God
is dead" are in place, then this sentence could be translated:
"Ours is the first attempt in recorded history to build a culture
upon the premise that it is not important for the workings of
man and society whether or not God is present." This may be
what Martin Buber calls "an epoch of homelessness," but humans prove to be durable beings and they soon cope with their
epoch, whether or not they consciously seek another kind of
time.

A culture without a consensus forces different kinds of tasks
on its citizens. Romano Guardini has prophesied:

> The rapid advance of a non-Christian ethos . . . will be
> crucial for the Christian sensibility. As unbelievers deny Rev-
> elation more decisively, as they put their denial into more
> consistent practice, it will become the more evident what it
> really means to be a Christian. At the same time, the unbe-
> liever will emerge from the fogs of secularism. He will cease
> to reap benefit from the values and forces developed by the
> very Revelation he denies. He must learn to exist honestly
> without Christ and without the God revealed through Him;
> he will have to learn to experience what this honesty means.
> . . . A new paganism differing from that of earlier ages will
> appear in the new world.

Christians of a pastoral inclination will concern themselves
most of all with the former problem. Thus Abbé Godin writes
in his book *France, Pagan?* of the problem of the believing
community:

It is not merely anarchists, or fallen girls, or professional boxers who cannot be integrated into a parochial community. It is the people of Paris as a whole—educated as they have been with no trace of Christianity. . . . It is almost every man we know in our regiment—and in the regiments of many of our fellow-priests—who will never become Christians by joining a group that they cannot help looking on as a world apart. . . .

Other Christians and self-conscious unbelievers will concern themselves with Romano Guardini's second group: those who must form society and build culture without a consensus based on a belief-system. What worries them is that "the 'age of disbelief' is . . . an age of 'disturbed or deformed belief,' " to quote F. H. Heinemann. It is too simple a matter to suggest that some monolith like "the scientific world view" can fuse society. We have been well reminded that such a view is also a fiction; not since Newton's time can we properly speak of *the* scientific world view. We possess a scientific method and many world views based on it, but they are not integrated. Others point to the fact that as the religious sphere lost importance, "work" took on incommensurate status. But work also is not all-embracing. Technology has its place as the basis of interpreting society; to the nations far removed from Euro-American religion, technology has been the most effective missionary force for the West. It, too, is merely another element which strives to be seen as basic but which, in part, contradicts other elements.[13]

13 Guardini's essay is reprinted in Barry Ulanov, *Contemporary Catholic Thought* (New York: Sheed & Ward, 1963), pp. 172 f. Tom Allan, *The Face of My Parish* (New York: Harper & Row, 1957), p. 38, reproduces the words of Abbé Godin. On the problem of deformed belief, see F. H. Heinemann, *Existentialism and the Modern Predicament* (New York: Harper & Row, 1958), especially pp. 7 f. Albert N. Wells, *The Christian Message in a Scientific Age* (Richmond, Va.: John Knox, 1962), p. 651, describes the absence of *the* scientific world view. Bruno Bettelheim stresses the failure of work to unify society in an essay, in Erik H. Erikson (ed.), *Youth: Change*

9

Insofar as community is based on communication, it is jeopardized by the pluralistic character of the modern secular culture; the symbolic order has disintegrated.

Federico Fellini's motion picture *La Dolce Vita* is a film whose form and content depict the confusion of modern community. In one scene, its central figure, the journalist Marcello, sits down at the organ in the church of his acquaintance Father Franz. After a few notes of jazz, followed by a frown from the priest, Marcello tries a few serious chords. Then his friend Steiner sits down at the organ and begins to play some Bach. He says as he plays, "These are sounds we have forgotten how to hear. What a mysterious voice; it seems to come from the bowels of the earth." The scene ends. The gesture and the words are typical of what is coming to be called "the breakdown of symbol." Man's relation to nature is broken, so that he cannot derive unifying symbols from it. The varieties of belief and unbelief in the society cause him to mistrust the central myths of his history. Real communication is rare, for in one sense, says Karl Jaspers, "only those with a belief can have effective communication."

The roots of the breakdown are deep and long; the historical occasion for the malaise developed over long periods of Christian history and in the experience of Europe. The nominalist philosophy, which kept or allowed for belief in a transcendent God, but which focused concerns on the empirical, on human particulars, helped to establish the problem: "Nominalism," says George Tavard, "tended to increase the distance between the word of God and the words of men," and God's speech seemed or was less audible.

---

and Challenge (New York: Basic Books, 1963), p. 91. Arnold Toynbee, *America and the World Revolution* (New York: Oxford University Press, 1962), p. 43, provides comment on the missionary success of technology.

As a corollary to man's disinterest in the transcendent order and his refusal to see the historical sign of God's activity in Jesus Christ, there developed a "natural" view of the world. This, coupled with the nominalist philosophy, served to sever man's daily consciousness from the sacral or sacramental order and to jeopardize the symbolic ties between the two. Literary historian Erich Heller has graphically illustrated the transition by reference to an event in 1529 at Marburg, Germany. There Martin Luther and Ulrich Zwingli, leaders of parallel church reform movements in Germany and Switzerland, met in the attempt to unite forces; they parted without agreement. Between them stood the issue of "the predicament of the symbol" and the split between reality and what it signifies. The only conceivable order of things among moderns is the "tidy relationship between things themselves," the "positivist-scientific." Zwingli was on the side of the future in anticipating this view.

In their discussion of the bread and wine of the Lord's Supper, Luther contended for a sacramental model of reality. This bread *is* Christ's body, Luther insisted; this wine *is* Christ's blood, through a sacramental union. Zwingli responded that they were allegories or representations, mere symbols. "From then onwards the word 'merely' has been attaching itself ever more firmly to the word 'symbol,' soon gaining sufficient strength to bring about a complete alienation between the two spheres. Finally a new order of things emerged." While at that time the transcendental order was allotted high honors, it was "skilfully deprived of a considerable measure of reality."

Without a commonly accepted order of interconnections between the mundane and the transcendent, and especially after loss of interest in the transcendent, art, literature, human communication, became problematic. Private symbols had to serve, and they serve less well than commonly accepted references to a reality behind appearances. Modern unbelief has

learned to live with this absence of universal symbols throughout culture.[14]

We have asked what are the original elements in modern unbelief, steadfastly refusing to place importance on the mere
statistical change or size of the believing communities. The
method used was one in which numbers of witnesses have
been called in. In general, this anthology of references has
leaned, where possible, to the most recent. It has been ecumenical; that is, the many kinds of subcultures in Europe and
America have been represented; Christian and non-Christian
have been welcomed. If there has been a preponderance, it has
been toward Roman Catholic churchmen and theologians.
They have been most concerned, presumably having the most
to see changed by modern unbelief. At the same time, their
credibility is enhanced by the fact that Catholics often tend to
view cultural crisis with less panic than do other Christians,
who may take foreshortened views of history. In general we
have extended preference toward moderate spokesmen, shun-
ning those who strive for effect by talk about "the death of
God" which may be legitimate but, in our context, is confusing.

Without doubt some historians, theologians, and social critics could be brought upon the scene who would view things in
a different way. There may be some who find only impotence in
unbelief, who see a worldwide surge of Christian belief. But I
believe our sources are both representative and responsible reporting. Similarly, some elements could be added and some sub-

14 See Federico Fellini, *La Dolce Vita,* trans. Oscar DeLiso and Bernard
Shir-Cliff (New York: Ballantine, 1961), p. 89. Jaspers is quoted in a mean-
ingful study of community and communication, in Rudolf Bultmann,
Essays Philosophical and Theological, trans. C. G. Greig (London and New
York: Macmillan, 1955), p. 300. The reference to nominalism is from
George Tavard, *Holy Writ or Holy Church* (New York: Harper & Row,
1959), p. 80. Erich Heller's full discussion should be read. The specific
references are from *The Disinherited Mind* (New York: Meridian, 1959),
pp. 212 f. and 267 ff.

tracted from the composite without doing violence to it. When one is forced to deal with generalizations of this scope, hazard is involved. Yet we are better off with some family portrait of modern unbelief, even if at certain points the lines are too bold; at others, too blurred; and at still others, somewhat distorted. We shall have occasion to test many features of this group picture in later chapters. Here we have been content to suggest the varieties of responses to modern unbelief and to show how, by the definition of belief in the previous chapter, its opposite, unbelief, does indeed exist in today's world.

5 Two Types of Unbelief

A host of witnesses can be invoked to suggest the extent and variety of unbeliefs in the contemporary world. The concurrence and consensus of such a varied group of students of the modern spirit may be impressive. The net result, in the mind of someone who surveys their evidences, may be paralyzing and defeating. How can one find his way through the bewildering variety? Must busy people, Christian believer and nonbeliever alike, in order to live out their practical lives and fulfill their vocations, become museum-keepers of the interesting specimens of unbelief? Is it important to be able to run around with labels to pin on every victim within easy range? To take a concrete example, should a Christian clergyman become a sort of "clerical snooper" who cannot satisfy himself until he has diagnosed every symptom of deviation from traditional faith? These are practical questions which should color the discussion in the rest of this book.

We should like to hypothesize a distinction between the types or varieties of unbelief, and test it later by examining certain phenomena today. By reducing the subject from the paralyzing variety depicted above to two broad possibilities, I am well aware that I am risking oversimplification and facile generalization. The risk seems necessary, but it can be minimized if the distinction is set forth with caution.[1]

The attempt to define two broad types of belief and unbelief is practical and justifies the risk of misunderstanding, for various reasons. The modern world is pluralistic—that is, a variety of belief-systems coexist. Adherents of competitive systems, as they choose to live in isolation by totally rejecting each other, are themselves better served if they understand alternatives. The vast majority of people in free societies will, if the responsibilities are presented to them, look for other alternatives than

1 At the very least, the attempt will redeem me in the eyes of any reader who may have felt that I failed to commit myself in the previous chapter!

those implied by the act of rejection. In a world of interaction, of criss-crossing purposes and alliances, it is difficult for anyone to be a complete person or to live in a sane society and still contend that he can "go it alone."

The coexisting believing and unbelieving communities, when they come into positive interaction, tend to do so in at least three ways. First, there are attempts by members of each to convert members of the other. Although these attempts can be portrayed as threats, they are often genuinely well meant and may proceed with a high regard for other persons. In such cases they are motivated by a kind of love which pictures another's state as improved if he should change his belief-system. They can be undertaken on lines that are considered by both parties to be ethically legitimate. All interaction, all dialogue, offers some risk. All announced openness to witness and conversion is an invitation to attempts to convert.

Where attempts are made to induce voluntary conversions, they will enhance the ability of members of two kinds of believing communities to have reasonably coherent views of themselves, their communities, and their beliefs. The process will also aid them in understanding others. Much misunderstanding can be prevented, and time and labor saved. Defining types of unbelief or belief means nothing more than circumscribing, limiting, and clarifying subjects.

Second, communication not accompanied by a desire to convert also demands some definition. Within the Christian community, conversations take place between Roman Catholics and Protestants. Great numbers of people take part in these without any conscious purpose of converting the other (though, admittedly, conversions would not always be rebuffed by either party should they be accidental by-products!). Here again the values of definition become clear. A working and simplifying typology helps people to produce somewhat coherent views of themselves so that these selves can be presented to others. The speaker of gibberish, the madman, the

devotee of chaos, can convey only a private vision. Those responsible for sustained communal life and habitual interrela-
tions of people seek clarity.

A third kind of relation is expressed in a variety of temporary, strategic, alliances between those who hold differing belief-systems. They unite for other goals and goods (whether
greater or smaller than those which hold the subcommunities
together). They are best served if, when the need for alliance
has passed, they remain intact communities. They will do so if
they have defined and understood each other. For example,
American Jews and secularists may creatively unite to gain a
certain legal goal in a free society which may limit the liberties
of either because neither belongs to a Christian majority. But
after the court cases are over, the Jew goes back to the community of his belief and the secularist to his. Neither has wanted,
or needed, to adopt the whole system of the other. Both may
serve the free society if they keep their identities and can form
different alliances on different issues. Thus the believing Jew
may unite with the Roman Catholic in his desire to infuse the
national life with spirituality; the secularist and the Protestant
may unite to see that Roman Catholicism does not establish itself in a way that may limit the particular liberties of others.
To form such alliances and later to break them, it is not necessary for all members of each community to be expert in the belief-systems of others. But they do need handles for holding,
instruments for reading the broad intention of those who hold
to other beliefs.

Any definition which is to serve in these three kinds of inter-
actions will need to bear certain characteristics or to fill certain
expectations. It should be *useful* for these purposes. It should
be *inclusive* enough that most of the important factors of a
system can be recognized when it is employed. Such a definition should be *exclusive* enough that it will represent real and
fundamental differences between value clusters, even though
minor exceptions or variants or coincidences prevail between

them. It should be *matter of fact*, not startlingly original; that
is, it should appeal to a consensus of observers of the systems in
question. It should not be part of a private and personal vocabulary, introduced as a carefully guarded contribution which is
of limited use the moment one steps outside the author's field
of interest. Thus it should be *recognizable* even where it is
never wholly satisfactory on the part of those who hold to the
beliefs which are being summarized. It should enable an ad-
herent to say, "Yes, that is I. Something of what my colleagues
and I profess is represented in that distinction." He who recognizes himself in the distinction, therefore, will also understand
—even where he does not fully agree—the outside observer's
impulse to see logical consequences attendant upon his basic
position. Finally, it should be *neutral*. In the mere stating of
the definitions, there should not be a prejudicing of a case.
People may legitimately opt for one or the other. No outsider's
definition will fully satisfy all these requirements. Who can
ever fully grasp the inner direction, even of a movement or an
impulse of which he is a part? How often is there total consensus between those who share the broad outlines of a system?

With these strictures in mind, we propose that the fundamental distinction between both—types of belief and types of
unbelief—can be summarized in the terms integral or closed
systems and nonintegral or open systems.

Begin with the word the two varieties share: system. Does its
use prejudice the case, in that open system seems to be a contradiction in terms? Not at all, if by system, something other is
understood besides a tight, logical, and wholly satisfying intellectual construct. By system, nothing more is meant than a
sustained, habitual, communal, pattern of a more or less predictable nature. Closed system does refer to the attempt to
tighten and render a whole way of life logically and psychologically valid. But both adjectives can legitimately be used with
the word system.

The terms open and closed are introduced to permit some

verbal variety, to open the door to relief from monotony. They add some color, but are less precise, to my mind, than the terms integral and nonintegral. Integrality is here to carry some of the nuance or weight of the French *intégral* or the German *vollständig*. These are words colored by a history in nations whose experience has allowed for integrality of a kind different from that customarily found on English or American soil; the experience has demanded a verbal accent on the absolute closed-offness of a reality. At the same time, the word integral can be easily understood in this context in its English lineage and on its own right.

Problems are connected with the introduction of this term. Those who are impatient with the applications will possibly feel that it can be used pejoratively. I should like to stress that it will be applied to belief-systems whose adherents would, we must presume, be pleased with its use. They are trying to live up to what the label implies. A Christian believer who hears that someone else is an integral atheist or an integral nationalist may feel that the person so labeled is being consigned to a status he would not seek. If to the Christian it appears as if adherence to a system which integrally closes off the Christian possibility should not be labeled, let us remind him, to borrow W. H. Auden's phrase, that if there are any souls in hell, it is not because they have been sent there, but because hell is where they insist upon being. And is this not the case with non- or anti-Christian patterns of belief? Most people who choose them consciously and hold to them systematically, after or in spite of the fact that they have been confronted with Christianity, are people who delight in taking the consequences of their position. This paragraph, of course, can be read from the opposite angle by a nonbeliever who may feel it unfair to consign anyone to a category such as "integral Christianity"! [2]

More serious problems are presented by the terms implying

2 W. H. Auden, from his chapter on "Anger," in Ian Fleming (ed.), *The Seven Deadly Sins* (New York: Morrow, 1962), p. 87.

integrality in the light of the fact that the author and many readers will readily agree that one must seek "social integration" or "integrity" or "personal integration" in all people, even in those who adhere to a system called nonintegral, or open. Admittedly there could be confusion in the fact that derivatives of the term "integral" may convey different shades of meaning. I shall try to live with the illnesses of the word, making a virtue of necessity in a later chapter when the problem arises of seeing integrated persons develop out of patterns of "open orthodoxy" (or nonintegral systems). Readers who are uneasy are asked to be patient to see the terms applied; to remember the caution with which we are using them; to recall that our first motivation is precision. Needless to say, if someone produces a different term which will as well convey the same general meaning as "integral" does, it should be employed.[3]

Integrality here implies that dictionary usage which speaks of anything that "lacks nothing of completeness; that which is complete or entire." The Oxford English Dictionary sees it "pertaining to a whole"; "made up of component parts which together constitute a unity"; "having no part or element separated, taken away, or lacking; unbroken, whole, entire, complete." Other terms could supplement what is implied when this relates to belief-systems. Those which are integral are in a sense organic; removal of any part would mean death of the whole. They are totalist in their claim upon life and intellect;

---

[3] This overapologetic note is introduced as a way of saying thanks to a discussant at the time of the Rauschenbusch Lectures, where I first made the observation that belief patterns could best be understood under these headings. The spokesman who was uneasy with the choice suggested that different terms be found. His orientation was toward the disciplines of Christian education and the personality sciences, where integrity is always a positive category. He provided me with a problem which consumed many hours of research and thought. Those whom I consulted, however, advised me that the term be retained and explained to avoid confusion.

doubt is destructive to integrality. It anticipates everything, foresees all possibilities and contingencies, attempts to eliminate surprise. As such, it may be a very satisfying vision. Christianity is often portrayed in this fashion as providing all the answers, anticipating *systematically* every eventuality. (Whether or not it is true to say that "Christianity alone has the answers" is a topic for another book.) That which is integral represents the impulse to the psychological closed circle of completeness.

Nonintegral approaches are characterized by their historical, contingent, somewhat more "loose-jointed" and even accidental features. They represent partial instead of total visions. (*"Unser Wissen ist Stückwerk"* is the German translation of Paul's testimony to partiality: "Our knowledge is piecework," spoken by the New Testament apostle in a specific context in I Cor. 13:9.) As such, they may seem less satisfying visions. They refuse to anticipate all possibilities, even when such anticipation may be desired or psychologically beneficial. A nonintegral attitude will tend to be somewhat more pragmatic as opposed to doctrinaire. It represents willingness to be psychologically content with the unfinished circle. If this seems unsatisfying, it may be so, but many psychologists have seen possibilities in it by relating it to the concept of growth. Thus Gordon Allport:

> Few if any of our value-orientations hold the prospect of complete fulfilment. Does any worker for the United Nations, however ardent, really expect a peaceful family of nations in his lifetime? Does the devotee of democracy expect to see his ideal fully realized? The devoutly religious person, however keen his hunger for God, knows that in this world his hunger will not be completely satisfied. Yet all such goals, unattainable as they are, exert a present dynamic effect upon daily conduct, and in so doing direct the course of becoming. How wrong we have been in viewing the process

of growth as a reaction to past and present stimuli, neglect-
ing the dynamics of futurity: of orientation, intention, and
valuation.[4]

It is possible that my choice of substantiating adjectives may
be prejudicing the case for the open systems. It is certainly true
that we shall see more possibility in open patterns. But we can
picture the dedicated Communist, atheist, or Catholic integralist welcoming most of these adjectives and recognizing them as
describing what it is that he accepts and, indeed, advertises. In
our historical moment it would seem as if the burden of ad-
vertisement will fall on those who offer the open systems.

The choice of these two inclusive types can be defended by
historical references. In the modern world the majority of
potent integral systems of politics can be traced to the systematic attempts of Hegel. Similarly, many of the impulses to
cope with unfinishedness or partiality in the world of theology
or philosophy—and even psychology—can be traced to Kierkegaard's rage against "the system." (It was Kierkegaard who, in
The Concept of Dread, showed an awareness of closed-system
unbelief when he spoke of unbelief's "shut-upness.") Kierkegaard spoke for history when he commented on Hegel, "His
work is full of syntheses, while life is full of choices." We hasten
to add that not all modern thought is consciously to be polarized around these two men, but rather that they are symbolic of
extremes in the post-Enlightenment history of ideas.

Integral tendencies may belong to the experiences of specific
peoples. Many have argued that Marxism as a closed view of
the historical process was welcomed on Russian soil because of
a predilection toward it in the Russian spirit. Dostoevsky detected evidences there of what Pascal had called "a Euclidean
intellect" or a geometric mind; that is, one which wants to see
things closed and finished. Pascal had distinguished between
l'esprit géométrique and *l'esprit de finesse,* or the spirit which

4 *Becoming* (New Haven: Yale University Press, 1955), p. 76.

is subtle or acute. The geometrical spirit aspires to those subjects that can be subjected to perfect analysis. Beginning with
certain axioms, it draws logical inferences. Clarity of principle
and necessity of consequence are the results. But, asked Pascal,
is everything capable of being treated in that way? Certainly,
to him, the human mind was not. The philosopher, he contended, should not construct an artificial or abstract man, but
should deal with real ones.

The Russian Nikolai Berdyaev never tired of pointing to
this Euclidean, or maximalist, tendency in Russia. In his study
of Dostoevsky he turned to the novelist's picture of the Grand
Inquisitor as embodying some of this integrality.

> The euclidian mind, full of revolt and self-limitation at
> the same time, tries to improve on the work of God. He cre-
> ated a universal order that is full of suffering and imposed
> on man the intolerable load of freedom and responsibility;
> in the euclidians' world there will be no suffering or respon-
> sibility—or freedom either. That mind necessarily leads to
> the Grand Inquisitor's system, the human ants' nest.[5]

If references to Russia cast the integral tendency in a wholly
unfavorable light, the French spirit can be viewed somewhat
more neutrally. There is broad agreement that the French
hunger for clarity, logic, and definition has inclined the mind
of France toward the closed system. On French soil, integral
nationalism has frequently appeared, and there the adjective
has been formally applied to parties in both state and church.
Charles Maurras, around the turn of the twentieth century,
spoke of his *Action Française* party as "integralist." It was
joined in uncreative alliance with its opposite number, Catholic integralism. The antimodernists "took pride in professing

5 *Dostoevsky,* trans. Donald Attwater (New York: Meridian, 1957), pp.
190 f.

an 'integral Catholicism' and described themselves as 'integral Catholics.' This earned for them and for their ideas the labels 'integrist' and 'integrism.' The object of integrism was to resist modernism by defending dogmatic truth against any attack to which it might be subjected. . . ." [6]

Integralism has remained in Franco-Spanish Catholicism; a Spanish party of *integristas* in the Roman Catholic Church has even at times asked for the condemnation of modern popes who, to their mind, deviated from hyper-traditionalist positions! Cardinal Suhard coped with enduring integrist tendencies in his famous pastoral letter at Paris in 1947.[7]

In Suhard's picture, authentic Catholicism is marked by temporality, contingency, growth, suffering, mystery, historical life. Therefore, it rejects integralism which would reduce the church's variety. The Cardinal saw three principal modes of error to be represented. The first was doctrinal integralism, an excessively dogmatic traditionalism. (It is interesting to note that Suhard sees integrity growing precisely where integralism is challenged.) Second, tactical integralism is found in the fanatic or crusading spirit. It misunderstands the world, the incarnate aspect of the church. Finally, there is moral integralism of the type associated historically (again, on French soil) with Quietism and Jansenism. It is particularly in the French experience that Étienne Borne has seen the pure development of integral atheism, too.[8] French philosophy, with its mathematical

---

[6] See Adrien Dansette, *Religious History of Modern France* (New York: Herder & Herder, 1961), trans. John Dingle, Vol. II, p. 309; see also Book 2, Chap. 7, "The Intellectual Renaissance of Catholicism and the Modernist Crisis." Book 3, Chap. 3, "The Church and the *Action Française* Movement," is an excellent description of Maurras' viewpoint and party.

[7] Suhard, *The Church Today, Growth or Decline*, trans. James J. Corbett (Notre Dame, Ind.: Fides, 1948), pp. 62 ff.

[8] Borne, *Atheism*, trans. S. J. Tester (New York: Hawthorn, 1961), pp. 79 ff., in a discussion of Jean-Paul Sartre, though the category is here ex-

bent (Descartes, Pascal, D'Alembert, Condorcet, Comte, and the amateur Fontenelle had all been mathematicians) bore the integralist stamp, too:

> [In the Enlightenment of Bayle, Voltaire, Fontenelle] apparent skepticism was in fact designed to establish an objective standard of truth to which even revelation would be constrained to bow.[9]

The foregoing references to Roman Catholicism or to Catholicism in general should not be construed to imply that to be Catholic involves one in dogmatic integralism. True, it can be presented as authoritarian to appeal to modern peoples' tendencies to "escape from freedom." Some apologists for Roman or Anglo-Catholicism can be found speaking in such terms. Rosalind Murray advertises "the totalitarian quality of Catholicism" as "its great attraction." [10] It may also be true that "the integrating power of doctrine" can be misconstrued as integralism in a negative sense, so that one "effectually disposes of an opponent and his religious convictions" with the words, "He is dogmatic." [11] Dogma or dogmatic system should not be understood to mean closed unless it so defines itself. Certainly St. Thomas Aquinas, Catholicism's universal teacher and supreme dogmatic systematician, was not an intellectual integralist. If by closed system, Hegel's standard ("The true form in which truth exists can only be the scientific system of truth") is applied, the *Summa theologica* fails to be truth. Thomas abruptly, deliberately, left his system unfinished. He decided to

---

tended to include non-Frenchmen such as Nietzsche and Marx, along with the native sociologist Comte.

9 Leonard M. Marsak (ed.), *French Philosophers from Descartes to Sartre* (New York: Meridian, 1961), pp. 14 f.

10 *The Good Pagan's Failure* (London: Fontana, 1962), p. 76.

11 Joachim Wach, *Sociology of Religion* (Chicago: University of Chicago Press, 1944), p. 38.

fall silent. He argued "within the mystery," and if Aymé Forest is accurate, he can be seen in *une extrême défiance des systèmes.* Despite all the proofs, all the logic, all the system, Thomas held, "We cannot know what God is, but rather only what He is not." "This is the extreme of human knowledge of God: to know that we do not know God, *quod homo sciat se Deum nescire.*" Nor can we get to the heart of history, nature, and creation. "The essence of things is unknown to us." This is not agnosticism; it is contentment with finitude.[12]

Protestantism cannot be seen simply as nonintegral or open; some of the phases of its own dogmatic scholasticism represented closed systems. There are those who argue that some forms of evangelicalism today are dogmatic in this sense. Sir John Wolfenden, of the University of Reading, spoke in detail of the "closed mind" as a Christian problem in an address in 1955. "Minds firmly closed, locked, bolted and barred" were purported to be the best defenders of scriptural revelation, complained Wolfenden.

> I am converted—the Bible is true—those who are converted are children of light, those who are not are in the darkness—the world lieth in the evil one—the wisdom of this world is foolishness with God—my teachers appear to be in the darkness, for they put across to me the world's science which is contrary to the Bible.

Each of these assertions may be based on Christian belief, set in a complicated historical matrix. Codified, they can be elevated to system and used to close off other possibilities.[13] If Russia

[12] Here we concur with, and are dependent upon, Josef Pieper, *Guide to Thomas Aquinas,* trans. Richard and Clara Winston (New York: Pantheon, 1962), pp. 157 ff.

[13] Quoted in A. G. Hebert, *Fundamentalism and the Church* (Philadelphia: Westminster, 1957), pp. 135 ff.

and France have been described as being integralist in instinct, practical-minded America has not been wholly exempt, either. Familiar descriptions of the "Gilded Age" or the period when Social Darwinism held sway (post-Civil War to pre-World War I), one could isolate an ideology:

> In religion, the "truths" were the "laws of God"; in biology or psychology, they were "objective fact"; in philosophy, law, politics, and economics, they were "natural laws." Always they were unchallengeable Truth, an ideological chain protecting America as it was with iron strength.[14]

No society fully develops integralism of either belief or unbelief. Ideologies which are intact on paper develop chinks and cracks and crannies when they are applied to people. Historical change, boredom with the old, wonder, surprise—each of these can induce the first elements of dis-integration. Just as a free society is not completely free and open, so "a completely controlled human society or even a severely controlled one has probably never existed outside of George Orwell's *1984*," [15] and societies which move by persuasion more than by control and coercion must be even more realistic about the degrees of integralism they can generate at best—or worst.

When the distinction between types of unbelief is to be ap-

[14] Eric F. Goldman, *Rendezvous with Destiny* (New York: Knopf, 1956), p. 70. Since several subsequent chapters will be given over to studies of American culture, religion, nationalism, etc., we shall not enlarge on this point here.

[15] Edward L. Walker and Roger W. Heyns, *An Anatomy for Conformity* (Englewood Cliffs, N.J.: Prentice-Hall, 1962), p. 2. The authors (on p. 98) provide a formula for inducing conformity as a system of control in open societies. If sufficiently practical goals are depicted, sufficiently vivid needs aroused, sufficient rewards proferred along the way to the goal, one can produce conformity on a specific issue without bringing about permanent ideological fusion.

plied, it is important to apply it equally to respectable intellectual movements and to practical modes of living. One handicap
in the past discussion of this subject has been the scholars'
predilection for intellectually satisfying integralist systems.
Henri de Lubac, in his haste to discuss the profound literary
expressions of unbelief in the nineteenth century, can bypass
"the everyday type of atheism which crops up in all ages and is
of no particular significance." [16] But if unbelief is sustained in a
way of life, even without an articulate ideology, it deserves the
same kind of serious attention devoted to the intellectual tradition. Millions of people who pay lip service to one system of
ideas may have integrated another system which actually moti-
vates them.

One could turn in a dozen directions for examples, but one is
sufficient: the closed-system hedonism, or sensuality, the popular cult of love that exists in the secularized Western world.
Richard Hoggart, in his excellent study of the popular culture
of Britain, has examined the effect of commercial popular
songs on the lower middle classes. The songs are rooted in
what were once genuine sentiments, and they are thus appre-
hended among the people. Later these sentiments are linked
into a pattern of attitudes which demand a total submission.
Finally,

one may doubt whether there is anything worth bothering
about in the world outside; one may be "cagey" about the
calls to one kind of belief or another; one may find oneself
often unable to cope with the outside world. But there is always love, as a warm burrow. . . .

If there are no values outside the present and the local, if
"religion is out-of-date," then for those whose sense of life is
essentially personal, love may perhaps be inflated to fill the

[16] *The Drama of Atheist Humanism,* trans. Edith M. Riley (New York:
World, 1963), p. vii.

gap, may be not merely linked with religion (as in the older songs) but made a substitute for religion.[17]

No one, no society, no tradition, is exempt from what Father Lynch calls "the totalistic temptation." The temptation offers what is intellectually appealing and psychologically satisfying. Whoever resists the temptation and organizes experience apart from its charms is faced with the task of "integrating the personality" without an integral system. Great numbers of people have been able to be open to history in this fashion, but the quest for the "clear or pure idea, . . . the univocal idea, born of the univocal intelligence, insisting as it does on a kind of absolute unity of thought or feeling and forbidding any muddying of the waters by the introduction of anything so crass or confusing as reality," preoccupies such great numbers of believing and unbelieving intellectuals in the once Christian world that the effects of the search must be scrutinized.

We shall examine two cultural contexts. One of these is conventionally pictured as providing few, if any, integral systems as living alternatives to Christian belief. The other is often seen as the milieu in which post-Christian ideologies close off not only the intellectual communities but the mass of people from the seriousness of Christian belief. Then we shall be free to test the typology of unbelief here depicted on a variety of systems which are present in both environments.

[17] *The Uses of Literacy* (Boston: Beacon, 1957), pp. 189 f. The obviousness, the everyday wisdom of this kind of assertion, should not detract from the fact that its wisdom is congruent with the kind of religion being depicted: obvious, everyday—but not less important than more formally constructed ideologies.

6 The Invisibility of Unbelief

The varieties of unbelief which occur in much of the Western world are obscured from view in the religious life of North America, particularly the United States. The basic distinction between the types of disbelief in Christian revelation seems hardly applicable where measurable disbelief is so rare. Whoever observes the scientific community or the academic, literary, artistic, political, entertainment, and business communities knows well that seldom are these established in such ways that Christian faith is evident. He is intensely aware of the problems and possibilities of secularization in these fields. Yet the secularization does not immediately reveal itself when individual persons are interviewed concerning the content of their beliefs about religion. The apparent absence of unbelief on a broad scale in contemporary America provides the problem which must now be faced: Is American orthodoxy broad enough to exempt one nation from the generally accepted picture of the extent of modern unbelief? Or is the generally accepted picture not valid?

Earlier, nine elements of originality in modern unbelief were isolated. These were derived from a reading of representative observers of the contemporary spiritual scene. If these are reviewed in the light of what is apparent in American religious life, five of the generalizations do not seem to apply; three can be read either way, and only one seems to conform to the worldwide picture.

The first feature was the growing Christian awareness of the extent of modern unbelief and of the non-Christian map. One must seriously question whether the present institutional make-up of culture and religion in the United States serves to intensify this awareness. The literature of the denominations and a content analysis of many sermons suggest that the numerical power of Christianity as a force in world population receives regular stress. "Christianity on the march" becomes a

84

slogan behind missionary motivational literature. Exceptions are numerous, but in general an "invisible shield" separates the faithful American churchgoer from an imaginative involvement in the world of unbelief, if measured from the viewpoint of Christian revelation. The corollary of religion's culturally favored position is the general absence of antitheism or atheism in the United States.

If the geographical extent of those areas of the world untouched by Christianity does not belong to the day-to-day consciousness of most Americans, neither does an awareness of the depth of penetration of the secularization process. Indeed, from the pulpit, "secularism," "materialism," and other vices are regularly scored. But most Americans define their nation and societal life in general in "godly" terms as a contrast to one disapproved form of political life, "atheistic" Communism. The tendency thus to divide the world into two camps does not evoke real self-criticism concerning the question: In what ways is American society an authentically godless society? Some months after the 1963 Supreme Court decision outlawing devotional Bible reading and prayer in public schools, 76 per cent of the people consulted in a Gallup poll disagreed with the decision. Clearly, the majority of the American people carry a national self-image in which religion is somehow a prime constituting element.

While the secularizing of society goes on in ways that are not often comprehensible inside pluralism, the desacralization of nature, of art and industry, of human endeavor, is not regularly perceived. The institutional weight of the churches may be a factor in the religious interpretation of life. At any rate, most Americans do not complain about the many favors shown the churches (tax-exemption, chaplaincies, etc.). These are considered not only a good thing but actually a payment by society to the churches as moral forces for services rendered. As a nation, Americans do not seem to experience the aloneness of man in the cosmos which most students of the West find to be prevalent today. To talk, as these students do, of the church being displaced among the powers has hardly made sense in a decade when the power of organized religion was growing. The Congress of the United States was careful not to offend religious blocs on issues such as Federal aid to parochial education. Voting analysts perceived a clear religious factor in many elections. Church affiliation was still considered an asset in the biography of any man seeking public office. More people joined, attended, supported, served, the churches than ever before. Was America in this respect also an island?

In still another respect the United States seemed superficially, at least, to be an exception. If many other societies were coming to the point of feeling content with an inability to find a religious consensus, this hardly seemed true of the United States. While it defined itself as a pluralistic society and granted great measures of religious freedom to its constituents, this variety appeared against the background of an implied unity. It was often suggested that all the religions at least had enough in common, and all shared enough of the national goals, to be considered part of an overarching spiritual and ideological consensus.

These signs could be read in support of the generalizations *or* in opposition to them. On the issue of the absence of the transcendent note, the evidence was unclear. Certainly there was widespread acceptance of traditional formulas concerning the God who is beyond the created order. But this could be countered by observations of the earthiness, pragmatism, and matter-of-factness of ethical life, which lacked any evidence of transcendent reference.

Nor can one read the process of secularization as a one-way process. If the whole trend of Western life for four centuries seems to be culminating in a time when the God of explanation has disappeared, is this true in America? Not only in the piety of Christian people but also in the sometimes surprising spirituality of the semicommitted, there seemed to be signs which reversed the trend. Many people were seeking God. The breakdown of the symbolic order and the ensuing problem of communication, the final motif in our summary, is a difficult measure to apply to the United States. Had it ever had a unifying order, since it was born in the modern period with its pervasive pluralism? How can one speak of a breakdown of an order which had never existed? How could one expect unifying symbols in a culture which was, from the first, made up of many cultures? From the beginning, the New England Puritan saw a different kind of symbolic tie between the transcendent and the mundane than did the Southern Anglican. How can one speak of an increase of the problem, especially if the long trend of national life was *toward* a sort of spiritual consensus with a development of national symbols?

Only on one point does there seem to be an obvious concurrence between the general views of modern life and the particularity of American detail. The United States has been rich in developing varieties of *ersatz* faiths alongside and inside the religious organizations. The half-belief in superstitions, the varieties of folk piety, the nationalist religions and patriotic sects which take on a quasi-religious character, the prevalence of interest in astrology, the general respect shown any kind of religious expression—all these suggest that Americans, if they deviate from historic Christian norms, exchange them for other theisms or for pantheism and not for atheism.

If on only one point America seems to be in close congruence with the imagery of post-Christian man, we must ask whether this nation is a mutation or an exception. Is it exempt from the spiritual stirrings of the European movements of the day? Many explanations are offered. American political isolationism, prevalent until World War II, may have ruled out some European influence. Anti-Catholicism in the nineteenth century may have trained Protestant America not to draw spiritual sustenance from the millennium and a half of European dominance. This could mean that inhabitants of the New

World would also be exempt from an anti-Christian expression of European provenance. The poet Archibald MacLeish described the frontiersmen's mood. Ahead of them was the grass. Behind were "dead kings and remembered sepulchres." This could be taken as a hypothesis in separating American from European spiritual culture.

Other explanations have been offered for the apparently isolated experience of the United States. The American temper, sometimes called anti-intellectual and always seen to be empirical, protected citizens from ideological expression. The American churches have been too busy caring for the obvious spiritual needs arising from the environment to have time to cope with European intellectual and literary currents (Marxism, Nietzschean thought) until they become incarnated or irretrievably bastardized in political movements (Soviet Communism, Nazism). The American predilection for such terms as "muddling through," "playing it by ear," "experimenting," or "experiencing," might explain how a private experience could be preserved into the latter decades of the twentieth century. The American Revolution was not ideologically as pure as the French or the Russian, and this is adduced as a typical factor. The overlapping of claims and the crowding of the center by the two major political parties is another illustration. In all these examples one sees an attempt to exempt America from the general and broadening European experience of secularization or godlessness.

The militant anti-Christian or antitheist organizations in the United States, usually in the past and certainly in the present, are inconsequential in the American intellectual mainstream. Few people have heard of the American Association for the Advancement of Atheism and its many ephemeral counterparts. Many Christian believers would be hard pressed to name one mature outspoken atheist among their acquaintances, though they may be surrounded by religiously unaffiliated persons or practical agnostics. If authentic unbelief on a broad scale is a possibility in America, it must be masked. If integral unbelief is to be perceived, it does not occur on the European scale or model (as in Marxism or the Sartrean emphases).

Up to this point, largely negative features have been used to depict American religious life. We can, however, turn the question upside down and be surprised to find a pervasive *Christian* kind of orthodoxy in the majority expression of the American people. This orthodoxy of expression is so widespread that even subtler forms of unbelief would hardly seem to be consequential in an understanding of America. We may rightfully wonder how the preachers and the spiritual leaders could be disturbed over many trends in society: They seem to have the sympathy of almost all and the participation of a majority of people in their depiction of needs and goals for man and society.

The question is not how this orthodoxy was arrived at or what occasioned it, but in what does it consist? What is the *content* of American belief? At present we stand between two sets of overly broad generalizations. One reproduces the scholarly consensus concerning modern trends of unbelief. The other reproduces the popular consensus concerning American exceptions to these. But the content of belief (belief that) can be measured where the focus of belief and the quality of faith (belief in) cannot. The modern techniques of interviewing, poll-taking, and analyzing have been of service here. Readers of this book need hardly be reminded of all the limitations of such a method. Errors in sampling, confused motivations in reply, misunderstanding of questions, misrepresentation of answers—all these serve as qualifications on the usefulness of polls and the statistics they produce.

The most ambitious and comprehensive measurement was taken in 1952 by Ben Gaffin Associates; the findings were reproduced by *Catholic Digest* soon after. The sociologist Will Herberg gave them wide and early publicity. More recently, they have been intensively studied and interpreted by the

Jesuit expert, John L. Thomas.[1] After reading Father Thomas' description of "sampling methods used" in an appendix of his book, most readers will have reason to be content with the reliability of the survey as being representative of much national religious opinion in 1952.

Where was unbelief in such a sample? Recalling the pro-

[1] *Religion and the American People* (Westminster, Md.: Newman, 1963). Father Thomas conceives of his book as a refutation of many of Will Herberg's and some of my deductions about American life. He proposes to show that it is a misreading of American life to see secularization as a supplanting of historic faith by generalized national and culture religions, and thus he accents (as does this chapter) the contentments which Americans show when they face the historic doctrinal positions of Christianity. Thomas' book is important, and its whole argument should be appropriated by American religious leaders. Herberg and others have suggested two kinds of secularization: one is the supplanting of historic faiths; the other, a subtle change and revision of their content while their terms are retained. See the chapter, "Religion and Social Change," in J. Milton Yinger, *Sociology Looks at Religion* (New York: Macmillan, 1963), especially pp. 68 ff.

Secularization, according to Yinger, can mean "the separation of religious motives, feelings, and decisions from other aspects of life" and it can also mean

> persons acting religiously in a way that does not express directly the faith they profess. These two processes are not the same; and I believe it is a mistake to use the same term with reference to them. It is one thing to have many of life's decisions carried out without reference to religion—the usual dictionary meaning of secularization. It is another thing to redefine one's religion while disguising or obscuring the process by holding, somewhat superficially, to many of the symbols of the earlier religious system. Religious change is usually a latent process, carried on beneath symbols of nonchange.

Thus Herberg and Peter Berger and others are seen to speak both of "the application of nonreligious standards to life" and "religious movements that lack 'authenticity'" under the term "secularization." It seems to me that the former sense applies to the main European development and the latter to the American. Some terminological confusion seems inevitable, and it will be necessary to define the usage in each context.

visional picture of the historic referents of Christian belief
(with the symbols Trinity and Incarnation), we shall look for
exceptions. How widespread are they? The survey, when projected on the national scale, finds little unbelief and much
"continuity of symbol." The religious preference of the sam-
pled group was as follows:

Protestant	68.3%
Roman Catholic	22.8%
Jewish	3.4%
Other, none	5.5%

Twenty-seven per cent reported that they were not active
church members; 32 per cent had not attended religious services in the previous three months. "What do [these] modern
Americans think of . . . traditional 'eternal verities'?" For-
get, for the moment, the Jewish minority which would naturally reject the two symbols Trinity and Incarnation. Only
1 per cent of all Americans stated that they are atheists, that
they do not believe. Even in the group which expressed no
religious preference, only 12 per cent were self-confessed nonbelievers. In the whole sample, only 2 per cent were not quite
sure whether God existed, but 87 per cent were absolutely certain that he did. Only one out of five in the whole sample
failed to see God as a loving Father.

What about the Trinity? "The adult American public holds
firmly to the belief." Only one in ten *in the whole sample*
(thus including the Jewish and the nonpreferring group) disbelieved, and only 6 per cent expressed clear nonbelief. Incarnation appeared in this survey under the symbol "divinity
of Christ." At most, one out of five disbelieved in his divinity.
Even 55 per cent of the "nonpreference" group believed in his
divinity. We have expressed curiosity about the witness, the
testimony to belief. The survey used the biblical revelation as
the symbol. Eighty-three per cent were content to call the Bible
the word of God. Others in the remaining 17 per cent showed

respect for the Bible, but in more qualified terms. Real deviation begins to occur only on the subject of a future life. "Immortality" was the symbol here. At this point, 23 per cent denied some sort of future life or were agnostic about it. Forty
per cent admitted that they never think about what may happen to them after death. The question of belief in heaven was
asked of the 77 per cent of the sample which believed in an
afterlife; the majority did believe. But of the *whole* sample, 28
per cent did not. Forty-two per cent did not believe in hell or
punishment for evildoers. Seven-eighths of those interviewed
did not "regard hell as a possible future alternative" for themselves.

The significance of the adaptation of Christian beliefs about
afterlife should not be underestimated, but immortality is not
among the chief symbols under scrutiny here. We shall leave
the Ben Gaffin Associates survey after a brief notice of regard
paid to the churches as witnesses. Only 5 per cent felt that religion is unimportant in their lives. Seventy-five per cent felt it
was "very important." Only 17 per cent felt the "most important
function of the church was to convert people to a spiritual belief; nearly one half (49 per cent) thought that it should
teach people how to live better with others; one third believed
that it was both." [2]

If this most-inclusive survey is accurate and if the climate has
not changed significantly since 1952, one may safely say that
Americans express their faith in continuity with historic symbols. If there is widespread unbelief in America, "the changes
are being obscured by the continuity of symbols; they are,
quite understandably, opposed by most religious professionals

2 Thomas' book reproduces results which subdivide the sample into denominations, sexes, regions, age-groups, levels of education, etc. These have
an intrinsic interest, but there is no merit in wearying the reader on the
topic of unbelief by detailing the samples on belief. We are reluctant to
elaborate on a subject so familiar as American orthodoxy. Yet reference
must be made to locate the whole argument. See Thomas, *op. cit.*, pp. 28,
51 ff.

—with the result that much of the new religion is developing at the hands of laymen—but the changes continue nevertheless." [3]

Yinger observes:

> If one defines religion statically—in terms of a system of beliefs and practices that emerged at a given time and were subject thereafter to no *essential* revision—religious change is nearly identical with secularization. It represents the falling away from the great tradition.

It should be noted that by this definition we are considering religion statically, by its historic Christian referents.

The Ben Gaffin Associates survey can be corroborated wherever one turns and sees subsamples taken by others. Some of these are noted here for comparison. Gerhard Lenski, in a heralded study of religion in metropolitan Detroit, studied both orthodoxy and devotionalism in religion. Those responding in Lenski's sample were asked six questions with orthodox Christian references: 62 per cent of the Catholics, 38 per cent of the Negro Protestants, 32 per cent of the white Protestants took an orthodox stance on all items. "Most of the heterodox accepted the majority of the six basic doctrines." The first and the fifth questions are nearest to our symbolic points, Trinity and Incarnation. But we reproduce the whole chart:

Question	White Catholics	White Protestants	Negro Protestants
Believe in God?	98%	97%	99%
God like a loving Heavenly Father?	95%	85%	97%
God responds to men's prayers?	90%	87%	97%
Belief that in life after death some will be punished?	75%	45%	52%
Jesus God's only Son?	93%	82%	89%
God expects men to worship Him every week, if able?	82%	54%	71%

3 Yinger, *op. cit.*, pp. 72 f.

These findings would lose some significance if the survey were concerned only with active, dedicated affiliates. However, it reckons with the inclusive preference groups, by which only 5 per cent of the whole population sample is ruled out: 41 per cent White Protestant, 35 per cent White Catholic, 15 per cent Negro Protestant, 4 per cent Jew were the preferences listed.[4] Thus we are dealing with a cross-section of 91 per cent of the population, omitting only Jews and the nonpreference groups.

An earlier comprehensive survey, before the touted religious revival of the 1950s, was taken by Gallup (Dec. 9, 1944). Then only 1 per cent of the American people expressed disbelief in God and only an additional 3 per cent were undecided. A similar percentage was turned up by Gallup on December 18, 1954. In 1948 Lincoln Barnett reported only 5 per cent expressing disbelief. A *British Weekly* report in December, 1952, corroborated the Gaffin survey on the divine inspiration of the Bible. Gaffin found 86 per cent concurrence; the British report gave 86.5 per cent in the same year.[5]

So far as youth is concerned, the widely recognized religious rebellion and search also seems to be undertaken with reasonable contentment with existing symbols. A Gallup survey of December, 1961, found in the 14-22 age-group that only 26 per cent had less than "very firm" belief in God; about 33 per cent failed to believe in the "complete truth" of the Bible.[6] In a collegiate survey of 1960, only 1 per cent chose to call themselves atheist and only 25 per cent failed to assent to either expression: "I believe in a divine God, Creator of the Universe, Who knows my innermost thoughts and feelings, and

[4] *The Religious Factor* (Garden City, N.Y.: Doubleday, 1961), pp. 23, 50 f., 53 f., 361.

[5] These findings were reported on and publicized by Will Herberg in his familiar *Protestant-Catholic-Jew* (Garden City, N.Y.: Doubleday, 1955), pp. 85-112.

[6] Reported in Leo Rosten, *Religions in America* (rev. ed.; New York: Simon and Schuster, 1963), pp. 302, 304.

to Whom one day I shall be accountable" or "I believe in a power greater than myself, which some people call God and some people call Nature" (48% were content with the former). This collegiate response of 2,795 undergraduates at eleven colleges is relatively high on the unorthodoxy scale.

One would expect a higher degree of orthodoxy in two conservative Lutheran groups of youth; Merton P. Strommen reports on their general consent to historic belief-items. Two surveys (1959, 1962) of two groups will be referred to.

Strommen includes the following as Trinitarian items:

	Percentage Responding in Agreement with Lutheran Pastors Youth		Per cent of Pastors Answering	Answer
	1959	1962		
3. To know Christ is to know God	90	92	99	Yes
11. I believe Jesus is both God and man but still only one person		84	96	Yes
19. The Holy Spirit can be called God	77	78	94	Yes
21. God the Father is more important than the Holy Spirit		76	98	No
22. Jesus differs from God in that God is stern and Jesus is gentle	75	81	98	No

Additional Christological (Incarnation) items were:

28. Christ was tempted just as we are by impure thoughts, resentments, and pride	72	65	66	Yes
31. There are other ways than through Christ by which the God of salvation can be found	70	78	96	No
46. Although there are many religions in the world, each one leads to the same God		60	97	No

Here we have a controlled group reporting on static positions, and we find considerable acceptance. In this case, however, the questions are more complicated and somewhat trickier. It is interesting to note how unorthodox Lutheran ministers were on the humanity of Christ (Incarnation). Polls such as this will suggest that, given a controlled environment, the historic faith can be inculcated in, and appropriated by, contemporary young people.[7]

In the Gallup surveys, reported on by Rosten, there were some differences on belief in God when men and women were consulted separately. Several of these surveys are consolidated here: [8]

	Percentage Affirming		
Do you believe in God?	Men	Women	Ratio
Gallup	95	97	1.02
Ross	70.4	81.6	1.16
Katz and Allport (1931, liberal arts students)	63	74	1.17
Allport et al.	62	66	1.06

One could extend the list indefinitely, to this effect: Virtually all Americans shun the label "atheist," and few express formal disbelief. Only about 10 per cent—including Jews and non-preference groups—are discontent with the Trinitarian symbol; not a large minority is impatient with Incarnation and the authority of the Bible as witnesses.

The purpose of this reproduction of materials citing American orthodoxy is clear and simple. It is necessary to suggest that whatever unbelief is occurring in the United States—whether of the closed or open variety—it will have to be sought not in overt expressions of atheism and disbelief but under

[7] Merton P. Strommen, *Profiles of Church Youth* (St. Louis: Concordia, 1963), pp. 50 f.

[8] See Michael Argyle, *Religious Behaviour* (Glencoe, Ill.: Free Press, 1959), p. 73. Referred to under "Ross" is a 1950 survey for Association Press. Katz and Allport is a survey published by Craftsman Press (Syracuse, N.Y., 1931). Allport *et al.* is a study in *Journal of Psychology*, XXV (1948), 3-33.

the symbols of continuity established by organized religious groups, particularly those with historic Christian reference. Unless this is remembered, the sermons one hears or the books one reads on the subject of faithlessness and contradictory beliefs will seem to refer only to species of unbelief discoverable anywhere *but* in orthodox America.

Unfortunately, I am not equipped to present or to comment on data concerning Latin America. Roman Catholic custodians of its future have spoken in terms of crisis on that continent. The strange fusion of assent to the main outlines of Catholic teaching and adaptation to pre-Columbian pagan traditions is well known. The acceptability of non- or anti-Christian quasi-religious political ideologies in many Latin American nations is also a familiar topic. The other area of focus for the background of our study, therefore, remains Western Europe. Eastern Europe expresses in boldest outline the post-Christian situation. The fact that it may prevail in part by coercion does not detract from the fact that the godless man and the godless society are—in Christian definition—present and existent there. Eastern Europe will be referred to throughout the remainder of this book whenever Marxist Communism as religion, political ideology, and political force is to be discussed. The particular interest will be in those instances where Marxism supplants Western Christianity. Eastern Christianity, like Latin American Western Christianity, is not under discussion in the formal sense.

Does the European scene present a different picture? Does it corroborate the generalizations we have made concerning the originality of unbelief?

One difficulty regularly experienced in the career of anyone who attempts to portray the depths of secularization to Americans is the inability to find models. Americans can be brought to recognize widespread disinterest in religion; indeed, most

Christians are aware of disaffection and apathy toward religion in Christian America. They can be brought to concur that religious change can take place while people retain continuity of symbols for expressing them. But to be told of really widespread and profound attempts by individuals and society to construct a whole life apart from God—this is less frequently understood because the phenomena are so rare or so remote.

If we suggest that Europe has had such an experience, there is immediate danger that the assertions are misread. From the Christian viewpoint, it may seem chauvinistic to compare the continents and to find Europe wanting. Are generalizations really useful if they are so broad as to suggest a continentwide temperament in each case? Is Europe more oriented toward ideology, as Americans are toward institutions and practice? We may make educated guesses or undertake extensive surveys. Rather than be unfair because of the size of generalizations necessary, it seems advisable to forgo them entirely and discipline ourselves to comment only about events.

Whereas the United States has only rarely seen formal, open, articulate unbelief; whereas it has never been institutionalized on a wide scale; whereas the nation's mores commit people toward religious expression, Europe has known widespread anticlerical, antichurch, and even anti-Christian expression and institutions. In recent decades the experience of church participation in Europe begins to suggest considerable differences from that in the United States. These are events, factors, documentable features which characterize the separate experiences. The integral forms of unbelief have taken more public form in Europe. The attempt to enclose personal and social life without reference to God is a more licit venture in Europe than in the United States, where such activity is screened from view by many devices.

This is not to suggest that Europe has failed to know spiritual vitality in recent times. The Roman Catholic and the Protestant-Orthodox ecumenical movements certainly point to the presence of hungers among the population. The recovery of disciplined life in Protestantism, even to the point of the establishment of monastic communities, is an indication of spiritual life. The renewal of the laity, the experience with lay academies for the reform of church life, the attempt to express a theology of the church that reckons with such renewal—these are also observable factors. The French Catholic openness to the dialogue with godless man and the fine example of some Catholic novelists should not be overlooked. England has seen surprising forms of renewal. Behind the Iron Curtain the churches, while suffering, are by no means dead. It would be as reckless to dismiss the Christian venture in post-Christian Europe as it would be to suggest the superiority of America.[9]

Although Europe experiences greatly different elements of spiritual climate than does America, it would be naïve to assume that no communication between the two and no potential change in either can be expected. Particularly in the spiritual realm, they have a common destiny. America is informed in decisive ways by European theology; Europeans have acknowledged indebtedness to some American forms of church life. Each mistrusts the ecclesiastical setting of the other, but the ecumenical movement has provided a forum for sharing

[9] On monastic renewal in Protestantism, see Olive Wyon, *Living Springs* (Philadelphia: Westminster, 1963); on the laity, see Margaret Frakes, *Bridges to Understanding* (Philadelphia: Muhlenberg, 1960); on Catholic penetration of the spiritual situation of Europe, see Louis and André Retif, *The Church's Mission in the World* (New York: Hawthorn, 1962). The literature on these subjects is enormous. Most of it is oriented toward the "phoenix" idea: that is, that the death of the churches in Europe was becoming known and that renewal comes in the form not of resuscitation but of resurrection, new creation, and new life. American renewal may have taken less radical form because the secular situation has been less radically perceived by Christians.

understanding. On the secular side, many Europeans complain that the American way of life is being exported, with all its materialist values. In America, European authors are read and films are seen, to the detriment of America—claims the American moralist—because of their secularist tendencies. Whether in these negations or in positive ways, the classic pictures of the nearness of belief and the remoteness of unbelief (as Americans perceive it) cannot be expected to remain intact.

When we mention events which show Europe's experience with unbelief, we can cite the whole four-centuries-long process of secularization as being largely of European origin. The political version, with the separation of church and state and the disestablishment of the churches, was an American contribution. But if we take the symbolic names for the many-formed movements, most of them will suggest an at-homeness with the central experience of Europe: Copernicus, Galileo, Machiavelli, Descartes, Hegel, Feuerbach, Marx, Darwin, Nietzsche, Comte, Schopenhauer, Voltaire, Freud, Camus, Sartre—few of these giants, these molders of the modern world, have intellectual counterparts in the United States.

Perhaps because the churches were not disestablished in most European nations, there were more widespread anticlerical or antichurch reactions. The numerous expulsions of the Jesuits from France, the *Kulturkampf* in Germany, the anti-Christian attitudes of the social revolutionists of the nineteenth century, are all dramatic contrasts to the American experience.

For the past century, most of the literature of the "godkillers" has originated in Europe. Some of the atheistic expression was institutionalized through Marxism, and made political in Russian Communism. Others have exercised widespread influence in a more subtle, uncoerced way, as with the following of Albert Camus and Jean-Paul Sartre. More disturbing to Christian missioners of Europe is the extensive apathy of the working people. More and more, and despite revivals of theology, preaching, and laity, the common men and women of Europe seem content to round off their lives without reference to God or their Christian traditions.

In Scandinavia, with its Lutheran establishment, and in England, with its Anglican one, only a very small percentage of the baptized population is actively involved. Abbé Godin, in his famous thesis, could have removed the question mark from his book title, *France, Pagan?* Germany, which has strong Catholic, Lutheran, and Reformed elements, also exposes to public view startling kinds of secularization and broad disinterest in the church. Italy houses not only the central See of Roman Catholicism but also the world's largest free-world Communist following. Spain combines uniform acceptance of Catholicism with an undercurrent of skepticism about Christian claims. There is no point in extending the list indefinitely; the tables of church attendance and involvement are readily accessible and, by United States standards, indicative of markedly low church interest.[10]

10 Robert B. Evans, *Let Europe Hear* (Chicago: Moody, 1963), is an inclusive survey. One hesitates to recommend the book because the author's theological bias (anti-Catholic, antiliberal Protestant) permits him to find precious few authentic Christians anywhere. However, if this bias is kept in mind, one can profit from the compilation of materials, of statistics, of literary references. For what it may be worth, we reproduce the results of a Gallup survey of January, 1948 (see Rosten, *op. cit.*, 1st ed., 1955), p. 247:

DO YOU, PERSONALLY, BELIEVE IN GOD?

Answers from Nations:	Percentages		
	Yes	No	???
United States	94	3	3
Norway	84	7	9
Finland	83	5	12
Holland	80	14	6
Sweden	80	8	12
Denmark	80	9	11
France	66	20	14

The purpose of this contrast has not been to suggest the spiritual superiority of the United States. Nor does it precommit European unbelief to integral or closed-system forms while the American version remains open. It has only tried to account to Americans for the apparent remoteness of radical forms of unbelief. If one generalization is to be risked, let it be this: Secularization is a universal Western phenomenon. In Europe, it tends to take the first form depicted by Yinger—the attempt to have many of life's decisions carried out without reference to religion. In the United States, it is more apt to be represented by the redefinition of religion, obscured or disguised by the process of holding, somewhat superficially, to many of the symbols of the earlier religious system.

The ensuing examination of varieties of unbelief in the two types will, however, be largely freed of mere geographical interest.

Unfortunately, we do not have similar comparisons on belief in the Trinity or the Incarnation. Since religious instruction is part of public-school training in most of these European nations and since almost all citizens are baptized, there may be instinctive resort to the category "belief in God," and the real nature of Europe's spiritual life is better perceived through indicators of religious participation. One comparison existed on another doctrinal referent: "Do you believe in life after death? Here Norway and Finland were slightly more confident—as represented in their samples— than were United States samples. The United States group gave a 68 per cent affirmation, with Holland also 68%. Following were: France (58%), Denmark (55%), Sweden (49%), Britain (49%). In each case the No answer was more decisive than with the United States, where nonaffirmation often meant indecision.

Evans, *ibid.*, p. 153, publicizes two French surveys which indicate considerable disbelief in God. If church attendance can be considered a factor in the faithfulness of people and an indicator that they attempt to be open to God in forming their lives, most European figures would lead one to conclude that secularization has advanced far. In many nations, less than one-tenth the proportion of the population which the United States claims within the church attends worship. Sweden and Great Britain produce particularly low scores.

7

The Secular
Varieties of Unbelief

Having established two types of unbelief over against historic
Christian norms and having defined the Euro-American milieu,
we are prepared to test the usefulness of the thesis by applying
it to a number of families, or clusters, of unbeliefs. Does the
distinction between integral and nonintegral, between closed
and open systems, further our understanding? Is it inclusive
enough to incorporate the clusters described below and exclusive enough to perform the function of definition: to
limit? Can it show different sets of possibilities (conversion,
communication, and conspiracy being our chosen examples)
between one set of systems as opposed to the other? While
the nine clusters we shall examine are representative of most
possibilities, no attempt is made to claim completeness and no
attempt will be made to imprison exceptions and further varieties under these categories. They are mere instruments or
handles.

**1. Unbelief which cancels out the seriousness of belief and
unbelief: anomie and accidie**

Christian belief begins with a response to a word of God.
That word is perceived as having two sides. One (Law) represents God's distance, his transcendence and his judgment on
man's life. It serves, from the human side, to create tension between imperfect man and his environment. The other (Gospel) represents God's nearness, his immanence, his action in
man's life, and his involvement in man's life. It serves, from the
human side, to integrate man into his environment and to
bring him to perfection. Different theological traditions may
state these matters with somewhat different accents, but each
has some corollary to them.

Modern unbelief, like every value-system, will also ordinarily offer counterparts to these. A value-system will suggest the
need for man to become more nearly perfect, to find progress.

As such, it will be a judgment upon his present state and attainments. Similarly, it will offer man social and personal integration, providing some coherent view of the universe and some sort of meaning or purpose in life. These are the positive contributions of most forms of unbelief. Some, however, have negative orientations which make little attempt to do these things. What happens if neither Law nor Gospel is heard in belief and unbelief; what if neither tension over against environment nor integration into it is sought or understood? Is there a form of unbelief which cancels out the whole seriousness of choice, of value, of life itself? If so, it represents a greater problem to faith than would atheism and antitheism, for these are serious systems.

Indeed, such forms do present themselves in modern life. Without doubt they have historical precedents, but we are interested only in their present-day contexts. For shorthand purposes, we shall refer to these as *anomie* and *accidie*. Neither of the words is really new. Anomie is closely related to the Greek word *anomia* which, in the Bible, frequently means simple lawlessness. The word now contains other overtones that suggest some originality to modern unbelief. Accidie can serve as a translation for sloth, one of the medieval world's seven capital sins. Here again, the word has a long history and a modern overtone. Anomie is a form of refusing to recognize the power of the Law of God or of judgment in human value-systems; accidie is a way of declining the power of the Gospel or the positive values of human offerings.

All humans experience the reality of dealing with others who are victims of anomie or accidie in temporary or superficial forms. The fanatic or the crusader may be anomic; the listless may be a victim of accidie. But the two are also cultural problems, incarnate and visible on a plural and semipermanent basis in the modern, pluralistic world. They may remain as long as culture bears many of its modern competitive features.

Most persons know how to deal with legalism, or *nomism*, which is a repressive and judgmental view of life. They know the phenomenon of antinomianism, in which a person consciously and with dedication rejects the Law in the name of the profession of liberty. Anomie differs from each, and refers to a state in society or to a human condition brought about by reaction to a state of society. The word was modernized in the 1890s by Emile Durkheim, though not all the implications of his sociological use need concern us in our theological or antitheological setting. He needed a word which would describe his culture's reaction to bewildering economic change. In 1893, in *De la division du travail social,* he spoke of a "disintegrated state of society that possesses no common values or morals which effectively govern conduct." Arnold Toynbee speaks of "drifting," or "on-the-run," cultures as being anomic.

In Durkheim's *Le suicide* (1897), the ideas were carried further. He pondered why there seemed to be an increase in suicide when conditions of economic life were either extremely depressed or extremely prosperous. (Oscar Wilde has said that there are two tragedies in life: not getting what we want and getting what we want.) Each, in an economic society, can produce anomie: a normless, rootless, standardless, state of society. People become unsure of their place in community change; they cannot value the activities of fellow men; *solidarité* breaks apart.

Today, issues besides the economic come into play, and they can be minimized here. One could use the experience of a competitive or pluralistic society. In it, many belief-systems are exposed to each other; they conflict or clash or overlap; they are interactive; each bids for attention.[1] This experience reaches Christians because of their intensified awareness of an

---

[1] In this section we shall rely on comparisons to the anomic state in political life as portrayed by Sebastian De Grazia, *The Political Community* (Chicago: University of Chicago Press, 1948).

unbelieving world (the first reference in our nine factors of originality in unbelief today).

Anomie is recognized in the personal life of young people. Why does the teen-ager "get that way"? Look at the development of a belief-system. The human infant, unlike many animals, is helpless, a parasite. Attendants must feed him, sanitize him, comfort and shelter him, or he will not survive. Physical dependence leads to psychic dependence. As the child becomes less helpless, he will begin to see withdrawal of attendants—long before he rebels against them. But during this period he remains in harmony with his environment; attendants exist only for him. Good and evil come and go at his command. When attendants take on separate identities and contradict him with their value-systems, his is threatened. Anxiety of separation occurs. Planned withdrawal by attendants follows. New adult influences come upon the scene, with conflicting views. The childhood gods crumble soon after their identities have been established.

In these years the child virtually inherits the religion or belief-system of the parents. Complete nonreligiousness at this stage—however heterodox the pattern of belief—is inconceivable. In a traditional society, culture helps to prepare the child for the next stage and leads him through it. He keeps his identity, traveling little, experiencing only his own family and his own neighborhood. The outside world is filtered and translated to him through the eyes of the community.

Modern society is modern to the degree that this noncompetitive value pattern disappears. A free society involves all in interinfluence. Anomie now occurs when the maturing person fails to choose any norms because there is conflict. Adults seem to be hypocritical. He experiences identity diffusion and does not know who he is. The modern world of communication, business, and politics enhances the problem. Man is a political animal and in many ways is determined by this characteristic. Anomie arises when classes or men are out of joint. The historic and early ideologies, the religion of the parent or sponsoring society may be left behind in the stress of competition and conflict. The old belief clashes with the new needs of life. Political anomie can lead to anarchy or totalitarianism.

In De Grazia's distinction, simple (as opposed to acute anomie) is a response to conflicting directives in social life. This is an inevitable condition of living, and maturity comes as one learns to cope with it. In our society, for instance—in religion and civil life especially—the directives to co-operate and to compete are in conflict ("Love thy neighbor; shove thy neighbor"). Political life enjoins people to work for common good but also to join a party. In economics a person is to work so that more may share earth's blessings, and at the same time he must compete economically. In religion he should love his brothers but still oppose them. When these directives are momentary or sporadic, timeless processes are being worked out. When they are institutionalized and taken for granted in society, anomie can result.

Acute anomie is the result of particularly profound problems and cannot be escaped unless the individual meets them maturely. The causes of anomie have to be understood and dealt with if man is to be "at home in the universe," to borrow Josiah Royce's phrase. The leaderless and valueless person in such a universe drifts into normlessness and spiritual death or becomes a victim of totalitarian attractions. Failures in political leadership can produce lawlessness. ("Too little, too late" on state and Federal levels of leadership in the American South has helped to produce normlessness in recent years.)

Anomie need not be a permanent state. Work, compulsive leisure, hedonism, and sense-experience can provide escapes. Acute anomie is escaped by many Americans when they join

clubs, churches, lodges. These provide group substitutes for
leadership, and a coherent if only illusory world view is presented. Others compartmentalize life and numb themselves in
the face of realities which are unsettling. Failure to reduce
anomie leads to crises such as war. One can minimize it or
let it rise to new crises, or he can maladapt into mental disor-
der or suicide. The American religious situation, with the
competitive directives (co-operate, compete) can contribute
to societal anomie, and the ecumenical movement is one means
of attempting to reduce the causes. Young people as they mature (the college generation is typical) find adults equivocat-
ing and competing over Christian truth. Some turn to sects,
which screen out competing directives. Others drift and are
normless; still others mature as their sense of history grows.
All are helped when the causes of anomie are minimized.

Anomie is not simple lawlessness. Gangsters have a code;
anomic persons reject even minimal attempts to organize experience. At most, the anomic type seeks escape and entertainment. His world is detached, rebellious. Anomie is the disease
of the postcivilized; it occurs only in the overorganized life. It
may form units which profess positive values, such as the "original" faith of the nation or club or church. But the negatives
of nihilism and the positives of the will to power may actually
be his only intrinsic values. "And slime had they for mortar."

Accidie has many of the same roots but is the opposite expression. Accidie is paralysis, or listlessness, in the face of potentially good acts or beliefs. The man of God is made
for joy but turns away. The man approached by the philosopher of value may be bored. When medieval theologians spoke
of this capital sin, they did not refer to the mere laziness implied in the modern translation, "sloth." They meant the
canceling-out of seriousness. "Count me out." "I'm all right,
Jack." "*Ohne mich.*" "Oh, yeah?"

Paul Elmen has described accidie.[2] The man possessed of it
has neither ambition nor curiosity. He is the spectator. If he
works, he works hard, without meaning, as on a treadmill. If
he plays, he plays hard—compulsively, without enjoyment.
He is bored. A belief-system meets him and, like *Hamlet*'s
Horatio, he asserts the creed: "So I have heard and do in part
believe." Elmen notes: Little wonder that Dante consigned the
bored to the fifth circle of the *Inferno*.

From Elmen we have learned a distinction between accidie
and simple or mere boredom (*demon meridianus*). The latter
is part of finitude. Time is the enemy; when it is not creatively
used, one is bored. Accidie is acute. The true spectator becomes
the "true believer" of Eric Hoffer's description. Having rejected a great good, he turns to great evils. "Strict orthodoxy"
is then "as much the result of mutual suspicion as of ardent
faith." [3]

St. Thomas Aquinas provided the classic definition of accidie from the Christian viewpoint: *Tristitia de bono spirituali*
—Sadness in the face of spiritual good.[4] Such sadness is not
merely oriented toward outward temporal evil but specifically
toward an inward spiritual good. Thus a belief-system can be
rejected for the same reasons in times of depression or prosperity.[5]

Enthusiasm wanes in the face of lack of theological curiosity
or central affirmations of belief or definitions of goal. Some

2 *The Restoration of Meaning to Contemporary Life* (Garden City, N.Y.:
Doubleday, 1958), pp. 19-74, includes a discussion from which we have
profited.

3 Eric Hoffer, *The True Believer* (New York: New American Library,
1958), p. 114.

4 *Disputationes* viii, *de Malo* 1, 4.

5 Father Andrew Greeley analyzes this mood in a segment of modern
American life in *The Church and the Suburbs* (New York: Sheed & Ward,
1959); see the chapter which denominates accidie, "The Waning of Enthusiasm," pp. 125 ff.

have spoken of "the suburban sadness," or "amiable low-keyed unpleasure," which results from trivial goals in the life of a group that holds a belief-system. There is what St. Gregory called "an aversion to openness," or what W. H. Auden's character Rosetta calls "a dowdy death for those who have so dimly lived."

As with anomie, so with accidie: it is apparent that when acute accidie is present, only a profound and uprooting crisis will lead a person to be open to a positive pattern of values. Evidently a more advisable course would, again, be the removal of the causes of accidie, insofar as this is possible. Stimulation of imagination may awaken curiosity; central affirmations and goals can be portrayed vividly and made central in institutional life. Since pluralism is not going to disappear in a free society, it seems important to prepare young adherents of a belief in community to anticipate those with which they will later come into contact. By definition the anomie-accidie polarity seems to elude classification within our basic typology. Neither is closed and neither is open, because each is too listless or heedless to care about forming patterns of belief.

Yet even on this scale, even in this family of unbeliefs which is the most serious problem for historic faiths, the shadows of system begin to fall. Few can permanently sustain the acute states of anomie or accidie; each keeps issuing either in escape or—Durkheim was figuratively correct, if we view the course of freedom in modern societies—in suicide! We could denominate acute anomie and acute accidie as integral or closed. The medieval theologians were conceptually precise when they listed the latter among the seven "capital" sins. That is, it stands at the head of a column; from it, other faults grow. Meanwhile, simple anomie and mere boredom are separate problems; they represent open systems even though, in their lack of moral or intellectual seriousness, they resist systematization. We have suggested that the causes of anomie and accidie can be minimized in society. The psychic damage to maturing humans can be lessened through anticipation and education. Institutional problems which foster each can be solved. It would seem that awareness of types within this family leads to understanding and—for believer and unbeliever alike—to some strategic possibilities.

2. Unbelief which rejects the possibility of positive belief: nihilism

Attempts have been made to establish the origins of the word "nihilism" as applied to features of modern life. The root of the word is, of course, *nihil*, "nothing," and a history of the idea of nothingness would certainly show that people of the past have often been able to develop philosophies of life which rule out the possibility of something positive or affirmative in the universe. But the modern use of the term relates not to temporary, individual, exceptional, instances of rejection. It is applied to the institutionalization of negation.

Friedrich H. Jacobi (d. 1819) is often credited with having coined the modern form of the word "nihilism" and, according to Ernst Benz, Franz Baader (d. 1841) gave it the connotations which have currency today. Turgenev's *Fathers and Sons* issued this currency in the literary world and through him, great numbers of people have become conscious of extensive attitudes and philosophies of devotion to nothing, to rejection.[6]

6 See Ernst Benz, *West-östlicher Nihilismus* (Stuttgart: Evangelisches Verlagswerk, 1949). Helmut Thielicke, in *Nihilism*, trans. John W. Doberstein (New York: Harper & Row, 1961), presents a popular development of the word in modern times. Thielicke does, I feel, apply the term rather imprecisely in areas that could better be covered by terms such as "atheism" or "moral agnosticism," but his attempt to define the theological and psychological meanings of "the absolutization of nothingness" commends the book to the general reader.

Nihilism presents entirely different problems than do anomie and accidie. The latter serve to cancel the seriousness
of choice between belief-systems; nihilism does not. It takes
the choice seriously, and has already made it. As such, it can
be and often is an intellectually serious form of unbelief. That
is not to say that it is as widespread a phenomenon as normlessness and spiritual listlessness, but only that it has defenses
and arguments which those numbed by anomie and accidie
cannot present. It is a literary, psychological, and sometimes
political phenomenon. [At its root it subtracts all elements of
affirmation in the universe,] leaving a vacuum which it cele-
brates as a doctrinal absolute. Nihilism is hard to sustain. Its
"ism" excludes the possibility of something happening. But
something does keep happening.

Not all forms of unbelief are nihilistic, but all nihilism is
a form of unbelief from the Christian viewpoint. It denies the
possibility of God's positive action in history (Incarnation).
It shares with all unbelief and all agonized belief two basic
visions: God is not apparent in the universe, and evil is.
Whereas the believer comes to accept the presence of God precisely through belief (as opposed to knowledge or pretending: "I must believe this testimony") and in spite of the presence of evil, the nihilist sees only the latter.

Nihilism in its pure form is always integral, a closed system,
the absolutization of nothingness. The nihilist may speak (and
many dramatists and novelists committed to its philosophy
have done so eloquently); but it is difficult for them to engage in real communication with those who affirm, since the
nihilist has already canceled their moral universe as a possibility. Integral nihilism sorts out all experience; since its a priori
statement rejects affirmation, whenever something bobs up it
must immediately be beaten down. It is antihistorical. It rules
out the absolute in advance—before, one might say, all the evidence is in. The nihilist sees the breakdown of the symbolic

universe as absolutely complete and rejects the attempt to find a new one or to reinstate old ones.[7]

The nihilist philosophy is difficult to carry out programmatically. It would be difficult to conceive of a society organized on its basis, though it may thrive in a disintegrative society. Thus Jean-Paul Sartre's absolutizing of the category of "the absurd" has nihilistic elements if it is seen as the basis of the universe. Yet as a judgment against some societal elements and living off others, it can be temporarily sustained. One confronts nihilism, then, more frequently in the literary and artistic world. There, men of genius or talent may be given over to it as an antispiritual vision which helps them to diagnose unequivocally the spiritual malaise of contemporary times. One confronts it less frequently in the political realm because the attempt to organize society begins to bring with it some affirmations, some senses of history and possibility.

Nihilism may occur in the mob or the crowd, though there it will often be obscured by temporary symbols which have a quasi-affirmative cause. Gustave Le Bon, the great student of crowd psychology, observed this:

> Crowds will hear no more of the words divinity and religion, in whose name they were so long enslaved; but they have never possessed so many fetishes as in the last hundred years, and the old divinities have never had so many statues and altars raised in their honor. . . . Were it possible to induce the masses to adopt atheism, this belief would exhibit all the intolerant ardour of a religious sentiment, and in its exterior forms would soon become a cult.[8]

---

[7] Ludwig von Bertalanffy, "Human Values in a Changing World," in Abraham H. Maslow (ed.), *New Knowledge in Human Values* (New York: Harper & Row, 1959), pp. 70-74.

[8] *The Crowd* (New York: Viking, 1960), pp. 75 f.

Nihilism may occur in an individual political leader if he does not need to sustain a positive program. The last days of Adolf Hitler's life portray the nihilistic temperament. He could no longer conquer, and had difficulty sustaining illusions that he could. His "moral" universe was crumbling. He could only wreak further destruction and bring down others with him.

Integral nihilism is not necessarily an alien or European phenomenon, even though it is observable in the rise and breakdown of totalitarian crowd movements. If Richard Rovere's portrayal of the late Senator Joseph McCarthy is accurate, we see in it the presence of nihilism on a personal scale in the political realm:

> He was not . . . totalitarian in any significant sense, or even reactionary. These terms apply mainly to the social and economic order, and the social and economic order didn't interest him in the slightest. If he was anything at all in the realm of ideas, principles, doctrines, he was a species of nihilist; he was an essentially destructive force, a revolutionist without any revolutionary vision, a rebel without a cause.[9]

Rovere summarizes nihilism: "McCarthy, though a demon himself, was not a man possessed by demons," for he had no positive convictions.

The literary world and the political world, then, can see momentary and personal incarnations of nihilism in one kind of crowd and another kind of demagogue. There are forces in society which can produce nihilistic responses. Gabriel Marcel finds the tendency of the technocratic order to be inevitably nihilistic: "Nothingness or mere negation is, as it were, the secret which technocracy jealously hides in its heart." [10] Technoc-

9 *Senator Joe McCarthy* (New York: Meridian, 1960), pp. 8, 253.
10 *Man Against Mass Society* (Chicago: Regnery, 1962), p. 261.

racy elevates technique at the expense of idea, and tries to organize society apart from gods or values. Political chaos, the
permanent clash of ideologies, the apparent removal of choice
between ideologies—these can produce nihilism in a maturing
generation. Thielicke's book, it should be remembered, was a
series of lectures to German youth the year after the war. Martin
Niemöller, another spiritual leader of Germany, surveyed
postwar youth as victims of totalitarianism and war and said,
"Youth of these days has inherited nothing but a pessimistic
view of the future and has accepted an attitude we have come
to call 'nihilism.' . . . all human endeavors will fail." [11]

Nihilism may, in some way or other, partly affect most powers. Ignazio Silone gives the most passionate definition of its
pervasiveness:

> I know of no party, no church, no institution that can at
> present be considered uncontaminated by this terrible
> scourge. Nihilism is making a pretence of a creed in which
> one does not believe; it is the smoke of incense before an
> empty shrine; it is the exaltation of self-sacrifice and heroism
> as ends in themselves; it is liberty that is not in the service
> of life; liberty that has to have recourse to suicide or crime
> in order to prove itself. It is the subordination of truth and
> justice to selfish utility; it is the primacy of tactics and cun-
> ning in every form of collective relationship.[12]

Silone's intention is admirable: he wants to call people from
the habit of finding scapegoats (Hitler, McCarthy), and so he
extends as far as possible the definition of nihilism. But,

[11] Quoted by Harry C. Spencer in *World Outlook* (September, 1957), and
reproduced in Stanley J. Rowland, Jr., *Land in Search of God* (New York:
Random House, 1958), p. 16.
[12] "On the Place of the Intellect and the Pretensions of the Intellectual,"
in George B. de Huszar (ed.), *The Intellectuals* (Glencoe, Ill.: The Free
Press, 1960), p. 265.

despite its eloquence, it begins to introduce elements of confusion. Certainly the phenomena he describes in church and state have a nihilistic bent. But they are not sufficiently worked out or sustained to deserve the appellation "nihilist" in every instance.

Therefore, a distinction between the form of closed-system nihilism, which has been defined, and the open systems, with some possibility for transcendence, should be sought and kept alive. Thielicke does this through the distinction between "naïve" and "reflective" nihilism. The reflective type has to be integral. It has thought things out and come to a conclusion; it "continues to stand its ground in the face of the question of meaning. . . . The question of meaning is faced in full and unflinching consciousness and then answered in despair with the words, 'There *is* no meaning!' " Naïve nihilism would be a better term for that described by Silone: This is, in Thielicke's words, "an attitude in which the question of meaning is no longer negated but is simply no longer allowed to appear. It is a matter of unquestioning surrender to the moment, to the immediate activity, the immediate duty, the immediate pleasure." [13]

Is not much of what is often pictured as nihilism unfairly lumped with reflective nihilism and thus paid an intellectual compliment it does not deserve and given an apparent moral insult it should not elicit? There seem to be good pastoral reasons for counselors not to impose an ideology on young "rebels without a cause"; for by typing them, counselors provide them with a creed, a confession, a church—and call it nihilism. Unquestionably the amiability of the suburban cocktail party, the vandalism of the teen-age gang, the boredom and the violence of slum and suburban youth, the identity diffusion of high-school students—all have elements of naïve nihilism. Sometimes the temporary psychological roots are obvious, and proper understanding will help the person come to a more

[13] Thielicke, *Nihilism,* pp. 159, 148.

positive system. The societal reasons can be diagnosed: a war between generations, a rebellion against perceived hypocrisy in the older generation.

The advice of social psychologists regarding anomie and accidie is applicable here, too: to remove or to minimize the *causes* of temporary and unsustained or noninstitutionalized naïve nihilism. Proper diagnoses, human understanding, improvement of the bad situation which causes naïve nihilism, the tactful portrayal of positive elements in the universe—each of these could lead to the first affirmation in whose presence reflective or integral nihilism is born. "The least touch of any theology which has a compensating Heaven to offer the tragic hero is fatal." [14]

Now and then, naïve and unreflective or open nihilism may conceal a metaphysical thirst or a spirit of longing. In such a case, the distinction between integral and nonintegral types of unbelief may be not only accurate but practical. In the criss-crossing of values or belief-systems, should conversion or communication or co-operation be a possibility, the attempt to keep systems fluid and open has a strategic usefulness. Integral nihilism is beyond the reach of "the least touch of any theology which has a compensating Heaven" and thus has moved beyond tragedy.[15]

[14] I. A. Richards, *Principles of Literary Criticism* (New York: Harcourt, Brace, 1926), p. 200. I am not for a moment suggesting that Richards herewith gives us the clue, the secret, the answer for taking the seriousness out of nihilistic tragedy. I quote the sentence only to show that *when* the "least touch" of compensating theology is accepted, integral nihilism is either hardened or shattered.

[15] For a detailed discussion of the modern temper viewed as a positive possibility disguised by negation, see Franklin L. Baumer, *Religion and the Rise of Scepticism* (New York: Harcourt, Brace, 1960), pp. 187 ff., in the chapter "The Age of Longing." Arthur Koestler, Carl Jung, Karl Jaspers, Nikolai Berdyaev, Miguel de Unamuno, C. E. M. Joad, Ignazio Silone, Martin Buber, Albert Camus, and Aldous Huxley, among others, provide sources for his view (which does not lead to Christian belief) that positive signs are disguised behind contemporary rejection.

3. Unbelief which rejects God and roots out the idea of God: atheism and antitheism

The temptations to detail the varieties of atheism are many, but they must be resisted for our single purpose: the attempt to test the usefulness of a basic distinction between varieties of unbelief. The literature on the subject is extensive, because integral atheism is a modern phenomenon and, as the most articulate and dramatic version of unbelief, it deserves to draw most attention to itself. Since it is also a literary expression, most persons' acquaintance with it is through novels, drama, and modern philosophy. We shall try to suggest why it is not present in pure form in political life on any extensive basis.

Atheism may be two steps up from anomie-accidie and one step up from nihilism. It is always intellectually serious and often morally serious. Quite frequently it is characterized by affirmative elements not found in some other forms of unbelief. It can develop explicit theologies (or better, antitheologies) and extensive systems of philosophy, morality, aesthetics. More than any other form of unbelief under discussion, it is shrouded from view so far as "the man on the street" is concerned. Attempts to found atheist associations have usually fallen ludicrously short of goals. A scant 1 per cent of the American population calls itself atheist, and probably many within that small percentage would not find it important to publicize the fact—indeed, may find it necessary not to. The atheism that is reckoned with in American life is of a practical, undercover type: subtle, temporary, unreflective. But atheism is a permanent theoretical possibility even where it is rare in practice, and in many parts of the world which were once called Christian, there are publicized spokesmen for, and cells of, "metaphysical" atheists.

Because the word "atheism" has taken on pejorative tones and because it often implies a moral condemnation, it has be-

come an all-purpose word for the many forms of unbelief. In
an important interview, "Is the Modern World Atheist?" Friedrich Heer has cautioned against lumping all forms of misbe-
lief, disbelief, nonbelief, and unbelief under this single head-
ing. "The word 'atheist' is a harmful and dangerous term."
Christians were seen to be atheist by the Romans, and in the
Reformation era the various church parties called each
other atheist. "There is consequently in Europe a long tradition of treating as 'atheists' those whose faith differs from one's
own." If the word were used carefully and descriptively, "we
would have to say something like this: in all of the great currents of our time there are both theistic and atheistic elements." Father M. D. Chenu concurs: The atheization of the
world has "touched not only individuals but even the very
structures of the new humanity," but this gives no license to
"lump together under the term 'atheism' too many disparate
elements." [16]

The term "atheist" is here applied only to the integral form,
the closed-system definition, which roots out God and the idea
of God from human existence. It denies his transcendence and
his action in history. Since it is surrounded by beliefs in gods,
to preserve its identity it must also be *antitheist;* that is, it must
reject the idea of God as a threat to human freedom.

Modern atheism or antitheism, then, must be regarded as an
event, just as the other original families of unbelief under discussion are. It occurs and can occur only where belief is or has
been.

> [This] explains why atheism, which . . . is to be met in
> history—though in a systematic form which indicates that
> it is of late and even accidental occurrence—is itself a proof,
> by reason of its invariably polemical character (witness Lu-

[16] *Cross Currents,* XI, No. 1 (Winter, 1961), 12.

cretius in antiquity, or Nietzsche and Marx in the modern
world), of the reality and depth of the religious impulse.[17]

The reader who desires to see the faces of atheism detailed
from the viewpoint of Christian (Catholic) belief, will do well
to consult Étienne Borne's *Atheism*. As Borne depicts it, atheism is dogmatic, as is nihilism; it also rules out the possibility a
priori of revelatory elements. But it differs from nihilism in
that it can construct—and indeed desires to construct—positive
views of history after the death of God. His corpse must be removed in order to make man free. Borne makes much of the
basic divisions within atheism. He distinguishes an atheism of
solitude and an atheism of solidarity, the former, Nietzschean
(God is dead, individual man becomes free), and the latter,
Marxist (God is dead, so man in the collective form becomes
free to fulfill the historical process). But atheism must also be
broken into what we would call nonintegral (e.g., pantheist)
forms and what he, too, calls integral ones.

Integral atheism seeks and claims to have found a decisive
proof against God in the order, or rather the absence of order, of this world. It sees discord and contradiction everywhere. . . . Sartre, with some insight, finds the negations
of God in the irreducible opposition between value, which
has so little strength it is confounded with nothingness, and
reality, which is so strong as to be altogether too much.
. . . It is from absolute evil that integral atheism infers the
impossibility of God. [Thus it refutes philosophies of history
such as those of Marx.] The supreme argument is between
Christianity and integral atheism.[18]

17 Regis Jolivet, *Man and Metaphysics,* trans. B. M. G. Reardon (New
York: Hawthorn, 1961), p. 24.
18 *Atheism,* trans. S. J. Tester (New York: Hawthorn, 1961), pp. 49-83,
and especially pp. 80-83.

Integral atheism is so sure of itself that assent to a belief-system which is open to the divine is always by its nature, to use Sartre's phrase, "bad faith." Integral atheism, it must be noted, is difficult to see incarnate and institutionalized. Some would go so far as to suggest that this form of atheism is impossible to sustain. Paul Tillich would see the reflective and impassioned atheist gripped by an attachment to "ultimate concern" and thus—by Tillich's definition—religious. The student of religions, Gerardus van der Leeuw, doubts its historic reference: "It has never, in any conditions whatever, acquired historical form." Individuals may run away but they end up in the jaws of the next power. "There is no religion of atheism: there is only the individual fleeing from God. . . ." Insofar as every religion experiences a flight from God, it has an atheistic dimension, but that is different from persistent atheism.[19]

When the definition of religion is as broad and dynamic as Tillich's and van der Leeuw's, unquestionably one cannot speak of atheism; atheists in their passion may often be the most religious. But it is a different matter to speak of atheism as an event on Christian soil. There, Christian proclamation can be an agent of reaction. According to Gerhard Ebeling:

> The source of modern atheism is closely connected with Christian faith. Only where God is so radically proclaimed and believed can he be so radically denied. . . . Furthermore, Christianity [in its failures] has also a guilty connection with the pre-history of modern atheism.[20]

Atheism as an event of reaction to Christian proclamation and life is still dependent on what it opposes, though this de-

19 *Religion in Essence and Manifestation*, trans. J. E. Turner (New York: Harper & Row, 1963), II, 600 f.
20 *The Nature of Faith*, trans. Ronald Gregor Smith (Philadelphia: Muhlenberg, 1961), p. 80.

posit may be less each year and atheism may be taking new
forms today—for example, in Sartre's dogmatic humanism
which begins to be affirmative without reference to Christianity.
Sartre does not need Nietzsche's dead God as a background;
Sartre is content: God may have spoken, but now he is silent.
Some Christians have begun to speculate about the character
of the new kind of atheist. Romano Guardini sees the development of a new kind of atheist in the "autonomous secular order." Hence, lines may be drawn more sharply between Christian and dedicated non-Christian.

> The unbeliever will emerge from the fogs of secularism.
> He will cease to reap benefit from the values and forces de-
> veloped by the very Revelation he denies. He must learn to
> exist honestly without Christ and without the God revealed
> through Him; he will have to learn to experience what this
> honesty means. . . . A new paganism differing from that of
> earlier ages will appear in the new world.[21]

Until atheism completely frees itself from Christian reminiscence, it will not be completely integral. Haunted as it
sometimes is by Christian appeals, tantalized by what it opposes, it remains open to dialogue, even at a great distance. As
time passes this dialogue breaks down. Many dedicated human-
ists in European intellectual circles claim to go through their
careers without meeting a confirmed Christian.

Some believers see positive elements in atheism. As judgment
on Christian inaction or as condemnation of Christian injus-
tice, it has a creative function. Often quoted is Martin Luther's
dramatic assertion that God might prefer the angry shout of
the atheist to the prattle of the pious. Atheism is greeted by
others for its rejection of a disfigured God and thus as a catalyst

---

[21] "The End of the Modern World," in Barry Ulanov, *Contemporary
Catholic Thought* (New York: Sheed & Ward, 1963), pp. 172 f.

for Christian redefinition.[22] Today's integral atheism, because
it remains a religion of rejection, is not as attractive as it
might be. Emmanuel Mounier has called its present form aus-
terely Calvinistic, cold, shuddering, morose, and even whiney
in tone. Atheism which moves beyond rejection to the point
where it does not care whether God ever lived or died is a more
perplexing problem for Christians.

Implied in these last words is a word of advice which many
students of unbelief give to believers: Do not let atheism become integral. Keep it open, uncertain. Subject it to the same
kind of systematic scrutiny to which it has subjected Christianity. The counsel to remain an irritant at the side of modern unbelief is frequently heard. Gabriel Marcel has served as one
of these questioners ("Has a philosophy the right to pass judgment on the universe as being absurd?"); so, as we have seen,
has de Rougemont, who wants documentation in history for
the event of the death of God. The open-system alternative to
atheism is agnosticism or radical skepticism. Like atheism, it
finds that God is not apparent, but evil is. Unlike atheism, it
does not make the absence of God an a priori in a dogmatic
method. When consistent with its own basis, it is historically
oriented and open: "I do not now know whether or not God
is and acts." The agnostic, from the Christian viewpoint, may
be as far from the kingdom of God as the atheist. But on the
human plane he presents a different set of problems.

Those who refuse to make distinctions between types of unbelief will be impelled to lump together both atheism and
agnosticism. When this is done, great numbers of self-admitted
and self-defining seekers are given a creed (atheism) which
they may not be seeking. This may be legitimate from the
viewpoint of the fullness of Christian belief, but it is an
imprecise way of dealing with matters. It is the opposite
counterpart of the tendency of religionists (Tillich, van der

22 See André Liégé, O.P., *What Is Christian Life?* Trans. A. Manson
(New York: Hawthorn, 1961), p. 40.

Leeuw) to "convert by definition," describing religion in such broad terms that it includes everyone. The majority in America's academic-scientific community might become atheist in such a designation, whereas the prevailing assumption and method is actually more agnostic or skeptical. Borne suggests that it is advisable for believers to separate agnostics from atheists to emphasize the fact that unbelief is a house divided against itself. Tactically, to incorporate all seems to him to give credence to the unbelievers' assumption that leaving Christian belief behind is somehow the natural thing to do. Agnosticism, the most prevalent form of intellectual unbelief, is often an embarrassment to other forms, just as the persistence of doubt is a problem for faith. Thus, we are often reminded, one cannot be an agnostic Marxist, and there was no such thing as an agnostic in the Nazi ideology. These philosophies of historical process and power purport to *know* where history is taking men. The agnostic does not know.

The agnostic vision begins with an awareness of "the benign indifference of the universe." The agnostic marvels at the persistence of the Christian enterprise, particularly when he finds it intellectually respectable. To him this seems to be like erecting a traditionally strong edifice on a metaphysically condemned site. He finds his freedom in an uncluttered laboratory, where the "God of explanation" would stand in his way. He needs no hypothetical God, no stop-gap God, no *deus ex machina* to be wheeled out when man is at the end of his intelligence. The scientific method and the historical sense are part of the agnostic temper. These are reasons why the agnostic is more at home in America than the atheist. He is active in both kinds of secularization: the attempt to separate life from religion and the attempt to transform religion under existing symbols.[23]

23 The agnostic temper is also at home in Christianity and particularly in Protestantism, though it may be mislabeled atheism. The nineteenth-century historian of theology, Albert Ritschl, once wrote, "Without [apart

Agnosticism is by its nature antidogmatic and thus oriented toward history. It may need reminders of its own first presupposition. Thus in a book of satire the agnostic is reminded of the dangers of overconfidence in the following definition:

> [Agnostic:] A two dollar word invented in the nineteenth century by Thomas Huxley. It served him and his time well, but it has no current use or validity. Nowadays we know

---

from] Christ I am an agnostic [or atheist]." There are many today who would readily subscribe to this remark. John Courtney Murray, S.J., "The Structure of the Problem of God," *Theological Studies*, XXIII, No. 1 (March, 1962), 20, quotes J. N. Findlay: "I am by temperament a Protestant, and I tend toward atheism as the purest form of Protestantism." Comments Murray:

> In other words, the religion of modernity, which was Protestantism, is atheist in its logic. . . . The tendency of his Protestant temperament is towards avoidance of idolatry; but in the logic of this tendency, pursued as a philosopher pursues logic, there lies the denial of the presence of God. This is biblical atheism. . . . In the modern context he who says to himself, "God is here," is the fool.

Protestant conservatives with a strong metaphysical viewpoint join extreme Protestant rationalists (Bartley was noted earlier) or agnostics (Kaufmann) and Thomist Catholics (Murray) in pointing to this logic. Thus Carl Henry, in John F. Walvoord (ed.), *Inspiration and Interpretation* (Grand Rapids, Mich.: Eerdmans, 1957), p. 268, in the context of the authority of Scripture: "The surrender [by neo-liberals] of conceptual knowledge of the metaphysical world inherits always the task of avoiding agnosticism as its discomforting estate." Among the best recent statements critical of Protestant atheism or agnosticism is Alasdair MacIntyre, "God and the Theologians," in *Encounter*, September, 1963. His essay was occasioned by John A. T. Robinson's book *Honest to God* (Philadelphia: Westminster, 1963) which, in the name of authentic Christianity, rejects ideas of transcendence and other Christian metaphysical statements. Citing these critics does not imply that they have caught the real intention of the Protestant theologians in question. But unquestionably, Protestantism does introduce an attitude against idolatry which can turn against symbols, and an attitude of criticism that can become skeptical.

everything; except who we are, where we are going, and
what we are doing here, wherever that is.[24]

Agnosticism as an event on post-Christian soil is open to
affirmation in ways that atheism is not. It exists in the world of
longing, which was the affirmative counterpart to nihilism. It
still is devoid of content, for it is a method. But it enables one
to stand, as Simone Weil found herself, "at the intersection of
Christianity and everything that is not Christianity." Of course,
there are psychological and intellectual dangers, as well as
spiritual problems, in agnosticism's intersectional position. One
may fail to derive the real benefits of either Christian belief or
unbelief. One may romanticize the attitude of doubt and become a permanent fence-sitter ("Do I dare?" "Notice my
doubts!" "What am I bid as I settle on a commitment?"). These
are not greater hazards than those which accompany any other
important commitment, and they are more fruitful than some
for those interested in communicating between believers and
unbelievers.

The agnostic may stand at the side of the believer as they together help "kill off Pan and Caesar" by dedivinizing nature
and desacralizing the state. The agnostic is quite sure that man
will then stand alone; the Christian has a different hope. Both
attitudes differ markedly from that of the atheist, who knows
and proclaims the freedom of man apart from God. John
Dewey saw the dangers in skepticism that becomes religious. It
must remain particular, not general; it must be historically,
not dogmatically oriented; it must constantly seek new goals.
"Skepticism that is not . . . a search [for new facts and ideas]
is as much a personal emotional indulgence as is dogmatism."
Therefore, Dewey rejects "the grounds upon which wholesale
skeptical and agnostic philosophies have rested" in the interest of experiment and the scientific or historical methods.

[24] Samuel Milton Elam, *Hornbook for the Double Damned* (New York:
Meridian, 1962), p. 13.

"Skepticism and agnosticism are particular and depend upon special conditions; they are not wholesale." [25] These expressions are far removed from those of integral atheism, and alert believers will notice the difference when they deal with the self-conscious agnostic. Perhaps nowhere among all the varieties of unbelief does the distinction "closed" versus "open" have more practical bearing.

In a remarkable statement the anthropologist Bronislaw Malinowski argues for an alliance between agnostic and Christian—the kind of working arrangement impossible with the integral atheist and the doctrinaire Christian.

> I, personally, am unable to accept any revealed religion, Christian or not. But even an agnostic has to live by faith— in the case of us, prewar rationalists and liberals, by the faith in humanity and its powers of improvement. This faith allowed us to work. . . . [Since World War I] science, like Christianity, has failed us as a foundation for ethics and for constructive action. So that as a rationalist and a believer in the development of human personality and of a liberal commonwealth of free men, I find myself in the same predicament as that of a believing Christian. It is high time that the old, now essentially unreal, feud between science and religion should be ended, and that both should join hands against the common enemy.[26]

Today the feud has moved on from the struggle between science and religion to the question of meaning and purpose in life in a universe where God is not apparent and evil is. The

[25] John Dewey, *The Quest for Certainty* (New York: Putnam, 1960), pp. 193, 228. Dewey did not always hold to these professions, but this is not more important than the fact that Christians are not always consistent, either.

[26] *Sex, Culture, and Myth* (New York: Harcourt, Brace, 1962), pp. 296 f. This statement was made originally in the Riddell Lectures of 1935.

atheist and the Christian dogmatist seldom find much to talk
about together, though they may shout. The agnostic and the
critical Christian are in much closer relation.

**4. Unbelief which supplants the God of Christian faith and
develops pantheisms and paganisms of history and power**

When religious people in America are told of the prevalence
of unbelief in the modern world, they often feel incredulous
and skeptical. Where are these unbelievers, these atheists? The
sense of Christian well-being is so regularly cultivated in religious organizations that one may be regarded as a pessimist
merely for tabulating the strength of the forces outside of world
Christianity.

If at such a moment one introduces that half of the world
which is not called "free," and points out that it has virtually
moved outside the reach of historic Christian belief, a startled
sense of recognition may dawn upon the audience. "We hadn't
thought of it that way." Nazism, Communism, and the new
nationalisms which parallel or lean toward them are so frequently perceived as political and military threats that their
character as belief-systems is undervalued. Yet in the various
pantheisms and paganisms of history and power are seen the
most powerful examples of Christianity's aftermath in unbelief. They are powerful because they are institutionalized, consolidated, operative. We of the West may assert that "half a
world" is involved involuntarily, by coercion. Without doubt
great numbers of people in the Soviet and Chinese Communist
orbits would prefer a different system and ideology. But it is
fatuous to assume that these are merely imposed systems. They
are also believed, and believed with passion that shames adherents of historic faiths. Even where they are not readily accepted as justifications of national goals, they serve to compli-
cate living witness to Christian belief.

Modern idolizations of history and power are not wholly

original. Greece and Rome and other pre- or para-Christian societies celebrated their military pretensions in pantheons and by adoration of Caesars. In the world hardly touched by Christianity, empires may bear some of the marks of post-Christian paganism. Still, it is possible to speak of these most powerfully organized phases of unbelief as original, as events which grew up on Christian soil and look different because of their experience. Since many protest when Communism is called a Christian heresy, it might be well to avoid the term in this context. But it is obvious that Communism is an event which exists in the face of Christianity, from whose history it has learned, and which it seeks to supplant.

Only the last two of the nine summary features we detected in treatments of modern unbelief are absent here. They are: (a) In the free world it is increasingly assumed that no single consensus is essential for political life; the Nazi and Communist worlds *know* that consensus is necessary. Where not accepted, it must be imposed. The Communist faith sees this view of history on its way to worldwide prevalence; (b) The breakdown of the symbolic universe is also more the experience of an open and pluralist society than of a closed, monolithic one. While dictators have difficulty enforcing their attempt to impose symbols (witness the German artistic underground of 1933-45 and the deviationism of Russian artists into "bourgeois" molds), symbols are widely recognized. In Communism this is possible because the historical process generates a kind of this-worldly transcendence which unifies the world of the mundane and the world of the ideal. In Nazism the folk-deities of the nation's past were artificially resurrected to provide symbolism.

On the other seven points, the originality of these modern events of unbelief is clear. With them Christians are made aware of the conflict of belief-systems in the world. (Where does one hear "everyday" Christians of the West speak of atheism except in connection with Communism?) Second, the aware-

ness of the depth of unbelief's penetration into all areas of life
is manifest in the totalitarian system which absorbs all a nation's activity. The transcendent note is lost. Man is not seen
to be alone in the cosmos as he serves the state or the process.
The churches are effectually or formally displaced. The political consolidation of these forms of unbelief is recognized as a
culmination of long historical processes of revolution or reaction on secular lines. The *ersatz* faiths which crowd in upon
the death of God are numerous.

Much of what was said throughout these chapters concerning the nature of unbelief can be tested in these historical
movements. That today's man may, in his heart of hearts, already have opted for pantheism against theism or atheism is
suggested. That real atheism is difficult is evident: Man flees
from one power to the jaws of another. The fact that these
movements may, like Communism, call themselves atheist is
not necessarily a reason for accepting the designation. On
Borne's terms, one would not worry about Communism if it
were atheism, for atheism, as such, has no program, no base for
consolidation in political and national life.

While mere nationalism and culture religion can become
integral and can bear similarities to these idolizations of the
historical process, they are not exact counterparts. Whereas
anomie-accidie, nihilism, and particularly atheism had open-
system counterparts or nonintegral opposite numbers, these
ideologies by definition leave no room for the nonintegral.
Deviationism there may be, but not so much because those at
the centers of power consider it to be advisable as because they
must permit it. Everything is worked out; the ideology has an
answer for everything because it knows and possesses the future.
The master race will prevail. The historical process will see
the defeat of capitalism.

It is not without significance that when a political ideology
of a quasi-religious character is imposed on a people with

strong Christian leanings or memories, the ideologists immediately sense the need of providing secular and social rites which parallel Christian baptism, confirmation, marriage, and burial. An incredible number of details of private life are made to serve the process. Both Nazi Germany and Communist China immediately found the existing family structure an impediment, and developed substitutes which would better serve the nation. Details of private lives are public to those who impose and control the ideology and are kept secret from the free world. In attention even to minor detail, the integral character of pantheisms and paganisms of the political world is made patent.

The presence of these idolizations of history and events is a warning to those who follow the argument of this book to note that devotion to history *as such* solves nothing, if humans are looking for protection against idolization. The Japanese, who lived under the post-Buddhist unbelief of World War II's warlords, saw the power of unbelief and new ideology in the Orient, where history was viewed less purposefully than in the West. The Germans, who lived under the post-Christian unbelief of Nazism's pagan militarists, saw the power of unbelief and new ideology in the Occident, where history was viewed more purposefully (beginning, middle, end) than in the East. Clearly, the "historylessness" of Eastern religion and the "sense of history" of Western Christianity were both absorbed, then displaced and ground up by different kinds of ideologies. History, when deified, can terrorize, and something else must be meant in this book when historical openness is cited as an element in open systems.[27] Albert Camus, as clearly as anyone, no-

---

[27] See Karl R. Popper, *The Open Society and Its Enemies*, Vol. II, which is subtitled, *The High Tide of Prophecy: Hegel, Marx, and the Aftermath* (New York: Harper & Row, 1963), for a full-length discussion of the integralists' misuses of history and prophecy. See especially Chap. 25, "Has History Any Meaning?"

ticed the dangers of the idolization of history when nature is desacralized ("the breakdown of the symbolic order") and politics is not dedivinized.

It is Christianity that began substituting the tragedy of the soul for contemplation of the world. But, at least, Christianity referred to a spiritual nature and thereby preserved a certain fixity. *With God dead, there remains only history and power.* For some time the entire effort of our philosophers has aimed solely at replacing the notion of human nature with that of situation, and replacing ancient harmony with the disorderly advance of chance or reason's pitiless progress. . . . Europe no longer philosophizes by striking a hammer, but by shooting a cannon.[28]

The power of ideologies of history translated to politics is most clearly seen in our context: It allows neither for nonintegral nor open participation. The characteristic term applied to a state built upon such an ideology is "totalitarian," and the description is precise. No area of life is exempt from its domain. There is no room for the half-believer, the dissenter, the heretic. The heretic becomes the martyr and the dissenter moves in secret; neither belongs to the society in which he lives. The answers to all conceivable questions of life are anticipated and solved in the simplicism of the totalitarian answer. The leader has ultimate self-confidence that his purposes are congruent with those of history, and the follower is led to share this belief. The judgment upon the forms of society implicit in Christian belief is rejected as an impossible intrusion. The redemption in and beyond society, which is the corollary element of Christian belief, is denied, for it provides exception to the single-minded purpose in history as perceived by the state.

Not even atheism pretends to such powers. Less potent, be-

[28] From "Helen's Exile" (1948) in *The Myth of Sisyphus*, trans. Justin O'Brien (New York: Vintage, 1959), pp. 136 f. (Italics added.)

cause it has never been consistently actualized in human society, atheism produces alongside itself a nervous uncertainty which is one of the forms of agnosticism. But an agnostic Nazi or an agnostic Leninist is a contradiction in terms.

The reasons for Christian concern over the development of such forms of belief in history and power are obvious. Christianity may be permitted to survive as a private element in life but not as an inclusive view of society, culture, or the state. More often, Christianity is transformed by force (as in Hitler's takeover of the hierarchy of the Evangelical churches and the development of the *Deutsche Christen* cult, and as in Red China's assumption of the hierarchical role in the Roman Catholic Church which is actually cut off from Rome) or by circumscription of the church's domains (as in Communist Poland or Hungary, where the churches are free to exist within certain boundaries).

Conversion from a totalitarian ideology to free and open Christianity is impossible because Christianity is limited and defined in such a society. Even where such an ideology is chosen—as in the American Communist party of the 1930s—conversion represents a possibility only because the party has not prevailed politically. In the free world, men who shared the ideology could leave it and write of "the God that failed," as many of them did. But when the ideology has taken complete power, conversion can mean only quiet dissent, a circumscribed Christianity, or martyrdom. Each represents a kind of rejection from society.

As with conversion, so with communication. Words ("people's democracy," "freedom," "peace," etc.) take on different colors and are used for different goals. Collaboration is not one between equals but between the ruling belief-system and the tolerated subordinate.

Since our only interest is in the integral-nonintegral distinction, it is not incumbent upon us to trace the whole history of these modern unbelief patterns. They have their roots in Hegel's dehistoricizing of Christianity in the name of history. For him, where God is master of history, there is no history. Where God intrudes upon history, there is no human history. Thus Trinity and Incarnation—the symbolic terms of Christian reference in this study of belief—cannot be part of the system.

What Hegel undertook to do, still showing some deference to Christian reminiscence, was shaken by his left-wing materialist successors, notably Feuerbach and his great heir Marx. The right-wing succession was consolidated in Nietzsche and given political incarnation in the Nazi movement, which, though no legitimate heir of Nietzsche, made its appeal to his vision of man in a universe where God is dead and man is free.[29]

The post-Hegelian offshoots sometimes call themselves atheist (Marx-Lenin) and sometimes veer off into more obvious kinds of paganism and thus cannot call themselves atheist (the Rosenberg mythos of Nazism). Both are convinced that the God of Christian worship and history is dead; his corpse is the stench among men; it must be dragged out so that the new can take its place. In Nietzsche and the bastard movements which appeal to him, individual man is freed to fulfill history; in the

---

[29] See Étienne Borne, *op. cit.*, pp. 35 ff. The chapter titled "In the Beginning Was Hegel" details the process from Hegel to today in terms congenial with the argument of this book. "This same Hegel, whom we can expect to find at the heart of all forms of modern atheism, is the very opposite of an atheist. Few philosophers have made more of God, even to the point of systematically taking the side of the infinite and absolute against the littleness of individual men. But Hegel, and this is surely the basis of his teaching, judged that the story of man, in which he thought that Christianity had its proper and necessary place, could not be rationally completed except by passing beyond Christianity. . . . Hegel undertook to reform the God of Christian experience, so that history could attain to its rational completion. . . ."

One might almost say that, to modern political ideologues, Incarnation as the historical and thus nonsystematic intrusion of God in the affairs of men is the really offensive point in Christianity. With it, history takes on surprise and particularity. It cannot be depended upon or brought to "its rational completion."

Marxist family, human solidarity fulfills history. Unbelief of the former kind is obvious because it calls itself atheist even where it is not; the unbelief of the latter is equally obvious. Where it is consistent, it militates against the God of Christian memory; where somewhat inconsistent (as paganisms always seem to be), Christian traces may be absorbed in a haphazard syncretistic process along with traces of other gods.

The German sociologist Spranger was the first to call Communism "a secular religion"; no one needed to think long to apply the term to Nazism and the pagan apotheoses of history and power. Communists, calling themselves atheist, may reject the word "religion" as inapplicable, but students of comparative religion do not shy away because of this. Jules Monnerot observes:

> A religion is seen as such only by those outside of it. For its adherents it is simply the highest form of truth. For the true believer Russia no longer exists as such; but he does not believe he is a believer; he believes he possesses the truth. In fact, he is *possessed* by something which he believes to be the truth. . . .[30]

[30] *Sociology and Psychology of Communism* (Boston: Beacon, 1960), pp. 16, 20. Monnerot's approach to integral unbelief is made clear on p. 123:
"What in Hegel was philosophy becomes, after Marx, religion. *A philosophy lived collectively cannot remain philosophy but is transformed into religion.*"
"[Now] it is here that Marxism, which takes up again on its own account the Hegelian search for the unity and homogeneity of the world, can make an ally of the need for intellectual unity, coherence, and tranquillity, which has moved men at different periods of history to look for a key and to believe that they have found one. The aim is to enclose everything within a circle, leaving nothing outside; to enclose literally everything, beginning with life itself. It is then no longer a question of a purely speculative system, but of an orthodoxy which shall be at one and the same time a vision of the world and a practical imperative, both science and conquest."
P. 131: "If intellectuals are easily attracted by Marxism and then by

While those forms of pantheism or paganism of history and power which grew up on Christian soil are doctrinaire and, at root, intellectualistic, one must not suppose that all participants in the system share it on the same level. There are two levels of obvious competition—between pantheisms and paganisms and within them. There is, for example, an individualistic and a collectivistic Hegelianism, a right and left wing. But more important is the actual historical situation in world politics. Here one sees that the integral attempts are themselves intruded

communism, it is because they are projecting an aspiration for orthodoxy upon an actual living phenomenon which combines within itself a doctrine, a church, and an army. This phenomenon possesses the attraction of totality and of unity; it is a new form which can present itself to our imagination, if we allow it, as an integrating force capable of embracing everything without exception, so that the historical nostalgia for orthodoxy and the human yearning for atonement can be merged together in it and find fulfilment.

"Existence, on the plane of lived experience, and science, on the plane of controlled experiment, are both of them by definition *open*, and, compared to them, the System has today the appearance of a closed sepulchre." But Marxism finds ways to integrate these, too!

After a discussion of Nazism's intricate disguises of its nihilism, p. 292: "History and the historical mind cannot be accused of making anyone a nihilist who was not already on the way to become one; for there is nothing that history more clearly emphasizes than man's inventiveness. Man is, above all, *the animal which finds a way out.*"

Monnerot's text is highly relevant, offering a full-scale development of one of the varieties of unbelief and one of the few that permits no open or nonintegral alternative.

See also Peter Viereck, *Meta-Politics: The Roots of the Nazi Mind* (New York: Capricorn, 1961), especially Chap. 13, "Nazi Religion versus Christian Religion," which discusses the Aryanized Christ, Hitler as Messiah, the new "chosen people," the militancy of the movement, and the renaissance of the dark, dead gods of German nationalism. Viereck's book first appeared in 1941.

On Hegel's glorification of History and a discussion of what he does with Incarnation, see Christopher Dawson, *Progress and Religion* (Garden City. N.Y.: Doubleday, 1960), pp. 32 ff., on "History and the Idea of Progress":

upon by combinations of motivations and goals. The break between the doctrinaire, intransigent Red Chinese Leninists and
the negotiating Russian Marxists of the early 1960s certainly
bore the mark of nationalism. Nationalism may be as strong a
driving force and may be the real religion of the modern world,
including the Marxist world. But at its best it does introduce
one more element into the house-divided estate of those who
had tried to complete a circle which would eliminate all possibilities but one. It is not our purpose to speculate as to which
tendency will prevail, but only to note their dual and conflicting presences. Søren Kierkegaard, with that amazing prescience
which characterized much of his work, noticed the dual tendencies. He surmised, when he read the Communist Manifesto of
1848, that although the Marxian revolution appeared to be
economic and social with a religious element it would, when
fulfilled, be seen as a religious revolution with economic and
social elements. In our context, Kierkegaard's observation
leans toward the proper religious interpretation of Marxism,
but the socioeconomic elements may, in turn, prove the basis of

---

Hegel regards History as the highest form of knowledge. Physical science
can only show us the eternal cyclic repetition of phenomenal change,
while universal History is the progressive manifestation and self-realiza-
tion of the absolute spirit in Time. Thus the reality and value of the
eternal world, which idealism had intended to deny in respect to Nature,
is restored and given a transcendent significance. For in History the Real
is the Ideal, "the rational necessary course of the World Spirit," and that
spirit whose nature is always one and the same, but which unfolds this
its one nature in the phenomena of the world's existence.

Two observations are in order here. First, one might almost say that, if
a reader wants to see whether or not a philosopher is tending to integralize
the historical process, he should note whether the philosopher actually
uses or seems to reach for a capital *H* for History. Second, after reading
the Hegelians, one might better understand why integralist Christians are
often the more strident enemies of atheistic Communism and why their
use of history does not differ too widely from the Marxist-Hegelian and
may not be so fruitful an alternative as are nonintegral systems. This will
be developed later.

the undoing or the transformation of a supposedly perfect ideology.[31]

The presence of an incarnate integral system on Russian soil over a period of decades invites a full-scale analysis which we must forgo in this book. A study of its self-proclaimed post-Christian atheism would involve the Russian totalist or maximalist temptation of which Berdyaev spoke and which Solovyov had earlier noted in his attacks on extreme Russian nationalism. We would see the "knowing" of the outcome of history, with the elimination of Incarnation and embarrassment and surprise. We would observe the absence of hesitation or inner conflict in the working-out of history.[32]

Development of these ideas belongs, however, in a book devoted specifically to complex questions such as those raised by Hegel, Nietzsche, and Marx, and by the historical existence of political Communism and Nazism. Nor does our topic permit us to examine those historical instances when Christianity tried to develop its dogmatic and ecclesiastical structure into a totalist political reality (as in the Inquisition). The integralist dangers of dogmatic Christianity have appeared repeatedly, but in this book we must restrict our inquiry to modern unbelief. The originality of modern pantheisms and paganisms of history and power which masquerade as atheism or nationalism lies in their rejection of the living God of Christian witness on once Christian soil.

The man of today may choose other than political versions of his option toward pantheism. But these remain either ill-

[31] Heiberg, Kuhr, and Torsting (eds.), *Søren Kierkegaard: Papirer,* *X6B40* (Copenhagen: Gyldendal, 1934). Quoted also in Carl Michalson, *The Hinge of History* (New York: Scribner, 1959), p. 243.

[32] See Hans Kohn, *The Mind of Modern Russia* (New York: Harper & Row, 1955), p. 223, for Solovyov; Walter Lippmann, *The Communist World and Ours* (Boston: Atlantic-Little, Brown, 1959), p. 51, for an American analyst's view of Leninist knowing; and Gustave Weigel, *The Modern God* (New York: Macmillan, 1963), p. 27, for the Communist world's self-consciousness and sureness as contrasted to the West's hesitations.

defined (as in hedonism and the pursuit of pleasure) or private visions. An example of the latter would be D. H. Lawrence's explicitly pagan philosophy:

> I know the greatness of Christianity: it is a past greatness. I know that, but for those early Christians, we should never have emerged from the chaos and hopeless disaster of the Dark Ages. If I had lived in the year 400, pray God, I should have been a true and passionate Christian. . . . But now I live in 1924, and the Christian venture is done. The adventure is gone out of Christianity. We must start on a new venture toward God.[33]

In William Butler Yeats's private vision, one sees the "start on a new venture toward God" by the development of a sort of neo-pagan mythology. Like Lawrence, Yeats bases his yearning on the death of the Christian God and the resulting "colorless, all-color of atheism from which we shrink." One critic has summarized Yeats's vision: "Better a malign God than no God at all; better to live in a universe of ordained torture, 'the invisible spheres formed in fright,' than in a universe of anarchic godlessness." [34]

Lawrence and Yeats and their colleagues, followers, and limited cults are original in that they must displace the dead God of Christian belief. However, they are of less interest here because in other respects their vision of history is not greatly different from earlier paganisms and because neither is associated with a totalitarian impulse of power.

One could dwell at greater length on Sigmund Freud, who also walked the terrain where the dead gods and especially the once living God of Christian belief lay reeking. Freud's man is

---

33 *Phoenix, the Posthumous Papers of D. H. Lawrence,* ed. Edward D. McDonald (New York: Viking, 1936), p. 734.

34 B. L. Reid, *William Butler Yeats: The Lyric of Tragedy* (Norman, Okla.: University of Oklahoma Press, 1961), pp. 12 f.

Nietzsche's superman, aborted. Freud's is an integralist vision: His a priori in religious matters is that religion, particularly Christian belief, is an illusion. He shared, from different motives, Feuerbach's view that the deity is man written large or projected on a cosmic screen. Freudianism in its orthodox, or closed, forms and in its various heretical (and open) offshoots, such as those of Carl Jung, may be as great a complication for historic Christian belief as is the ideology of Marxism. Freud is an example of the organicist's view of religion: it would pass away inevitably and by a process as inexorable as growth. But Freud should not be associated with Marx and with the various political movements cited above. He was not interested in consolidating his views in actual power movements, believing that science and the scientific method would confirm them. By introducing the empirical possibility, however, his a priori was called into question. Some of his disciples were less sure that religion *had* to be an illusion, and not all of the Freudian heritage represents closed-system complications to Christian belief.

5. Unbelief based on methodological preoccupations which casually crowd historic belief patterns

The four clusters of unbelief which have already been cited have a permanence, a durability of intention, a persistence that characterizes their every element. As a threat to the believing community, each of them seems to be marked by a sense of inevitability. The first family (anomie-accidie) is a form of paralysis which is not open to authentic belief. All forms of nihilism rule out a priori the possibility of ententes with positive faith. Atheism has a polemical character which is integral to its position in the form which appears in modern Western history. The ideologies of history and power of the post-Christian West must, with determination, supplant the community of Christian belief.

Over against these are forms of unbelief which may be described as accidental or casual. It may seem strange thus to classify them, for these may be most extensive of all, most full of practical effects for the daily life of free men. What is more, the historical development of each has seen decades, if not centuries, of warfare with theology; how can they be classified as casual or accidental? If in this family we include such features of modern life as scientism and the technological world view; secularization of the historical method and of politics—how can these be seen to be marked by anything but insistent opposition to historic faith? Does calling these "casual" in any way reduce their power as alternatives to Christian belief?

The answer to these questions begins with the reminder that throughout this study, unbelief is being regarded as an event, an historic episode in Euro-American experience. In this context one may say that the clash between the methods of science and technology, critical history, political and social sciences and, on the other hand, Christian theology and life has been episodic. Many have moved beyond mere clash, finding ways of bringing the two outlooks together. This has been done not only by an unsatisfying compartmentalization of life. The methods have been many: adaptation, moving to higher syntheses, clarifying the intention of language in each, and so forth. Historians of modern unbelief regularly date the crest of the clash between science and theology in the nineteenth century; today the question of meaning in life predominates over the scientific problem. Yet both science and theology have survived, the scientific method and the life of faith coexisting in the same communities and the same individuals. If the clash were inevitable, permanent, and inclusive, such a situation would not exist today.

In no wise should this observation minimize the enduring power of methods which crowd historic ways of looking at faith. Alfred North Whitehead's familiar observation remains true: "Each age has its dominant preoccupation, and during the three [modern] centuries . . . the cosmology derived from science has been asserting itself at the expense of older points of view with their origins elsewhere.[35] Nor has much of anything happened to minimize the psychic dislocation implied in the scientific method since this dislocation was described by Walter Lippmann a third of a century ago: "The radical novelty of modern science lies precisely in the rejection of the belief, which is at the heart of all popular religion, that the forces which move the stars and atoms are contingent upon the preferences of the human heart."

The dominance of a new cosmology and its shattering effects on man produced the well-known "warfare of science with theology." Science, in order to define itself as it confronted Christianity, has regularly had to elbow its way into respectability and alternately to ward off embrace by believers who would misuse the scientific method. The warfare is stated in dramatic terms when it is regarded as a conflict of orthodoxies. Thus André Gide claimed that Christian orthodoxy is exclusive; belief in its truth excludes belief in any other truth. "Culture must understand that by trying to absorb Christianity it is absorbing something that is mortal for it." [36]

The difference between the original forms of unbelief based broadly on the scientific method and those previously cited can be stated simply: The nihilist, atheist, consistent Nazi or Communist, may not become Christian without ceasing to be nihilist, atheist, or consistent ideologue. The scientist, tech-

---

[35] *Science and the Modern World* (New York: Macmillan, 1927), p. ix.

[36] Lippmann is quoted from *A Preface to Morals* (Boston: Beacon, 1960), p. 127; see André Gide, in Justin O'Brien (ed.), *The Journals of André Gide* (New York: Knopf, 1948), II, 380. H. G. Wood, *Belief and Unbelief Since 1850* (Cambridge: Cambridge University Press, 1955), is a brief but still sufficiently detailed study of the episodic clash between modern critical and scientific methods and historic faith. His account should be consulted by those readers who wish to explore further the specific problem of science versus faith. The setting of his book is Great Britain, but the character of the struggle there has been paralleled elsewhere.

nologist, or secular politician may become, may be, and often is a believing Christian. His styles of living in the two spheres may often clash, but they need not do so inevitably. The practical effects of living in two spheres may often be paralyzing to the life of faith, but these can theoretically be transcended.[37]

The scientific method, modern cosmologies, the secularization of politics, and the critical approach to human relations have had to do without "the God of explanation," and where Christianity stands at its (his?) side it is threatened. The adaptation of Christianity to the modern scientific situation has meant definite changes in historic ways of looking at faith. But it has not in every such instance of clash failed to produce coexistence or synthesis. Perhaps one reason for this is that the scientific method *is* a method. As a method it is agnostic; it does not know. Through hypotheses and experiment it seeks to affirm and may make many provisional assertions. Most details of daily life may be based on these assertions. But insofar as the method remains critical and agnostic, it also remains open or nonintegral and thus does not a priori rule out Christian belief. It alters the human context of faith, forces a reappraisal of the history of faith, and threatens many expressions of belief. But it does not necessarily close itself off in such a way as to rule out belief "before all the returns are in."

An integral parallel to the scientific method does exist. For

37 It is interesting to note that in some surveys students of natural and physical sciences are more predisposed to being Christian believers than are those in historical and social sciences. They may even be attracted to the more literalistic biblical attitudes, according to a University of Chicago survey. See Albert Rasmussen, "Contemporary Religious Appeals and Who Responds," in Jane C. Zahn (ed.), *Religion and the Face of America* (Berkeley: University of California Press, 1959), p. 11. The *rapprochement* may occur not only on the level where two materialistic views of truth are compatible but also on levels of synthesis. The lifework of Pierre Teilhard de Chardin suggests one such synthesis which is provocative if not always completely orthodox.

some people it can be summarized in the phrase "the scientific world view." But we may question whether *the* scientific world view has existed since the days of Newton. Today something more dynamic and competitive is evident: the presence of fluid scientific world *views*, among them forms open to Christianity. When the scientific world view closes itself into scientism and seeks to offer the answers to ultimate questions, or rules out the legitimacy of asking ultimate questions, it moves, of course, into the realm of permanent and necessary incompatibility with belief.

Science must be the destroyer of faith when it absolutely dehumanizes. It creates disaster when it enters into a tragic fusion with politics and loses its own freedom. Faith is in jeopardy when scientism produces the kind of technology in which the entire human landscape seems to be man-made and man thus absolutely holds control of the future, or believes he does. When the scientist becomes "priest and savior" and a chaos without meaning results, faith is lost.[38] While these evidences may be prevalent in culture, they are the fruit of scientism (integral) and not of the scientific method, precisely defined.

The scientific method may come to be integral if other forms of viewing evidence (historical, experiential) are completely displaced and if the secular communion of saints disintegrates. Faith is a fragile growth, and human experience ("the heart has its reasons") seems frail in the face of the promises and performances of science and technology. The transcendent loses power and men turn to inventions.[39] Technology, as H. Richard Niebuhr has observed, gains power because it gives

[38] For a book-length discussion of this topic and an extension of the points in this paragraph, see Harold K. Schilling, *Science and Religion: An Interpretation of Two Communities* (New York: Scribner, 1962), especially pp. 233 ff.

[39] See J. H. Oldham, *Work in Modern Society* (Richmond, Va.: John Knox, 1961), p. 18.

us signs, makes predictions, comes through to fulfillment, and is somehow thus seen to be faithful to man.[40]

We have chosen to refer particularly to the scientific method (versus integral scientism) and, in passing, to technological interests (if not technology), though these are but part of a larger revolution in man's coming of age, his emergence from religious adolescence. Actually, the complicated process of secularization represents a form of unbelief which methodologically crowds historic faith. Viewing the process as a whole, one must ask the same question that was asked of the scientific-critical method. Can one apply the terms "casual" and "accidental" to the crowding and the clash? If the modern world does contain people of real faith and if these people are sophisticated enough also to breathe the air of the secular world, then one must answer that secularization as an event is not necessarily integral or closed to faith. Secular*ism* is. Secularism permits no transcendent reference, no witness to the activity of God in history, no possibility of "belief *that*" he is or "belief *in*" his actions or belief in the witnesses to him in the human sphere. It is self-contained, self-explanatory, self-enclosed. It can very well be the real religion of the modern world, incorporating most elements of what belonged to life in historic religions.

If we take seriously the testimony of Christian thinkers in the secular era, even though we do not agree with it, we will discover people who affirm their belief in God and who move with real freedom and finesse in modern culture. Such a culture is marked, then, by secularity: a carefully cultivated and self-critical (nonintegral) base of neutrality which withholds judgments until "after the returns are in." Such a culture may pose deadening effects to faith. It may mean that year by year

[40] *Radical Monotheism and Western Culture* (New York: Harper & Row, 1960). See especially pp. 79 ff., although the whole essay has a bearing on this topic.

the returns will further convince man of the meaninglessness of the Christian residue in personal and social experience. But this kind of threat is very different from one posed by a closed system of secularism. A neutral secularity, for instance, may state that it is legally necessary in a modern pluralistic state *not* to permit prayers in public schools. The deadening corollary may be the logical deduction that the God once prayed to is silent or dead. But actually the practice of the state is not to pass this judgment; it makes no comment on God's existence or activity but only on the legality of imposing a spiritual climate on all schoolchildren.

Max Weber contended that "all phenomena that originated in religious conceptions succumb" to the steady "progress of the characteristic process of 'secularization.'" He noticed this particularly in American life.[41] Without doubt there has been a four-centuries-long drift in the direction Weber describes, although it is questionable whether *all* signs on all fronts at all times belong to this drift. Again, one must observe that there is a difference between historical tendencies with their ambiguous developments (scientific method, secularity) and philosophical a prioristic systems which cancel each other out (scientism, secularism). There are many Christians who, having reflected on the situation, would not choose to "push the world back into adolescence" and resurrect the "God of explanation" as being a desirable way to propagate the faith. Most unreflective Christians have also somehow come to terms with secularization and in many cases have held to a kind of faith which can bear scrutiny. If this is true, the issues over casual or accidental clashes must be resolved on the practical front: How is life really lived?

Answers or attempts at answers to this question can best be examined in the political sphere, which is the real base of secu-

41 In H. H. Gerth and C. Wright Mills (eds.), *From Max Weber: Essays in Sociology* (New York: Oxford University Press, 1958), p. 307.

lar life and society.[42] In this sphere the mainstream of development in the West for over four centuries, and particularly in the last two, has been toward secularization, and the trend is continuing. It is another question whether the trend rules out real Christian belief or whether it actually liberates, defines, and sets in bolder relief the believing community.

The secular society arose out of a combination of practical circumstances, conflicting ideologies and church acquiescence. In the United States the fact that the several colonies had differing religious establishments or none made a particular establishment impossible as the nation was formed. The presence of an American Enlightenment or natural religion made public profession of particular Christian truths unnecessary or complicated. The fact that some churches such as Baptist and Quaker fellowships were being persecuted by the establishments and the fact that their theology allowed for separating the spheres of church and state promoted secularization because the state took on a kind of autonomy. Beginning in 1774 in Virginia, the New World produced a separated situation in which church and state legally went their own ways even though their relations were congenial.

The passing of the years and the growing articulateness of the competing religious and nonreligious groups in the United States has produced a self-consciously pluralistic society. As a result, the nation as such has had to be ever more neutral toward the churches and religion itself. Surveying the result, Gustave Weigel, S.J., says that no society has ever made God totally active in all its realms. But "all will admit that we are a far cry from the days when the will of the revealing God was considered normative for the heads of governments and for the framers of public policy. . . . Our governments operate

---

[42] See Isaac Rosenfeld, *An Age of Enormity* (New York: World, 1962), p. 332.

without reference to the will of God." In the Marxist and demo-
cratic worlds there is agreement "that God must not have a
place in the political life of a nation. In one case it is a matter
of philosophic principle and in the other it is the pragmatic
necessity of political action in a religiously pluralistic society." [43]

That this kind of practical secularity may have Christian
potential is clear from the fact that most churches consciously
embrace it as the best option for society and for the churches.
"When the king went, the couplet of God and king went too,"
says Weigel and, he implies, good riddance! But the result has
been one great legal base for what Arnold Toynbee calls "a
great secular revolution."

A secular society is one which refuses to commit itself as a
whole to one particular view of nature or the universe; it is
open and heterogeneous, and it will tend to be (for it will have
to be) tolerant. That is, its basic assumption will not permit it
to enforce or coerce belief in a single religious view. It must
unify differing groups of people for some common goals. [44]

What worries Weigel and others who look for sacral elements
in society is the tendency that through the legal attempts to
produce a neutral society and through the prohibition to
teach religion in public schools, a secularistic society will form.
Such a society can develop without a legal base. Great Britain
may have a legally established church and yet know a great
measure of secularization. "God is not allowed in our laboratories" was the motto of integral nationalists in France at the
turn of the century. The legislature becomes the laboratory
for working out a godless society. Students of such societies are
usually careful to point out that they do not necessarily guaran-

[43] *The Modern God* (New York: Macmillan, 1963), pp. 67-71.
[44] These and other features of a pluralist-secular society are spelled
out by Dennis Munby, *The Idea of a Secular Society* (London: Oxford
University Press, 1963), especially pp. 9 ff.

tee more freedom than the Christian societies they supplant. They merely refuse to commit themselves religiously.

Secularity is not always and wholly hostile to biblical religion. The prophets' prohibition of images can be extended into the political sphere: the really neutral societies in a secular era also fail to develop unifying images or discourage their development. Protestantism contributes to secularity by declaring that "there are no holy places" (even though it may originally have meant "all places are holy") and by introducing a critical and skeptical spirit. Protestantism in particular has felt at home with what Gustaf Aulén calls a "more or less secularized humanity," while Catholic thought has worked more toward a fusion of culture and religion. The Protestant Christian reads his Bible in such a way that he may see that his faith in a living God desecrates nature and desacralizes history and is thus committed to a secular culture just as his whole witness would be crowded out by a secularistic one.

Merely to keep the word "secular" open and its kinds of culture systematically nonintegral does not mean that the modern forms of secularity create no problems for faith. The maturing person who sees that the state can be operated as well through practical atheism as through recourse to the deity may begin to wonder in what realms such recourse is necessary or possible. Even more, the secular spirit can produce habits of mind that make the act of believing and being open to belief more difficult. At the very least, secularization means that the areas of life in which religion is dominant are reduced. It is active at the edges, or tangentially, or on a fraction of the social life of those who believe. Religion is given a section in the press; the name of God appears as invocation but not centrally in political ritual. "The world of religion has been confined within constantly narrowing limits." [45] The "sense of wonder"

[45] Bernhard Groethuysen, quoted in Walter Nigg, *The Heretics*, trans. Richard and Clara Winston (New York: Knopf, 1962), p. 401.

that Josef Pieper speaks of tends to disappear. "The threat to the religious attitude," then, says Erich Fromm, "lies not in science but in the predominant practices of daily life." [46]

Casual, incidental, or accidental unbelief which is associated with methods of arranging social life or of perceiving the physical universe can be devastating to faith. But it is so in a different way than is planned and integral unbelief, and the difference is important for anyone who wishes to study "the varieties of unbelief." In Bernanos' words on this form of secularization (which we have had occasion to quote once before): "One does not lose faith; it simply ceases to inform one's life." In the end, says Samuel Miller, man "is not hostile to religion, or even concerned. He simply does not raise the religious question at all, not even in church." [47]

The five families of unbelief cited thus far do not begin to exhaust the possibilities, and within them there are infinite varieties. They do provide some illustration of the distinctions between integral and nonintegral systems. We could summarize these in a table:

Integral or Closed	Neither	Nonintegral or Open
1. ———	anomie-accidie	———
2. Nihilism		"Longing"
3. Atheism		Agnosticism
4. Pantheisms of history and power		———
5. Scientism-secularism		Scientific method-secularity

If the distinctions have merit and if it is true that open systems offer most possibility for interaction—conversion, communication, conspiracy—then it can be seen that, even within

[46] *Psychoanalysis and Religion* (New Haven: Yale University Press, 1950), p. 100.

[47] *The Death of God.* Quoted in Gabriel Vahanian (New York: Braziller, 1961), p. 148.

the world of unbelief, some options are more fruitful than others. The wise affirmer or rejecter of Christian belief will therefore acquaint himself with these choices.

Two clusters of unbelief create special difficulties for understanding and they shall be isolated in the next two chapters. The first cluster consists of syncretistic forms which share many elements with Christianity. The second includes those forms which appear specifically within Western Christianity in the modern world.

8

The Syncretistic Varieties of Unbelief

Not all of the modern varieties of unbelief occur in the apparently "pure" forms which we have called secular. We turn now to the "mixed" forms which are equally common.

6. Syncretistic unbelief which combines elements of Christian belief with contradictory cultural features

Conceptual and linguistic propriety requires us to acknowledge that all religion is syncretistic and all religions are culture religions. That is, each system of belief, worship and life tends to mingle elements of other systems picked up—usually unconsciously—from the environment. The milieu is the raw material out of which religious response is born. This is true even where one faith is official and supposedly universal: there will always be cultural accretions. So, too, even first-generation movements of prophecy or mysticism are dependent in many ways upon the culture they reject and whose language, tools and instruments they use. We shall therefore be discussing relative scales of appropriation of culture into religion, and not entertaining the possibility of "pure" religion. We shall ask at what point cultural appropriation becomes dangerous to the life of faith and what elements in culture can compromise the central realities of belief.

As we move from the terrain of atheism, Nazism, Communism, formal secularism, and nihilism to that of culture religion, the mood seems to change. The American reader, who may have felt secure in his sense of distance from dramatic unbelief, may now not welcome becoming involved in new ways. He who may have been bored by the remoteness and apparent irrelevance of distinctions applied to unbelief may be threatened by the nearness of unbelief and may more seriously question the importance of distinctions. At this point it will again be necessary to note that we have no interest in the quantity of culture religion today as opposed to the good or bad old days of the past. The only concern is with its quality, its originality, its character as an event of the recent past. The method is more analytic than judgmental or pastoral. The first task is to try to define and isolate the modern form of culture religion as unbelief.

At the same time, the dramatic features of such unbelief must not be minimized. We cannot apply a different set of standards to those forms of rivalry to Christianity which appear where the faith is institutionalized and strong. It is unwise to call something "weak faith" when it is actually unfaith. From the viewpoint of Christian revelation the nearer and apparently more subtle rivals may be at least as devastating as the remote and radical ones. These forms—apart from artificial elements like coercion (toward Christianity in Spain; away from it in East Germany)—will be more prevalent and more serious rivals wherever Christian institutions are most vital. They will inevitably adopt Christian forms and terms (without the substance), whereas in cultures lacking these institutions, other patterns would be fitted.

For the sake of simplicity, we shall confine ourselves for the most part to the American setting. However, parallels may be seen in other countries where Christian institutions are likewise strong and their protective coloration is attractive.

Culture religion may be open and consider itself under the judgment of distinctive Christianity. Or it may be closed, having worked out a coherent universe of belief on an integral basis. One constant element in both types is this: Culture religion wants to have its generalizing word before the particular word of Christianity is asserted and heard. It may permit varying degrees of subsequent attempts to articulate Christianity, as long as it has been permitted the first word. Thus it appears to be congenial to Christian belief and practice, and it may appear to be a strong defender of "the old ways" in religion. Yet it represents change.

If this form of unbelief be called secularization, it belongs to the second type as described by both J. Milton Yinger and Father John L. Thomas, who argue, as has been noted, that secularization refers only to systematic attempts to exclude God and religious concern from areas of life. In their view it does not apply to the change of religious sentiment and practical life under the guise of continuity of symbols. The words, the formal assents to doctrines, do not change, though the heart of what is actually believed may be undergoing radical change.

For Yinger, religious change is possibly creative as compared with "static religion," a term which—if his categories were inclusive—would have to be applied to our references (belief *in* God as existing Trinity and belief *that* God acts in Incarnation and is heard through witnesses). Religious change may be good for society and for spiritual life. For Thomas, on the other hand, religious change from these static norms and beliefs portends serious consequences for the Christian future. Yinger and Thomas simply unite in polemic against those who do not distinguish to their satisfaction between authentic secularization and disguised religious change.[1] It remains for the reader to choose between these two viewpoints, once the basic distinction has been made.

Culture religion, which wants the first word before particular faiths assert themselves, is syncretistic in both senses of that word's root. Some find its base to be pragmatic, goal-oriented, partly accidental. Plutarch used it to describe the warring Cretan brothers who united against common enemies. Others locate it in ideological, source-oriented, conscious choice. They

[1] See Yinger (ed.), "Religion and Social Change," *Sociology Looks at Religion* (New York: Macmillan, 1963), pp. 67 ff., and Thomas, *Religion and the American People* (Westminster, Md.: Newman, 1963), pp. 1 ff. Both illustrate their cases by pointing to disagreements with Will Herberg in particular. The distinctions they formulate are valuable, but I am not sure they do justice to the degree to which Herberg himself renders the same distinction; perhaps the only real disagreement is over the actual application of the term "secularization" to the second form.

base it on the Greek words for mixing together or mingling. In a complex, pluralistic culture there is an inevitable development of the first kind just as there are champions of the second.[2]

In a pluralistic culture it is impossible to conceive of a durable culture religion which is authoritarian, exclusivist, absolutist, intolerant, lending itself to immorality in the civil sphere or fanatically spiritual. Such a religion is unlikely to develop in the erosively competitive experience, and most citizens would find it undesirable. The developing American forms are, indeed, largely the opposite of each of these.

Instead of being authoritarian and professing confidence in one uniquely mediated source of revelation (e.g., the historic picture of Roman Catholicism) the American culture religion is openly syncretistic. Many truths are presented by a pluralistic people and most of them, it is conceived, can be appropriated into one consensus. A mixed culture becomes, then, a blurred culture. "We expect to go to a 'church of our choice' and yet feel its guiding power over us; to revere God and to be God. . . . We expect everybody to believe deeply in his religion, yet not to think less of others for not believing." [3]

Only in a profoundly syncretistic culture could an anthropologist call our culture "profoundly irreligious" and typically religious in the same passage:

> More than half of our people still occasionally go through the forms, and there are rural and ethnic islands in our population where religion is still a vital force.

The pattern of the implicit American creed seems to embrace the following recurrent elements: faith in the rational,

[2] See Hendrik Kraemer, *Religion and the Christian Faith* (Philadelphia: Westminster, 1957), pp. 392 ff., in the chapter "Syncretism as a Missionary Problem."

[3] Daniel J. Boorstin, *The Image* (New York: Atheneum, 1962), p. 4.

a need for moralistic rationalization, an optimistic conviction that rational effort counts, romantic individualism and
the cult of the common man, high valuation of change, . . .
the conscious quest for pleasure.[4]

The details provided by Clyde Kluckhohn are not important
here, and we need not accept all of them. What is characteristic
is that he sees the same culture (and the same people in it) as
at once profoundly irreligious and typically inclined to religion. One would expect this in a syncretistic complex as opposed to a purer cultural strand. The paradox of such an apparent increase of both religiousness and secularism, seen in
the revival of religion in the 1950s, is typical of this complex.
Its paradoxicality occasioned some of the studies referred to in
this book and is behind many of our immediate concerns.

As opposed to exclusivism, American culture encourages universalism. Only unbelief "looks bad"; any sort of belief is acceptable. We need not ponder long what such an attitude does
to any particular interest (belief *in;* belief *that* something is
true). As the world becomes interactive in new ways, on an
international and intercultural basis, the tendency toward in-
creasing the value of universalism as a step toward concord
may very well be enhanced. We may be seeing a sophistication
of what Jules Monnerot in another context called "the still in-
choate aspiration towards a religion of the Species" which rela-
tivizes the truth of particular witnesses.[5]

The third characteristic of such a culture religion is therefore a widespread relativism. As a first word spoken religiously,
before the theological or moral quest is seriously undertaken,
it reassures the seeker that the quest is indeed not serious. Its a
priori points to the truthfulness of all congenial belief-systems.
Whether the witness to the Christian Gospel would be neces-

[4] Clyde Kluckhohn, *Mirror for Man* (New York: Fawcett, 1957), pp. 189,
178.

[5] *Sociology and Psychology of Communism* (Boston: Beacon, 1960), p. 279.

sary in an environment where the Gospel's benefits are witnessed to in advance is a disturbing question to Christian missionaries and a reassuring one to everyone else.

Such relativizing paves the way for the development of a national religion. It is a widely accepted sociological maxim that every functioning society has to an important degree a *common* religion. American pluralism, while informed by Christianity, is not decisively Christian; accordingly, some other common religion is gradually taking its place. That common religion may be called a "common-value system" or "moral solidarity" or "a shared religious orientation." But none of these terms takes its root *only* in Christian resources.[6] Charles Frankel, who does not look to Christianity as the basic integrating faith, asks:

> Must there not be in any society some basic integrating faith, some unquestioned commitment to first principles and ultimate ends? Can men live together cheerfully and peacefully in society, can they work together with spirit on common projects, unless they agree on final values? [7]

Such a syncretistic culture religion inevitably professes tolerance. Intolerance, of course, cannot be lauded as a virtue, nor can it be reasonably defended in the light of historical experiences with persecution by prevailing believers. (Whether these two polarities can serve together to form the best single base for asking the question of a pluralistic society is another question.) The tolerance which must be shown people in practical living circumstances is then logically carried over to the beliefs which underlie norms and values of life. The churches

[6] Robin Williams, quoted approvingly by J. Paul Williams, *What Americans Believe and How They Worship* (rev. ed.; New York: Harper & Row, 1962), p. 478. Robin Williams, *American Society* (New York: Knopf, 1951), pp. 312, 342, develops the argument.

[7] *The Case for Modern Man* (Boston: Beacon, 1959), p. 78.

are subtly coerced to choose to bless (or they compete for the
honor of blessing) whatever in the current culture is attractive.
Robin Williams is suspicious of the roots of this kind of tolerance. It may be "a sign that the crucial values of our system
are no longer couched in a religious framework." [8] Whether indifference to beliefs is actually the soundest permanent basis
for interpersonal relations is questioned by many, and indifferentism as such is sometimes responsible for the breakdown of
tolerance in times of testing.

Since the culture religion is devised for the sake of organizing
and motivating society, it is unthinkable that society would en-
courage immorality as an element in that consensus. Indeed,
the American product is highly moralistic. The historic roots
for this go deep, at least back to the era of Benjamin Franklin
who first perceived the extent of America's chartered pluralism.
Sects may hold what they wish in particular, so long as in general they serve the common good and produce the good man.
What does this do to Christian belief? Christians do not want
to be thought of as on the side of immorality. But just as in the
early church they had to call themselves "atheists" over against
culture's gods, so in modern society they need freedom to be
called "immoralists" in the event that the word they receive
calls them away from society's norms. Many prophetic Christians protest the injection of "moraline" into their own veins.
Thus Emmanuel Mounier complains:

> The bourgeois house is a shuttered house, the bourgeois
> heart, a heart circumspect and cautious. The bourgeois
> would like to turn the catholic, apostolic Church into the
> back parlor of a shop, a confidential salon where anemic
> virtues stagnated in a curtained half-light, ignorant of every-

[8] Quoted in Stuart Chase, *American Credos* (New York: Harper & Row,
1962), p. 167, in a passage on indifferentism as a basis for extending civil
liberties.

thing unconnected with ecclesiastical gossip, the troubles of a pious clique and the sterile confidences of lonely lives.[9]

This is the kind of moral contribution to a moral society which the prophets of the past have been reluctant to make.

Needless to say, the spiritual values promoted in a highly instrumental culture religion will be heavily materialist in their basis. Substance rather than meaning is offered. Comfort rather than service is touted. Such a materialism develops its own new mythologies. A New Testament scholar can compare these with historic mythologies and find them incompatible.

It is impossible to interpret a mythology in which there is a place for transcendence in terms of one in which there is not . . . [such as] the American way of life, with its proclamation of the inalienable rights of life, liberty and the pursuit of happiness [as] simply the expression of a more humanely beneficent but equally Promethean determination of man to treat as ultimate his desires to keep on living, to do what he likes and to have a good time.[10]

If the six features of American culture religion which we have described are problematical, they seem superior to their opposites. Because they are generally attractive they pose perplexing questions for believers in particular faiths. What is more, American history is on the side of the syncretists. The impact of the Enlightenment, associated here with Benjamin Franklin,

9 Quoted by Alec Vidler, "Holy Worldliness," *Christian News-Letter*, IV, No. 4 (October, 1956), 16. For an agnostic's view of the same subject, see Norman Birnbaum, "An Agnostic Looks at the Church," *Frontier*, II, No. 1 (June, 1959): "Nothing . . . is as illustrative of the secular corrosion of religion as the revival of the American churches."

10 Ian Henderson, *Myth in the New Testament* (London: S.C.M. Press, 1952), pp. 52-53. The mythology to which the author is comparing America's is the less beneficent Nazi one.

is largely seen to be salutary in the civil order. The optimistic temper and the frequent successes of the American experience make citizens reluctant to tamper with its results. Many people "do so well" in this pluralistic climate, they deduce that therefore their churches or clubs must "be so good"—and true.

Evidently the most fruitful distinction to be applied is, again, that between open and closed systems of culture religion. An integrally worked-out culture religion would be unbelief of a high order. However much it would borrow Christian terms and rely on Christian reminiscence, its first word would render unnecessary and nonunderstandable all subsequent specific Christian judgments.

An open system of culture religion offers several possibilities. If properly understood, it can represent an inevitable and even salutary aspect of corporate life, as Robin Williams has pointed out. If it remains nonintegral, such a system leaves room for distinctive belief-systems to feed into the national consensus, to profit from the resultant good will of the society, and still to be free to stand apart from a society which it conceives as being in need of judgment and redemption.[11]

To understand the specifically Protestant critique of culture religion, one would have to enter with some patience the precincts occupied by the concept "justification by faith." Historically this teaching was regarded as a judgment on man and society not only when they were sinful and unbelieving but especially when they were religious and moral. This teaching, muffled in the context of culture religion, was designed negatively—in St. Paul's terms—to eliminate "boasting." Man was

[11] For a clear and concise statement of what such an integral and formally established (in the schools) culture religion could look like, see J. Paul Williams, *op. cit.*, Chap. 18, "The Role of Religion in Shaping American Destiny," pp. 472 ff. My *The New Shape of American Religion* (New York: Harper & Row, 1959) was a full-length description of open- and closed-system culture religion in the United States during the religious revival of the 1950s.

not to have a claim upon God; his efforts and his thoughts could not achieve one. God's activity initiated a new relation with man. In the context of modern forms of unbelief, God's activity disappears from the human horizon and with it the teaching that man is justified by faith. Extensive surveys reveal that it is not well understood even in the churches which purport to stand or fall on the purity of that teaching.

The question of man's justification by faith appeared in a decisively different context in the Reformation period, when both Catholic and Protestant lived in a world where the transcendent order was very vivid and the immanence of God more widely recognized. The attempt to apply the issues of that era —just before secularization began to be perceived—to our era is at the base of much misunderstanding. Without this teaching, culture religion cannot easily be brought under judgment. If a syncretistic culture religion is widely enough diffused, one is justified by his act of being born into the society, and excommunicated only if he engages in anarchic or treasonous activities.

When culture religion takes on many aspects of the syndrome described above, it must—from the viewpoint of historic Christian references—be classified not as a kind of weak faith but as a parafaith or competitive belief or unbelief. This form of unbelief does not necessarily discourage ancient organized religions. It ordinarily encourages them. The historic forms provide continuity and the important conservative base for sane social change. Their institutions no longer dominate and set the terms or give the name to a culture (e.g., a "Christian society"). But instead of penetrating into it, they react and adapt to the autonomy of the surrounding culture, and believers then narrow their concern to private, familial, interior, and spiritual aspects of life.

Defenders of the national culture religion ordinarily do not feel jostled if the churches "set out to save individual souls" so long as the culture religionists can control all the rest of life and world. The presence of strong religious institutions may serve to further justify the larger society, but these institutions would not dare to assert their real independence or superiority. We cannot overlook the validities of the larger culture serving as judge over ecclesiastical pretension, but clearly we are on original ground as we perceive the situation of the churches in the West today. The members of the larger society strike a bargain: If you grant us the role of establishing the religion of the public realm, you may have the private sphere of some lives. Only if there is overt clash between the two (nineteenth-century Mormons on polygamy; Jehovah's Witnesses on blood transfusions) will we intrude.

In the coercive world where pantheisms of history and power prevail, Christianity may be permitted to survive to the extent that it conforms to the state and contents itself with individual salvation. In the free world a subtler but no less extensive kind of dynamic comes into play. However many favors the religious institutions receive (tax exemption, etc.), they are automatically and effectually disestablished from the task of unifying public life.

Religious institutions are not necessarily rendered impotent in such a situation. They may serve to integrate their members when secularity bewilders them. They can provide people with identity and motivation to serve the whole culture. At the same time, it is normally incumbent upon such institutions to be the most loyal, most patriotic supporters of the civil state. In national crisis they tend to look like the most warlike element, no matter what their peacetime pretensions. They serve to bless the weapons and to denominate each war as "just" or "justified."

When the sense of transcendence was more markedly felt, religious institutions which specialized in witnessing to it could escape into apocalypticism. On the national scale the eschatological note does not prevail in today's America, and the churches have the problem of disestablishing themselves from the roles which society provides them and which they do not always choose.

There seem to be no good reasons for organized religious elements to be in total and permanent opposition to their culture. They may have left a creative deposit in it; they may see in it the raw material for redemption. Many of them recognize that their God works outside their own context of witness. The perplexing task for historic churches in congenial secular cultures is to carry on positive relations with what is good in the environment and yet to be free to step back and utter a transcendent word when called to by their witnesses. For this task of extrication, Christians can find company in some of the other nonintegral systems: agnosticism, the critical method, and a creative secularity which also tries to keep some distance from an all-embracing culture religion. One might even say that, in the dynamics of this picture, the more explicitly secular the culture, the freer the church is to carry on its witness there.

7. Syncretistic unbelief which combines elements of Christian belief with contradictory political features

Christian believers in every age have had tremendous positive and negative respect for the reality now called the state. The biblical revelation cultivates respect for both the God-ordered society (the Old Testament theocracy) and the God-ordained society (the New Testament Roman establishment, see Rom. 13). They have been aware of the great influence on all of life exercised by the civil body. They have, as citizens, usually shared the mystique of their own nation. For a millennium and a half in the West they provided the adjective "Christian" to describe the civil society. But the development of modern nationalism is an event with original features, and the political element in modern syncretisms deserves treatment separate from that accorded the cultural.

Where culture religion is an ill-organized creed with ill-defined acts of worship, nationalism attempts to produce some articulate doctrines and worship; it more effectively produces imagery and symbolism. But what most sharply separates modern nationalism from culture religion is the coercive element. This does not mean that the state always recognizes or desires to use its power. Certainly, not all nations at all times want to exercise it, nor is nationalism always a threat to Christian institutions and belief. The free society which specifically issues charters of religious freedom is a product of the same age which produces the spirit of nationalism. What must be noted, however, is the inescapability of nationalism and the tendency it has to produce religions which are different from Christianity although they adopt some Christian modes of expression and attract the Christian faithful.

At the same time that we note the ubiquity and power of nationalism, we must distinguish between its types of possibilities. Nationalism differs from the pantheisms of history and power because one can withhold co-operation from its ultimate demands. One can resist its integrating tendencies. Modern nationalism which becomes closed *is* an ideology of power and history which has shut out Christian judgment. Many believers whose faith is oriented to the Bible find in it resources for being loyal to the civil body and its imagery while keeping alive the means to transcend this loyalty when necessary.

In discussing nationalism we must return to the reminder at the beginning of the book that "one man's belief is another's unbelief." Therefore, technically, nationalism can be described as a religion in its own terms, and it becomes unbelief only when viewed as an event which has occurred where Christianity has held power. More often in such a case it is called idolatry or some sort of parareligion. Some years ago, when I first read Paul Tillich's *The Dynamics of Faith,* I was struck that on the first page this great philosopher of religion chose nationalism as his prime illustration of a belief-system in the world today.

If a national group makes the life and growth of the nation its ultimate concern, it demands that all other concerns, economic well-being, health and life, family, aesthetic and cognitive truth, justice and humanity, be sacrificed. The extreme nationalisms of our century are laboratories for the study of what ultimate concern means in all aspects of human existence, including the smallest concern of one's daily life. Everything is centered in the only god, the nation—a god who certainly proves to be a demon, but who shows clearly the unconditional character of an ultimate concern.[12]

At the time, these words seemed to be the understandable reaction of a refugee from Nazism. What did this have to do with the free world? As time passed, however, nationalism showed its many faces around the world in Asia, Africa, the Americas, and repeatedly in Europe. It has such power that it seems at times to be capable of displacing the ideological tie between nations which profess devotion to Marxism-Leninism! In Tillich's terms, nationalism can produce an ecstasy which few other idolatries can. The more I reflected on his illustration, the more its aptness stood out, and I have come to agree with those who think of nationalism as "the real religion of the modern world." It is not unbelief in the way that atheism is but in the way that ideologies of power are. It claims positive values and produces idols of its own. In its modern form it is demonstrably an heir, if not wholly a legitimate one, of the

[12] New York: Harper & Row, 1957, p. 1. Later Tillich goes on to define the state's power as one which calls forth "false ultimacy." "The finite which claims infinity without having it (as, e.g., a nation) . . ." is seen to be capable of producing, in the end, only idolatry (pp. 11 f.).

Christian tradition. It first occurred and spread from places where Christian views of meaning in history had prevailed.

The nation can claim to be a community in many ways. It sees itself as a natural community, claiming a rightful bond with an environment within certain natural boundaries. It is a historical community, evoking recall of heroes and saints and holy wars. It is an intellectual community, as it is in part sustained by the endeavor of man's mind. It tends to become a mystical community, and there is no modern nation which does not somehow rely on a mystique and seek to produce ecstasy. It can call forth voluntary support (one enlists in military service or buys defense bonds) and it can coerce (one is drafted, and, of course, taxed). It is capable of indoctrinating, particularly in state-supported schools. Unchecked, it can make total claims upon the allegiance of man as can no other widespread network of institutions. It subsumes both nonreligions and religions and is in this sense syncretistic.

Not all of these powers and attractions always take on a religious guise, nor is the final product always a form of unbelief which must prevail over the historic communities of belief. But nationalism is better poised to do so than are mere secularism or scientism or other entities which lack coercive power. The "man without a country" and "World Citizen No. 1" both learned the impossibility of escaping nation and nationalism. True, there can be international loyalties. Just as there can be an ecumenical movement among Christians who seek to transcend parochial and denominational boundaries, there can be a concern for world community, for a United Nations. But this concern lacks symbolism and coercive power. There can be subnational loyalties, such as those of party politics. Again, these must yield when nationalism asserts itself. It has been said that, in this belief-system, one can change his sect but not his religion. The choices represent actual differences in a way that choices between religious denominations rarely do. The modern integral state has preserved the concept of the heretic or the traitor where churches have not. The one who deviates from the nation's mystique is seen to be an actual threat to belief and life, and he can be put to death; those who deviate from historic religious patterns are seen to be threats only to those who choose to remain supporters of such patterns.

Professor Carlton J. H. Hayes virtually made a life work of the study of nationalism as religion. He sees it as a phenomenon born on the post-Christian terrain of Western Europe and from the first (Milton and Bolingbroke, Mazzini, "Vater" Jahn) it took on religious characteristics. Now it has spread around the world. "Modern nationalism first arose among peoples that were traditionally Christian, and as a religion it has naturally borrowed and adapted to its own purposes many customs and usages of historic Christianity." From Hayes's generalizations about the historic development we can form a composite that reveals features which nationalism has in common with established religions.

In its modern form, nationalism always works with a sense of "chosen people," set aside to fulfill the purposes of God or history. This concept of chosenness is often tempered with a secular element, a sort of Darwinian justification of survival of the fittest which legitimatizes war. There is a *Heilsgeschichte,* or salvation-history, in which man is somehow redeemed, or a cosmic fulfillment is found by participation in the life of the nation. A sense of destiny made manifest gives each nation a sense of eschatology, a radical control of the future or a hope beyond the future even when such hope seems implausible. The god of the *patria* is a jealous god, permitting no opposition; he is militant, calling men to battle. A conscious development of a mythos or mystique parallels the unconscious nurture as generations pass.

Nationalism, while actually particular, is universalist in pretensions: it would extend its salvation. There is a xenophobia in all nationalism: a "foreign devil" exists or must be

invented. The power of nationalism can best be seen in the
ways it demands ultimate sacrifice of its citizens. Men have
long been at the mercy of the pride of their military leaders,
but in the modern era the national purpose becomes a justification for the wiping out of whole enemy populations and
the surrender of one's own. As a religion it is careful to nurture
its young, to develop ceremonial undergirding, and even some
metaphysical pretension. There are shrines and holy places,
saints and heroes.

Not all evidences of nationalism contain all these elements
and, in context, not all of them need stand under judgment
from the perspective of historic faiths. These faiths have ordinarily professed the divine origin of order, law, and the
state. They have produced people who recognize that law and
order are somehow dependent upon the acceptance of leadership, a leadership enhanced in the loyalty of people through
the development of a common history and symbolism.

As Hayes sees it, in secular terms both pacifism and internationalism are forces which help to keep nationalism as religion from becoming integral. But pressures tend to dissolve
pacifism when war threatens (revealing the ecstatic power of
nationalism) and internationalism crumbles and becomes
nothing more than the basis of practical military alliances.

What, then, of historic religions like Christianity?

[Nationalism] offers a substitute for, or supplement to,
historic supernatural religion. Persons indifferent or hostile
to the latter are apt to find a compensatory satisfaction and
devotion in this-worldly nationalism, that is, *in what is essentially a religion of modern secularism.*

Nationalism, being also a very sectarian religion, tends to
be intolerant of any possible rival religion. . . .

The religion of nationalism . . . has borrowed from
older world religions, especially the Christian. In turn, the
older religions show a tendency to accept and even forward

nationalism. This develops a religious syncretism, or ad-
mixture, by virtue of which multitudes of people throughout
the world continue at least nominally to adhere to the faith
of their ancestors and to practice its cult while they adapt
it to the exigencies of nationalist worship and discipline. . . .

Syncretism of nationalism and Christianity is strikingly
noticeable in the United States.[13]

Hayes is a fair-minded historian, however, and notices not
only the syncretism of Christianity with nationalism. He sees
Christianity as an enduringly effective religion which can "ex-
ert a most important moderating influence on nationalism."
Nationalism owes some of its better features to Christianity.
The catholic or universal claims of Christianity, the residue of
belief in a transcendent order ("We ought to obey God rather
than men") and the sometimes-heard command to render to
God the things that are God's help set self-critical Christianity
apart from integral nationalism.

Hayes, as a Christian, expresses worry lest nationalism be
unchecked in Asia or Africa where such belief has no historic
root. He expresses the hope that Christians in Euro-America
will take their religion seriously and maintain it as a world
religion in order to leaven nationalism and limit its excesses.
Whether his worries or hopes are well-founded cannot be discussed here. But equally important is his account of the development of the historic forms of nationalism on Christian soil
until they gain independent power and cut themselves off
from their sources. What follows is "integral" or "totalitarian"
nationalism. (His illustration is the instance of Charles Maurras in France. "Integral nationalism," in Maurras' definition,
calls on its adherents to be ultimately concerned and sees them
placing their country above everything; the nationalist "con-

[13] Carlton J. H. Hayes, *Nationalism: A Religion* (New York: Macmillan,
1960), p. 180. (Italics added.)

ceives, treats, and resolves all questions in their relation to the national interest." [14]

The transcendent reference is not wholly lost in nationalism, but God is so confidently controlled that the sense of distance between his purposes and man's disappears. As a saying of some decades ago went:

> Gott strafe England, and God save the King.
> God this, and God that, and God the other thing.
> "Good God," said God, "I've got my work cut out."

The United States is a mixed culture, in which secular forces and religious forces alike are divided between support of integral nationalism and critical patriotism. The issues will no doubt be sharpened in the decades ahead as the legally secular basis of the culture is extended into other realms. The Supreme Court decisions which rule out imposed prayers in public schools produced double reactions among nationalists. Some who were determinedly secularist would like to see an integral religion of democracy become formally established, and they regard the removal of historic forms of devotion as a step in this direction. Others who interpret culture sacrally want to see religious and specifically Christian elements reintroduced in the culture, partly in order to continue justifying the Christianity-and-nationalism tie. The former does it out of an interest to see America move from a secular to a secularist position, the latter to see it return from the secular to a religious and even Judeo-Christian self-definition. The issue is per-

---

14 Carlton J. H. Hayes, *Nationalism: A Religion* (New York: Macmillan, 1960), especially pp. 164-182 and 136 ff. We have chosen to conserve space by referring only to Hayes's summary and may thus seem dependent on it. But there is little of idiosyncracy about Hayes's conclusions. The literature on the religious dimensions of nationalism is extensive, and it is unanimous on this point: No other rival to the historic faiths is better organized on a worldwide scale or more acceptable as a parallel religion to adherents of historic faiths.

haps more intense in the United States than in some other
nations where secularization is obvious because the process
was made most vivid and patent in the years of America's
purportedly highest religious interest. Why, it was asked,
when more people than ever were interested in religion in
America, should the nation define itself in more neutral or
secular terms?

Not only because of the United States' position of power
in the world but because of its historic situation it will be
watched. Gertrude Stein once called America "the oldest nation." In a sense it is, for it was first to possess the modern
experience of pluralism and permanent legal separation of
church and state. How it defines its nationalism and keeps it
from becoming integral—if it does—will be of interest to Christian minorities in Ceylon, Nigeria, and other nations whose integral nationalism is a religion which hampers Christian
proclamation. Nietzsche once spoke of man as an "indeterminate being"; America has been a sort of indeterminate nation. No one yet knows how it will define itself vis-à-vis modern
nationalism. Some Christians, fundamentalist and modernist
alike, seem to bid for a closed system that mingles Christianity
with nationalism. At the same time, a nation which in the modern era has produced an Abraham Lincoln in the secular
sphere and a Reinhold Niebuhr in the religious sphere also
understands that a religiously transcendent note can judge the
pride of nations. "The Almighty has his own purposes"; "He
that sitteth in the heavens shall laugh." A free society permits
these reminders as a check on nationalism; a totalitarian
one does not.

From the viewpoint of Christian belief the problem with nationalism is its capture of the transcendent note, rendering
irrelevant the witness to God's action in history outside the immediacy of the nation. Such a religion justifies man as it produces cohesiveness for the pluralist experience. Many Christians have looked hopefully to certain kinds of secular forces

for alliance against integral nationalism on either a secular or
a Christian base. Such an alliance is seen to provide a ground
on which Christians can stand as they seek to work out the
biblical injunctions to support the state and to leave them
free to assert with their greatest President that "the Almighty
has his own purposes" which may not coincide with the manip-
ulations of men. Open-system or extremely self-critical nationalism seems the more fruitful alternative in a free society
where communication and conspiracy must occur and where
conversion is a possibility. Once again, at the very least an understanding of the quasi-religious (and thus, from the Christian
viewpoint, partly unbelieving) character of nationalism is an
aid to creative relationships. Out of such an understanding
men may come to conscious choices in a bewildering world.[15]

15 The best discussion of Abraham Lincoln and one which illustrates the
critical dialectic in the life of a man who also shared a nationalist mys-
tique is William J. Wolf's *The Almost Chosen People* (Garden City, N.Y.:
Doubleday, 1959); reissued as *The Religion of Abraham Lincoln* (New
York: Seabury, 1963). See also Reinhold Niebuhr, *The Irony of American
History* (New York: Scribner, 1952) and the discussion of henotheism in
H. Richard Niebuhr, *Radical Monotheism and Western Culture* (New
York: Harper & Row, 1960).

9 The Religious Varieties of Unbelief

It is one thing to discuss unbelief as a worldwide or Euro-American evidence of change. It is another to bring unbelief into the range of culture religion and nationalism as Christians ordinarily experience these. It is still another to apply the same standards within the orbit of Christian institutions and spiritual expression. The dangers of being misunderstood are many and there are strong temptations to overstate the issues in order to draw attention to subtler phenomena. The necessity for careful expression is obvious and a plea for thoughtful reading is hardly gratuitous. Yet setting forth the varieties of unbelief in the Christian orbit and attempting to apply our basic distinction are required not only for consistency but because it may help Christian and non-Christian alike to understand the religious enterprise.

The suggestion that religious institutions and expression may be the chief locus for unbelief is not new, nor is the idea that at least unbelief is a more significant threat among them than "in the world." The greatest of the prophets spent most of their energies on precisely these realities. Jesus was little concerned with Greco-Roman paganism, but he stormed against the pretensions of religious people and upbraided his disciples for their unbelief. Later generations of believers know this and assent to the earlier enterprises of criticism, consolidating their insights into later positive expressions of religion. But these are not so regularly transformed into criticism of contemporary religious forms. It may well be presupposed that religion as a problem to faith—if it was vividly a problem to the prophets—may be a permanent reality. Those interested in understanding the faith and its cultural setting can therefore hardly avoid facing the newer forms of the permanent realities. Insofar as we shall devote time to the matter we shall once more avoid reference to the question of whether there is more or less institutionalized unbelief in the churches today.

The only question will be: What is original about today's forms?

In other words, the same standard applied to the environment is now applied to the churches. They are supposed to be most responsive to a transcendent word and most alert to God's activity in history. This, in the United States at least, is implied in the public expressions of faith of that majority of the population which calls itself Christian. When religious forms and expressions obscure the witness to these dimensions of religion, we may say that man justifies himself and that God's activity is not really necessary.

If the Christian grants the theoretical possibility that unbelief may be incarnate in his own religious forms, then he is justified to look for its actual and historical presence. If unbelief is seen to be a permanent corollary of faith, just as doubt is, he should not be surprised when examples are pointed to in the social setting of the churches. Other words may be chosen besides the inclusive ones which appear in this study. Some reach for more dramatic ones. Thus William Stringfellow speaks of "The Agnosticism of Religion" and "The Atheism of Religion." [1] Others seek to remove the subject from discussion, attacking its legitimacy in the public sphere even if it is part of the daily diagnosis of the Christian in private.

Whoever has met the Grand Inquisitor has met with integral unbelief in the church. He is the man wholly given over to religion,

> but he has a secret: he does not believe in God or in any meaning in life which alone could give sense to people suffering in his name. . . . Not believing in God, the Grand Inquisitor also ceases to believe in man, for they are two aspects of the same faith.[2]

1 William Stringfellow, *A Private and Public Faith* (Grand Rapids, Mich.: Eerdmans, 1962), Parts 2 and 3 of Chap. 1, pp. 25 ff.

2 Nikolai Berdyaev, *Dostoevsky,* trans. Donald Attwater (New York: Meridian, 1957), p. 189.

Presumably the church which produces the type of the Grand Inquisitor also produces lesser inquisitors in real life, and the unbelief built into religious institutionalism remains a legitimate subject of inquiry.[3]

It is difficult to isolate unbelief within the church because, viewed as weak faith, as existential doubt or even as mere faithlessness and human failure, it will be found everywhere. Yet the Christian faith asserts that the word of God is audible, will be heard and does not return void. God does not leave himself without witness; belief therefore must also be present. It is also difficult to isolate unbelief because empirical observation says that the visible effects and fruits of faith are present in the world. The task is further complicated because of the essential hiddenness of much of Christian life. Christianity must take scorn for weakness rather than boast over its hidden strengths. The task is hedged in with hazard because of the frailty of the tools with which it is approached: the measures of social science seem incongruous with the theological realities implied.

---

[3] No theologian of our day has discussed this characteristic of institutionalism with more frequency than Emil Brunner, who does so with almost wearying regularity. The most systematic statement runs through his discussion of the church in *The Christian Doctrine of the Church, Faith and the Consummation*, in *Dogmatics*, trans. David Cairns (Philadelphia: Westminster, 1960), III, 3-133 and especially 66 ff.

Many a sociologist or social analyst in the service of religion must wonder from time to time whether the topic of "institutionalism as unbelief" is sufficiently profound to summon so much attention as it has in recent years. Yet it would seem that the complex of institutionalism in the world and in the church today is an original feature of life and that, until creative measures for facing it are found, the analysis must continue. At least there must be evidence that it is noted. So as not to risk wearying anyone who has followed the argument up to this point, however, we shall restrict our attention to the central material point of each study from which illustrations are taken. Those who wish to pursue the subject further will have a ready-made bibliography and those who are interested in it only as a subsample of modern unbelief will not be overburdened.

It is necessary to isolate unbelief in religious institutions because its presence is known and affirmed as a corollary to authentic belief which is also forged in them. It is necessary that
there be complete frankness in the church because bad faith is
a particular temptation there; one must be oversuspicious
where faith is confessed. The attempt is necessary because it
safeguards against the use of a double standard. Shall a higher
standard be applied to the world, which is hardly expected
to be responsive, and a more lenient one to the church, where
responsiveness should be primary? The task is complicated by
the fact that any terms chosen will be partly confusing. Finally,
just as faith is elusive and hidden, so secularization of the forms
of faith may be so subtle as to go unnoticed.

A personal illustration may well point to the confusion
which must be faced. After speaking to a group of ministers
on these subjects, I was asked by one of them, "Surely, you
do not mean that we must look out over our congregations
on Sunday morning as if they were gatherings of unbelievers?"
In a sense, he was right—a congregation is first of all one of
believers. But it had never occurred to me not to think of them
also as unbelievers. That is, each Christian confesses his sins,
including those of want of faith. Why confess them if he has
no lack? Christian faith is born in the presence of each hearing of a word which calls it out of the nothingness of unbelief
and doubt. Protestant Christians treat man as being at the
same time justified and a sinner in the moral sphere. Why
not, then, in both the intellectual and practical spheres, regard
him as believer and unbeliever? The minister assented to this
position eventually. But he was unwilling to go a step further
and to see that personal unbelief is related to social unbelief,
that individual man's struggle for faith is related to the congregation's struggle. He was unwilling to see how unbelief may
be a special temptation in the church and how it may be consolidated particularly in the constructs of Christian institutions
and expressions. Neither he nor I prevailed that day, but I

did learn that in many ears unbelief is identified only with metaphysical atheism and formal proclamation of disbelief. Here, as previously noted, it applies to all sustained and actualized attempts to form the fullness of life apart from the activity of God. The crucial question is: Does *that* occur in religious institutions; is it a widespread danger?

8. Unbelief within the Christian orbit: the institutional aspect

Institutionalism cannot be understood apart from the positive understanding that all belief held by more than one person and sustained in time is institutionalized and that institutions are necessary to sane existence. The balanced social analyst seldom makes the mistake of underestimating the degree to which religion legitimately serves to give people a coherent view of the universe and to bring them into creative relations with each other. In other words, it is not always and only prophetic, seeking to create tension between the man of faith and his environment. In this sense, noninstitutionalism is impossible and anti-institutionalism is its own kind of idolatry. Pure individualism and the dogmatic profession of personal autonomy may be not only heretical in the light of the Christian doctrine of the church, but also may be unbelief as it becomes self-justifying and integral.

The integrative aspects of Christian institutions may, however, serve permanently to obscure the tension-creating aspects of a revealed word and to promote secularization by cutting off religion from many spheres of life. These dangers are apparent in the familiar justifications for religion, typified by one from the pen of David Nicholls:

> The Church is primarily a religious organization, and the Christian gospel caters for the religious needs of men. . . . It is the job of the church to preach, to pray, to sing hymns and to encourage and develop the pious feelings of its mem-

bers. . . . Religion is not concerned with the whole of life,
but with a part of life.[4]

Here is religion as a personally integrating feature of life seen
to be working against itself: it is then cut off from the wholeness of life. But religion can also prepare one for life, can organize the person for participation. Peter Berger, a severe critic
of existing religious and social institutions in America, says:
"The experience of conversion to a meaning system that is
capable of ordering the scattered data of one's biography is
liberating and profoundly satisfying." [5]

Institutions professedly exist or can exist to help provide
meaning-systems of that type. In the religious sphere they do
not differ from the secular as such. The Faith and Order Com-
mission of the World Council of Churches has come to speak of
an institution as "a definite and established structure, built
around and sustaining one or more social functions, and characterized by such traits as durability, persistence, and stabil-
ity." [6]

In the modern world these established structures grow inevitably more complex. A technical society assigns a specialized function to each. Efforts to simplify lead to new complications, as is evident in the numerous committees which are
formed to eliminate committees. One may blockade and quar-
antine religious institutions, but without outside help they
manage to produce new complexities to serve the several functions asked of them. Even criticism of institutions becomes
stabilized and institutionalized. Religious organizations are
not exempt from most of the pressures which are operative in
secular institutions and, to the social thinkers, appear to be

[4] "Your God Is Too Big," *Prism* (July, 1961), p. 22.

[5] *Introduction to Sociology: A Humanistic Perspective* (Garden City,
N.Y.: Doubleday, 1963), p. 63.

[6] Quoted by Nils Ehrenstrom, *The Quest for Ecumenical Institutionalization* (New York: Association Press, 1963), p. 27.

highly predictable. In an awesome typological study of institutions, Amitai Etzioni classifies religious organizations as normative—that is, they rely on high commitment to the organization on the part of highly controlled "lower participants." They do this because the directives received by participants seem legitimate as they are exercised through leadership, rituals, and shuffling of social and prestige symbols. But along with churches, other groups such as general hospitals, voluntary associations, and fraternal organizations do not exercise a basically different system of controls and appeals. The sociological perspective says little about churches that is unique to them.[7]

Theological assertion, by contrast, tends to claim too much in the way of uniqueness. To fail to see the church as subject to the secularization of forms leads to what has been called a "subliminal secularism," more potent because unrecognized. It is delusive to exempt the church from the pressures which push integral secularization on other forms of social life or, in the words of M. Holmes Hartshorne, "to suppose that because a man is a church-goer he is insulated from his world's fate." [8] The more the churches share of the institutional power of the secular society, the more they take on its secular guise. Karl Jaspers complained of this historical phenomenon in a passage which we have already cited. Looking for some spiritual future for mankind, he turned hopefully to the churches and saw that their "material power—their influence on education and legislation, for example, or their political patronage—has risen, and their authority is more frequently invoked than in past decades," but at the same time "their spiritual power has decreased tremendously in the past century." [9]

[7] A Comparative Analysis of Complex Organizations (Glencoe, Ill.: Free Press, 1961), pp. 40 ff.

[8] The Faith to Doubt (Englewood Cliffs, N.J.: Prentice-Hall, 1963), p. 92.

[9] The Future of Mankind, trans. E. B. Ashton (Chicago: University of Chicago Press, 1961), p. 256.

Tom Allan has quoted a study of the Secretariat for Evangelism of the World Council of Churches, on evangelism in France, to reveal the ways in which institutionalism becomes secularized in churches. These features, among others, could be culled from it:

a) Whenever the church is *enclosed* as a community, not in the sense of having disciplines but in the sense of excluding the outsider who does not make sense of codes whose biblical foundation and Christian meaning are doubtful;

b) whenever *acculturation* to the day-to-day modes of church life becomes a demanding project;

c) whenever the church's first concern is for its own *respectability* and when it seeks only to find "good" families for membership;

d) whenever the church's first concern is *self-perpetuation* and thus when it rejects reform as being revolution;

e) whenever it succumbs to the substantive reality of the *nation* and takes an adjectival role in relation to it (as in a "Christian nation");

f) whenever it must resort to *slogans* about social justice as a disguise for its own sentimental philanthropy;

g) whenever it is characterized by *introversion* and fear of the outsider—

—it then takes on an integral character which is closed to the word and activity of God and his witnesses because they are irrelevant. Man is justified, then, by affiliating with such an institution.

All of these tendencies are regularly noted in American religion, which we have chosen as our laboratory. America's is a "measuring culture," and it may have an impulse to measure too precisely some of the evanescences of spirit which elude the polltaker. Still, when samples are taken on many different premises by many different kinds of people in many different settings and they tend toward unanimity, they must be taken seriously. The pressures on religious institutions in America may be stronger than in Europe. As voluntary organizations— not established by the state—they are highly visible. In the bewildering pluralism of America, there are strong tendencies to cause people to affiliate in order to overcome anxieties.[10]

Ultimately, these institutions may outlive their promise and people move on to other gods. A practicing minister with a good historical sense has observed that the very institutions which attracted people in America in the 1950s have led the same people to reject them in the 1960s.[11] Yet no one foresees the disintegration of these institutions, no matter how secular the surrounding society becomes.

Gerhard Lenski, reversing the habitual Marxist interpretation of religion and returning to Max Weber for inspiration, found that religious institutions have tremendous power in shaping daily life. But the net result of his study remains disturbing to those who look with hope to the believing community. For most of the signals the community receives have little to do with the sacred norms which the community ostensibly professes. The institutions Lenski studied seemed to fill very well David Nicholls' picture of what churches were for. That is, they fostered compartmentalized and provincial views of life; their vision was narrow. Both Gibson Winter and Peter Berger have found religious institutions in America to be thoroughly secularized, functioning to justify the people who undertook nothing more than to look them up and affiliate with them. They were almost wholly enclosed, acculturated and adapted to the socio-economic class of the people who made them up.

10 See Stanley Schachter, *The Psychology of Affiliation* (Stanford: Stanford University Press, 1959), pp. 19, 43. H. Richard Niebuhr, *Radical Monotheism and Western Culture* (New York: Harper & Row, 1960), p. 58, suggests the henotheistic character of these institutions in American life.

11 John W. Meister, "Requirements for Renewal" in *Union Seminary Quarterly Review* XVI, No. 3 (March, 1961), 255 ff.

What is true of the church in the beleaguered suburbs also applies to it in rural areas or small towns. Victor Obenhaus found Illinois town-and-country churches to be almost wholly the products of their environment. The churches' belief-systems were virtually unknown to their members and were not a subject of curiosity to them. Arthur J. Vidich and Joseph Bensman surveyed a small town in upstate New York, where churches represented more stable elements in society than those in the suburbs. The picture that emerged was the same: only the religious professional is supposed to know what the belief-system of the church is about. To the mere members the systems are assumed to be important, but no one talks about them. Fairchild and Wynn roamed the pastures and parishes of Presbyterianism and found that active and leadership families had an almost wholly institutional and instrumental view of their parishes and the church. Ranking only fifth in their system of values, and a weak fifth at that, was the view that the church was somehow a redemptive fellowship. Charles Y. Glock, Samuel Blizzard, and others have found that the spiritual side of church life is secondary in pastors' allocation of their time, and that devotion to administration is so demanded in even the smallest of parishes that other concerns are obscured.

The authors of *Crestwood Heights* saw the religious institutions as being typically accepted but without molding power. John R. Fry contends that adult education suffers because institutionalized church people are not curious about self-knowledge in the light of theology, and Bruce Reinhart learned that most Christian education exists to equip people better to be members of the institution. Merton Strommen worked with young people in a denomination whose doctrinal insistences are well known. The young people had almost no idea of those teachings which set them apart from other denominations. The specifics of study after study could continue indefinitely; I know of no exception on a broad scale. Each study, no matter where it was made, tends to find: (*a*) a generally "orthodox" attachment to the asserted teachings of the religious group; (*b*) a general lack of knowledge about the meaning of these teachings; (*c*) a lack of curiosity about informing oneself in relation to them; (*d*) considerable loyalty to the institution in question and concern for its future; (*e*) assent to the main elements of the surrounding culture religion and a lack of awareness that it may be in conflict with some Christian beliefs; and (*f*) mistrust of obviously conflicting belief patterns (e.g., atheistic Communism, secularism).

Even if it is remembered that the measuring devices are not perfect and that exceptions are reported, the composite is clear: Attachment to the institution and participation in its forms is considered to be justifying in the sight of God, as far as most participants are concerned. So generally accepted is this composite that many students of the culture, as curious as they are about voluntary associations and religious organizations, lose their curiosity about the beliefs which stand behind values and norms. Thus Robert O. Blood Jr., and Donald M. Wolfe, in their study of marriage, minimize the question of religion as a shaping influence, and even church membership is subsumed under the general category of "formal organizations":

> Church membership was excluded [from a graph] because sociologists have traditionally viewed church membership as a conventional matter unlikely to signify much about the persons involved. The separate analysis of comparative church attendance . . . suggests that separation is unnecessary—churches should be looked upon as another example of a formal organization.[12]

Some people may say that such a passage tells a great deal about the secularization of sociology and about deficiencies in its method. This may be true, but the fact remains that sociologists are professionally involved in a commitment to accuracy;

12 *Husbands and Wives* (Glencoe, Ill.: Free Press, 1960), p. 39.

they work under "the watchful severity of their colleagues" and are open to many kinds of evidence.[13]

The study of institutionalism as a problem to faith remains superficial so long as we see institutions as arbitrary and regard life apart from organization as a possibility for the Christian. It dissipates into pettiness if we immediately focus on the malevolence of those who staff and control these structures. Complaints about "the hierarchy" and "the bureaus" may have legitimate bases: the study of the misuses of power is always in place. But how pivotal are these factors? The most benevolent and creative of leaders cannot wholly reform institutions of religious life.

The more creative efforts are those directed to understanding the ways in which the institution becomes closed and in-

---

[13] Those who wish to explore the concerns hinted at in this chapter may consult:

Peter Berger, *The Noise of Solemn Assemblies* (Garden City, N.Y.: Doubleday, 1961) and *The Precarious Vision* (Garden City, N.Y.: Doubleday, 1961).

John R. Fry, *A Hard Look at Adult Christian Education* (Philadelphia: Westminster, 1961).

Charles Y. Glock's chapter in Walter Kloetzli (ed.), *The City Church—Death or Renewal* (Philadelphia: Muhlenberg, 1961), pp. 177 ff.

Gerhard Lenski, *The Religious Factor* (Garden City, N.Y.: Doubleday, 1961).

Victor Obenhaus, *The Church and Faith in Mid-America* (Philadelphia: Westminster, 1963).

Bruce Reinhart, *The Institutional Nature of Adult Christian Education* (Philadelphia: Westminster, 1962).

John R. Seeley *et. al., Crestwood Heights* (New York: Basic Books, 1956).

Merton P. Strommen, *Profiles of Church Youth* (St. Louis: Concordia, 1963).

Arthur J. Vidich and Joseph Bensman, *Small Town in Mass Society* (Princeton: Princeton University Press, 1958).

Gibson Winter, *The Suburban Captivity of the Churches* (Garden City, N.Y.: Doubleday, 1961) and *The New Creation as Metropolis* (New York: Macmillan, 1963).

tegral or self-justifying. Carlton J. H. Hayes found in pacifism, internationalism, and Christian belief some checks against nationalism. Where are the checks against religious institutionalism of a type that eliminates the necessity for faith? Among those most regularly listed are: prophets and critics who recall institutions to congruence with their own professed and original purposes; outside pressures which change cultural expectations extended to them; self-reforming cells and units within larger institutions; and charismatic leaders. So long as the institution's charter is compared with its practice and the institution is not permitted to become enclosed and inclusive; so long as it is actually subjected to the possibility of change, it has not become integral and does not itself become the all-encompassing and demanding idol which eliminates faith.

Institutionalism becomes idolatrous in the ultimate sense when a new and independent ideology develops to justify its transformed action: this is the position of the Grand Inquisitor's life. When religious people defend the beliefs behind the forms but refuse to do more than acknowledge the faults of the institutions as such, they do well to listen to their critics. Isaac Rosenfeld, wearied of hearing a defense of the original intention of institutions that bore no trace of actual "good faith," typifies the sweeping answer of rejection:

> The doctrines of all present-day religions, as understood and observed throughout the world, justify most of the institutional practices which one might call them to correct; . . . it is impossible to separate the beliefs from the institutions in which they are formalized in any way which would be significant for culture. So far as the culture is concerned, religion is the sum of religious institutions.[14]

---

[14] Isaac Rosenfeld, *An Age of Enormity* (New York: World, 1962), p. 219.

The Christian may not have to accept the first part of this statement, but he can hardly escape the cultural judgment of the second part. At the very least, this kind of view by a "cultured despiser" indicates the necessity of bringing religious institutions under the most radical kind of judgment.

If the students of American religious institutions are correct, these are today the real loci of "bad faith," for they offer an unreal world in which the question of authentic faith is not raised. Nowhere does this characteristic reveal itself more than in the finesse with which religious organizations indoctrinate members about the organizations themselves, while interest in the beliefs which are supposedly agents of the institutions can be obscured. One joins the church by agreeing with its constitution but without being open to transcendent judgment, without being called to witness to the activity of God who disrupts even the most sacrosanct of men's forms of life.[15]

To point to institutionalism as an idolatrous or self-justifying problem in the church is not to say that everyone in the church has succumbed to the particular daimon of the institution or that widespread change cannot occur in the nature of given institutions. So long as devotion to them is of a nonintegral type, so long as people withhold co-operation from their strange and inclusive power, so long as an interrupting word is heard, institutionalism has not been closed off into self-sustaining unbelief. Nor is institutionalism the only reality of the church's life. The forms of the church as problems to the church are timeless. What is original is the increase of devotion to these complex forms in a technical society and the passion devoted to them whenever real faith is diminished or relinquished.

---

[15] On "bad faith" in religious institutions, see Peter Berger, *The Precarious Vision*. The fact that Berger may overstate the case does not mean that he fundamentally has misstated it.

9. Unbelief in the Christian orbit: the religious aspect

Christian belief begins with a vision of a gulf between a transcendent God and finite man; different ages may need different symbolic terms to express the gulf, the difference. But that God is "other" and that man is separated from him is a first assertion about faith. The term "Incarnation" represents an inclusive symbol for the fact that it is God's loving activity which bridges the gulf, overleaps the difference and encompasses man. The initiative by which man is justified is basically with God.

Whenever man so understands Christianity and so acts upon such understanding that God's activity becomes secondary or unnecessary, he is seen to be engaged in self-justification. In recent years theologians have begun to apply a dramatic definition of the term "religion" to cover this self-justifying activity. When they use the term in this sense, a precarious one to be sure, they do not refer to every kind of spirituality in the human sphere or to every impulse which can be classified as religious. They refer to a permanent, sustaining outlook and way of life. Such a view is obsessed with man in the act of being religious or pious. It identifies Christianity with any norm not dictated by the nature of faith itself: a specific kind of piety, a specific kind of metaphysic, etc. Whenever man's obsession with his own conscience, his own spirituality or his own inwardness preoccupies him, he is involved in "religion."

A better term is needed for this reality, but this is not the place to develop it or to make judgments about man's general religious impulse or even about "the great religions of the world." Here we are called only to report on the way that self-justifying religion has come to be regarded as unbelief by theologians, with sole reference to events and episodes that are original on the Christian scene.

Typical of the expressions which see religion as a problem for faith because it removes the necessity for witness or the pos-

sibility of hearing is that of the great missionary theologian
Walter Freytag:

> A man's religious life imprisons him against Christ. His
> religiousness, far from causing him to be open, makes him
> on the contrary as if obsessed. His ears are stopped to the
> message of Christ. . . . The more religious a man is, the
> less prepared he is to hear.[16]

Originally this kind of language was applied in modern theology by the circle of men influenced by Karl Barth. No one
has extended it further into missionary thought than the
Dutch missionary scholar Hendrik Kraemer who, using the
dramatic definition of religion and stressing the activity of God
toward man, states baldly: The Bible is not a book about religion. The Bible lacks the term itself, and is too theocentric to
be preoccupied with the reality to which the term points. The
word as we use it today "got the upper hand" in the anthropo-
centrism of the Enlightenment. There it was given the quality
of a category and Christianity became a subsection of that
category.[17]

It has become fashionable to say that Christianity is a faith
and the world religions are religions. I have heard Wilfred
Cantwell Smith, the Canadian student of religion, criticize this.
When religion is thus defined, he argues, none of the faiths of
the world is necessarily a religion.

Nowhere did the problem receive more radical treatment
than in Karl Barth's long discussion of "religion as unbelief"
in "The Revelation of God as the Abolition of Religion," a
section of his *Church Dogmatics*. What does Barth mean? In
what way is religion unbelief? Religion is a human construct
which makes God's activity (Incarnation) unnecessary and in-

---

[16] *The Gospel and the Religions* (London: S.C.M. Press, 1957), p. 43.

[17] *Religion and the Christian Faith* (Philadelphia: Westminster, 1957),
pp. 237-241.

comprehensible. To speak of religion as unbelief is not to despise the greatness of human spirituality but to see it as man's attempt to cover his godlessness on his own terms. Barth says:

> If man believed, he would listen, but in religion he talks. If he believed, he would accept a gift; but in religion he takes something for himself. If he believed, he would let God himself intercede for God; but in religion he ventures to grasp at God.

Therefore religion becomes human artifact and, since so much faith is invested in it, idolatry. It is unbelief because it represents man's attempt to obscure God's activity and to find God on man's terms. The Bible makes it clear that such rejection of God's activity is always sin, which, says Barth,

> is always unbelief. And unbelief is always man's faith in himself. And this faith invariably consists in the fact that man makes the mystery of his responsibility his own mystery, instead of accepting it as the mystery of God. It is this faith which is religion. It is contradicted by the revelation attested in the New Testament, which is identical with Jesus Christ as the one who acts for us and on us. This stamps religion as unbelief.

Religion need not become integral or closed off; even on its own terms it can produce checks against closure. Barth cites mysticism and, strangely, atheism! These are religious revolts against pseudo religion. But they remain largely negative. Barth, a theologian given to paradoxical talk, is soon speaking of "true religion" or Christianity, a faith which annihilates human religiousness but takes permanent forms that look something like religion.

The conservative and ill-tempered continentals of the Barthian school are by no means the only ones who are prone to such language, and the insight will not disappear merely because it is sometimes associated with Barth's name. For a century, British thinkers have expressed uneasiness; a century ago, F. D. Maurice could say:

> Religion against God. This is the heresy of our age. . . . We are turning the Gospel into one of the religions of the world, which is to be proved by endless argumentations and confutations to be better than other religions, when, if it is a Gospel of God, it should meet all other religions, it should satisfy all their craving. . . .

In modern England, Christians of both Barthian and "Mauritian" schools have continued this tradition. One thinks of Father Herbert Kelly, founder of the Society of the Sacred Mission at Kelham, who a generation ago said that "the worship of 'Religion' has become a great stumbling-block in the way of the worship of God." In our time, Alec Vidler, Daniel Jenkins, John A. T. Robinson, Ronald Gregor Smith, and a host of others see religion as unbelief or as a comparable problem for the presentation of the Gospel. In the United States this application of the term is so general among younger theologians that one may soon expect some reaction and rescue of the category.

Certainly such language is confusing to the non-Christian or to the student of the religious impulse. Their complaints about the term are warranted; but they must be asked to be patient, too, while the problem for faith which is constituted by man's religion is isolated and faced.[18]

18 See Karl Barth, *Church Dogmatics*, I, Part 2, trans. G. T. Thomson and Harold Knight (Edinburgh: T. and T. Clark, 1956), 280-361, and see especially 302-307, 314, 331 ff. Maurice is quoted by Alec Vidler, "Religion and the National Church," in *Soundings* (New York: Cambridge University Press, 1962), pp. 241 f. Herbert Kelly, *The Gospel of God* (London:

There is good historical warrant both in the Bible and in the thought of the Reformation for the attack on religion as unbelief. Jesus devoted most of the polemical energies of his ministry to attacking the human constructs of piety and metaphysics which closed off their lives to the possibility of divine intrusion, or which justified them. John Calvin and even more Martin Luther carried their concern for justification by faith (the most radical up to that date in Christian history) to the problem of spirituality and piety. Precisely when man is being religious does he most close himself off from God.

In terms of our distinction, religion is a problem when it becomes integral, organic, intact, whole. Perhaps some other word should be used for nonintegral religiousness; I personally prefer to speak of human spirituality, by which I mean only an element of human greatness, a raw material with which God works, a factor that may be appropriated in the act of belief in God but which may also be exercised as a dimension of personality by people who belong chiefly in the secular order of things. We see secular spirituality in those "saints" of human thought and action who are not believers in the historic sense. We see secular religion as an entirely different problem; it existed in the *ersatz* and pseudo religions, the pantheisms and paganisms which enslave man.

Christian ministers who in their pastoral life use dramatic

S.C.M. Press, 1959), is a book-length polemic against religion as unbelief. A simple, moderating summary is Daniel Jenkins, *Beyond Religion* (Westminster: Philadelphia, 1962). Dietrich Bonhoeffer, in *Prisoner for God,* trans. Reginald H. Fuller (New York: Macmillan, 1956), pp. 122 ff., has provided the most sweeping, and the most radical attack on religion. However, he sees religion as a passing phase in man's development; it is part of his adolescence and he is now outgrowing it. Bonhoeffer calls for a religionless Christianity. The argument is both too tentative and too intricate to be detailed here, but readers on this subject will find Bonhoeffer's work basic.

definitions of religion with great caution actually become quite proficient when, in their pastoral diagnoses, they locate religion as unbelief. They have all confronted people whose piety, whose chosen ways of worshiping or belonging to the church or establishing moral patterns and metaphysical positions, make it impossible for them to hear the Gospel. They also know of some character dimension, which we are calling spirituality, that they regard as transformed when one becomes a Christian. Readers who are uneasy at seeing religion classified as unbelief might try to substitute the adjective "integral" and then apply the test.[19]

If the distinction is forgotten, it is hard to do justice to an element of human response.

Despite Bonhoeffer's prophecy of a completely adult or non-religious world, there has been a proliferation of interest in religions and the nurture of the altar to the unknown God which seems to reside in every breast, as well as the development of secular religions. Here Paul Tillich, Mircea Eliade, and the Roman Catholic apologists have a point: Man seems to be incurably religious, whenever he is grasped by what he recognizes as a matter of "ultimate concern." And no Christian expresses his faith fully without seeing the introduction of religious elements. But these can be kept open, unfinished, receptive. Calvin may be correct: the human mind is an idol factory in constant operation. But the responsible believer's mind is also an idol-smasher. So the religious elements which are necessary (as institutions are inevitable) are less hazardous to faith when they are kept nonintegral.

Religion, according to Hegel,

[19] For a thoughtful criticism of the Barthian dramatic definition from the psychological point of view, see David E. Roberts, *Psychotherapy and a Christian View of Man* (New York: Scribner, 1950), pp. 149 ff. An astute criticism of Calvin, Kraemer, and especially Barth on religion as unbelief from the viewpoint of Christian apology is to be found in John Baillie, *The Sense of the Presence of God* (New York: Scribner, 1962), pp. 174-188.

is the region where all the enigmas of life and all the contradictions of reason find their solution; where all the sorrows of the sentiments are appeased—the region of everlasting truth and everlasting peace. There flows the stream of Lethe, where the soul drinks forgetfulness of all troubles; there all the lights of time are dissolved in the brightness of the infinite. In the mind of God, the spirit casts off all its finite clothing; it is mind completely free, mind which is the knowledge of absolute truth.[20]

The Christian believer in the Incarnation sees the jagged contradictions of God's action in history and sees anything *but* Hegel's all-embracing Absolute. Because religion as the solver of enigmas and contradictions thus obscures God's activity and eliminates the need for hearing, the Christian pastor, preacher, and theologian alike—no matter what terms they use—find integral religion to be the most perplexing if most subtle form of unbelief.

[20] Quoted by Martin C. D'Arcy, S.J., *No Absent God* (New York: Harper & Row, 1962), p. 26.

10 The Relation of Belief to Unbelief

No attempt has been made to delineate all the families of unbelief from the Christian viewpoint. We have chosen to represent five clusters from the secular world (reviewed on p. 150); two from the syncretistic or mixed religious-secular scene; two from the specifically religious setting. Integral culture religion and nationalism were seen to be syncretisms as devastating to faith as are nihilism, atheism, pantheisms, and secularism. Over against these we have placed open possibilities based on the necessity to live the Christian life both in culture and in the nation. Integral institutionalism and religion in the Christian sphere were found to be as debilitating as were their integral cousins. We recognized, however, that the Christian life is always lived in institutions despite their tendencies to idolatry and their need for criticism. We have also seen the need for an open category, such as "spiritual," to provide a nonintegral but manifest alternative to religion as unbelief.

To be a believer means to be in history. To be in history means to be called to faith out of one or another kind of unbelief. One kind presented almost insuperable barriers for interaction with believers on the levels of conversion, communication, or common action. The other kind seemed to offer possibilities. We have resisted the temptation to measure whether there is more or less real faith, whether there are more or fewer believers than in the past. The interest has been in the quality and not the quantity of unbelief, the originality of modern unbelief.

In the light of our discussion, a number of crucial questions arise concerning the future of faith in the world. Is it or can it be present in the world today at all? What kind of expressions of faith are depicted by Christian theologians as most hopeful, most fruitful, most full of possibility? In relation to the world of unbelief is there such a thing as integral faith and will it be more productive or will a more historically oriented and open approach better serve Christianity and the people with which it interacts?

Such questions, no doubt, are of more interest to Christians than to non-Christians. But anyone who has followed our discussion of the varieties of unbelief may also wonder how Christians propose to face a world of unbelief. It is not within the province of this book to present an apology for Christianity; it is rather pre-apologetic by definition, design, and self-discipline. Perhaps it would be best to describe what ensues as reporting on options which are being presented as clues today.

In one word, an *historical* understanding of faith is most regularly presented as a protection for its nonintegral character, which is considered most conducive to creative relations with unbelief as well as faithful to the tradition of belief. It would be unfair to describe this prevalent view as the only one. William Warren Bartley III, whose argument against commitment was cited earlier (p. 18), typifies those who prefer to see Christianity stated as a new and consistent kind of rational liberalism. Within Catholicism and Protestant Fundamentalism there is a broad tendency to state dogmatic propositions out of historical context and provide an authoritarian or integral system of faith. Protestantism's extremely liberal wing sometimes describes a form of faith which is not informed by history but which is chiefly a system of morals or eternal principles of religion. But the whole trend of Christian theology, preaching, and pastoral life has tended in recent years to stress the historical, the personal, the unfinished form of Christian witness. Whether it does so on a passionately theocentric base (as in the early Karl Barth) or on a more consistently anthropocentric one (as in the later Rudolf Bultmann), the historical, hence nonintegral, character of believing has thereby found new stress.

When these terms are introduced, dangers of misunderstanding come in the door with them. "Nonintegral" can be reread to mean noncommittal. It can be used to idolize the stance of nonassessment, to idealize indecision and finally apathy. Similarly, "historical," as such, achieves nothing certain as a safeguard to faith. We have seen that history *qua* history can also be idolatrous and is at the base of ideologies of power in the modern world.

In the nineteenth century there was a constant danger that Christians look for one more "wedge for God," one more *x* in the equation of human ignorance where one would find God. The church took "a series of hedgehog positions," tried to allow for a "God of the gaps" or a *"deus ex machina"*—to borrow the familiar terms of opprobrium. Even in the twentieth century there is an understandable impulse among Christian apologists in the world of science to look for such gaps to keep science from becoming integral as a world view. Thus in recent years Werner Heisenberg's "principle of indeterminacy" has become for many a place where God can re-enter. The principle states that both the position and the speed of an electron cannot be determined at one and the same time, and thus an unpredictable element is introduced into the atomic natural order of the universe.

Whatever legitimacy such impulses may have, they do not result in the Christian apologists suddenly producing God on the scene. If God is not apparent but evil is, it does not somehow solve the problem if we simply point to faith as an event and establish its historical origin and character. And it is this problem which gives rise to all forms of unbelief. God is not dependent upon man's "oddments, inklings, omens, moments, and poems" (to borrow Alastair Reid's delightful terminology). In the Christian witness, God himself takes action; man can only work to keep his ears open to hear if God chooses to speak.

Faith, in any biblical sense, is an event in the real world. In the Psalm, the issue of belief and unbelief is decided in man's moral action before God or in his delusion that "there is no God." In the Fourth Gospel the decision is made in the face of the flesh, or historical presence, of Jesus. It is made because of, or in spite of, the scandal of God's action (Incarnation) in the life of Christ. Most of all, the decision of faith is made in relation to his cross as a transection of history. The historical signals were never seen to be unambiguous: God conceals as he reveals, is *velatus* even as he is *revelatus*, and faith is born in the face of Christ's incognito. Sir James Jeans has spoken in scientific terms of this "gossamer universe"; in the historical sense its texture is also uncertain and unfinished from the Christian point of view.

Today's Christians who are concerned with integral forms of unbelief cultivate an historical sense for many reasons, including those of the heart which, in Pascal's phrase, "reason knows not of." Basic is the confrontation with scientific method and its claim to truth. Stephen Neill has frequently pointed to this problem for faith:

> Modern physical science . . . relies for its spectacular results on the evidence of that which can be measured, numbered and weighed. It is well known that those trained to use only one kind of evidence find it hard to adjust their minds to assess the weight of evidence of a different category. The kind of evidence that the Christian faith can produce is ruled out by many scientists as irrelevant. The kind of proof that science calls for is mostly of the kind that Christian faith ought not to be expected to produce.[1]

On this ground alone, alert Christians might justify the liberal educational endeavor because it stimulates minds to examine many kinds of evidence. But the historically (or existentially) oriented mind, which examines the evidence of events, and events that happen to "me," does not produce God. It opens

[1] *The Christian Society* (New York: Harper & Row, 1952), pp. 277 f.

man to more possibilities. This is true not only of history but of the literary dimension of liberal education.

Developing an historical and literary sense, a witness to God's action is a project of many of those who wish to see the reform of Christian institutions. For example, adult education is almost universally stressed among these reformers. When they speak on its behalf, they refer to biblical literacy, critical analysis of the church's tradition, and informed assessment of its status in the world today. They must believe that such study does not harm faith. This means that in their minds faith is not built on pretense, gullibility, or naïveté but is forged when other faculties of mind and spirit are intensified. This openness to history and literature is seen as the best check on integral institutionalism and religion.[2]

This view is not original as a counter to modern unbelief, but persists wherever reform is a possibility. Thus Martin Luther, speaking in the cultural tradition of the West, could say:

I am persuaded that without knowledge of literature pure theology cannot at all endure, just as heretofore, when letters have declined and lain prostrate, theology, too, has wretchedly fallen and lain prostrate; nay, I see that there has never been a great revelation of the Word of God unless He has first prepared the way by the rise and prosperity of languages and letters, as though they were John the Baptists. . . . Certainly it is my desire that there shall be as many poets and rhetoricians as possible, because I see that by these studies, as by no other means, people are wonder-

2 See Bruce Reinhart, *The Institutional Nature of Adult Christian Education* (Philadelphia: Westminster, 1962), and John R. Fry, *A Hard Look at Adult Christian Education* (Philadelphia: Westminster, 1961), for book-length depictions of a church which is perversely and willfully ignorant of its beliefs and traditions in order better to propagate its institutions and develop man-centered religion.

fully fitted for the grasping of sacred truth and for handling it skillfully and happily.[3]

Sectarian reform, which envisions no cultural responsibility, does not need such a view; but any revival of the church which must sustain a share in creating culture will develop these interests. Also, to call for a revival of theology is not exactly the same thing as calling for a renewal of belief, and Luther may have been somewhat sanguine about the regard people of letters would show the sacred text. But the basic principle remains: In a literate culture one must develop an openness to the breadth of human strivings if he wishes to be able to evaluate the activity of God in history.

In a day when the "warfare between science and theology" has lessened and the "warfare between secular interpretations of the meaning of life and theology" has intensified, it is interesting that the greater interest is no longer in natural theology but in the productions of artists and authors. Their intuitions and their assessments of the spiritual condition of man provide both more alarming and more positive bases for understanding Christian concerns than do "proofs" from natural theology. Christian campus ministries are strongly oriented to the work of men like Albert Camus, Arthur Miller, Georges Rouault, Paul Hindemith, and others. As an English theologian, H. E. Root, puts it:

Before natural theology can begin to function in our day it must have a sense of the inwardness of the lives we lead. Where do we look now for faithful, stimulating, profound accounts of what it is to be alive in the twentieth century?

[3] Letter to Eoban Hess, March 29, 1523. *Luther's Correspondence*, trans. Preserved Smith and Charles M. Jacobs (Philadelphia: United Lutheran Publication House, 1918), II, 176-177. This text becomes fundamental to Roland Mushat Frye, *Perspective on Man* (Philadelphia: Westminster, 1961).

The inevitable answer to that question carries a judgment. We look to the poet or novelist or dramatist or film producer. In creative works of art we see ourselves anew, come to understand ourselves better and come into touch with just those sources of imagination which should nourish efforts in natural theology. The best textbooks for contemporary natural theologians are not the second-hand theological treatises but the living works of artists who are in touch with the springs of creative imagination. This is only another way of saying that theologians cannot direct men's minds to God until they are themselves steeped in God's world and in the imaginative productions of his most sensitive and articulate creatures. That in turn is only another way of saying that the enterprise of theology cannot come to life until it takes to heart the principle of Incarnation.[4]

If the Christian sees a need for developing a sense of openness to history both so that he can bring a critical sense to bear and so that he can develop an imaginative view of self and world, he also knows the positive aspects of history. "History is something more than a process of ripping open dolls and turning them over to shake out the sawdust; it is also the midwife of values." [5]

When the Christian examines the Scripture, witnesses to the Trinity or Incarnation, listens to witnesses, responds to the tradition of the church, examines the believing community and his own heart, he is using history as a midwife of values. He becomes open to faith. According to Gerhard Ebeling:

It is noteworthy that faith today, as always, appears as an event. . . . Faith comes to us out of history, and it takes us

4 "Beginning All Over Again," in Alec Vidler (ed.), *Soundings* (New York: Cambridge University Press, 1962), p. 18.

5 Jules Monnerot, *Sociology and Psychology of Communism,* trans. Jane Degras and Richard Rees (Boston: Beacon, 1960), p. 291.

into its history. . . . Faith is not some kind of innate truth of reason, which we may come upon of ourselves and which we can recall as we please. Nor is it a purely inward happening. . . . Rather, faith comes into being as the consequence of the witness of faith. . . . That is to say, it comes into being, and continues in being, when it is handed on, in tradition. . . . Scripture bears witness to Jesus as the "pioneer and perfecter of faith" (Heb. 12:2).[6]

The man whom Roman Catholic Josef Pieper calls "the last great teacher of a still undivided Christendom," Thomas Aquinas, provides a reference point for history as the midwife of values. In our context it is not necessary to share his attack on "speculation about the deity" in order to concentrate on its alternative: relishing of history, event, decision. His theology of the cross represented the Christian belief that an integrated personality could develop without an integral or closed-off faith. Instead, "he [alone] is worth calling a theologian who understands the visible and hinder parts of God to mean the passion and the cross." [7]

For Luther and the Reformers, history itself is seen as the work of God; there is no dead history and no flight from history. God does not become obvious or apparent in history. He voluntarily conceals himself to preserve his omnipotence and to guarantee the reality of historical existence. Therefore, for Luther the themes of history were always "faith" and "unbelief." [8] These are not merely Protestant themes: on this subject

6 *The Nature of Faith,* trans. Ronald Gregor Smith (Philadelphia: Muhlenberg, 1961). See Chap. 2, "The History of Faith," and especially pp. 25 f.

7 "Heidelberg Disputation of 1518, Thesis XX," trans. James Atkinson in *Luther: Early Theological Works* (Philadelphia: Westminster, 1962), pp. 290-291. The reference to the "hinder parts of God" is based on Exod. 33:20: Man cannot see God and live. He is given only a trace of God from behind or below in history.

8 See John M. Headley, *Luther's View of Church History* (New Haven: Yale University Press, 1963), pp. 1-18, 267.

there is no basic disagreement in Western Christianity. Thus in our day Christopher Dawson can summarize: "A religion without Revelation is a religion without History, and it is just the historical element in Christianity which gives it its peculiar character." [9]

What in history gives it importance to the Christian? Why should there be an interest in keeping matters open? The answer must begin in reference to Josef Pieper's description of "the usual counterpoise to belief" which was "inveterate inattentiveness." That is, when a man closes off his life—whether in atheism or pantheism, whether by attaching his ultimate devotion to religious institutions or his own religiousness—he will be "inveterately inattentive." Such a closed-off life provides him, so to speak, with a creed or confession or church and aborts any possibility of inquiry or curiosity concerning Christian belief.

To look to history as a context for faith cannot mean that "belief that" is the basis for "belief in" or that faith rests on historical certitude. Historical security is the death of belief because belief is to be spoken of only when other terms do not suffice. Historical certitude leads to knowledge; acting as if historical certitude were present when it is not is bad faith or pretense. As Paul Tillich has noted:

> Faith includes certitude about its own foundation—for example, an event in history which has transformed history —for the faithful. But faith does not include historical knowledge about the way in which this event took place.

The introduction of historical openness is always a threat of death to Christian integralism of belief. Integralism is perfectly systematic and, when it is based in history, depends upon what Tillich calls "unbroken myth."

[9] *Progress and Religion* (Garden City, N.Y.: Doubleday, 1960), p. 192.

Christianity . . . by its very nature [is not an] unbroken myth, because its presupposition is the first commandment: the affirmation of the ultimate as ultimate and the rejection of any kind of idolatry. . . . Those who live in an unbroken mythological world feel safe and certain. They resist, often fanatically, any attempt to introduce an element of uncertainty by "breaking the myth," namely, by making conscious its symbolic character. Such resistance is supported by authoritarian systems, religious or political, in order to give security to the people under their control and unchallenged power to those who exercise the control.

Christianity is described by Tillich as an historical myth as opposed to a natural one:

If the Christ—a transcendent, divine being—appears in the fullness of time, lives, dies and is resurrected, this is an historical myth. . . . Christianity speaks the mythological language like every other religion. It is a broken myth. . . .

Tillich's use of the term "myth" is complicated and may cause confusion unless it is explained. What keeps Christianity a "broken myth," and therefore forces a nonintegral view of history, is the cross of Jesus Christ. It does not make God apparent or remove the immediacy of evil, and thus does not permit a closed-system satisfaction.

Christianity expresses itself in . . . a symbol in contrast to all other religions, namely, in the Cross of the Christ. Jesus could not have been the Christ without sacrificing himself as Jesus to himself as the Christ. Any acceptance of Jesus as the Christ which is not the acceptance of Jesus the crucified is a form of idolatry.

This brokenness also provides the basis for shattering the forms of unbelief which we saw extant in Christian orbits:

> From the Christian point of view, one would say that the Church with all its doctrines and institutions and authorities stands under the prophetic judgment and not above it. Criticism and doubt show that the community of faith stands "under the Cross," if the Cross is understood as the divine judgment over man's religious life, and even over Christianity, though it has accepted the sign of the Cross. . . . The life of a community of faith is a continuous risk, if faith itself is understood as a risk.[10]

In a linguistic study, Rudolf Bultmann also indicates, but in different terms, the ways in which knowledge (which implies integrality) is destructive of belief. Discussing the Johannine literature in the Bible, Bultmann writes:

[10] Paul Tillich, *The Dynamics of Faith* (New York: Harper & Row, 1957), pp. 89, 50 f., 97 f., 29. I have deliberately chosen to illustrate this point with the instance of Paul Tillich because he is often regarded as a philosopher of religion who is less interested in the historical dimension of faith than are the majority of contemporary Christian thinkers. His book, however, deals chiefly with what might be called existential doubt and the dynamics of faith. We have not included such doubt among the varieties of unbelief. Also, Tillich's strictures against equating Christian faith with "belief that" are not applicable in our context for two reasons. First, we are not ourselves saying that "belief that" constitutes faith; such belief (referring to Josef Pieper's analysis) only indicates that the witness has been attended to and reckoned with. Second, Tillich opposes "belief that" as a destruction of faith if it means that one thus accepts with historical or scientific certitude the truth of propositions about God. That is not meant in the reference points Trinity or Incarnation throughout this book. They provide a means of symbolizing the divine reality toward whom "belief in" is directed. See Tillich, *ibid.*, p. 19, for his discussion of the ways in which "belief that something is true" is incompatible with doubt and thus with faith.

There is a peculiar connection between believing and knowing. Knowledge represents the perfect relation between subject and object; this is shown by the fact that it, and not faith, is given as describing the mutual relation between the Father and the Son. Faith is man's first step towards God, or the revelation of God; if it is maintained it will be rewarded with knowledge (John 8.31 f.; 10:30). Faith, which Jesus is always demanding, is that doing of God's will which leads to knowledge (7:17). . . . This does not mean that faith and knowledge have different objects, or that knowledge stands on a higher level or is in possession of that which is known. . . . True faith, which "abideth," as such contains knowledge as one of its components; this is faith's own understanding, identical with that joy which has no more need to ask, because the word of Jesus is no longer parabolic, but perfectly plain.[11]

None of this means that Christian belief cannot be expressed systematically; the dogmatician must only remember what he is being systematic about: an historical experience transected by the cross of Jesus Christ. In it God both reveals and conceals himself. So long as this is true, God does not become immediately apparent, and evil remains apparent. Thus the occasion for unbelief remains and the Christian can empathize with the unbeliever. When this historical element in systematics disappears, Christian certitude becomes as intellectually arrogant and destructive of faith (though not necessarily so ill-mannered) as the assertion of Eunomius, Bishop of Cyzicus (d. 395) in the creed-making period: "I know God as well as He knows Himself." Such an integralism rightfully occasions from the unbelieving world some nontheological analogies to

---

[11] "Gnosis" in Bible Key Words, II, 50 f., trans. J. R. Coates and H. P. Kingdon (New York: Harper & Row, 1948).

Oliver Cromwell's famed plea: "By the bowels of Christ remember that you may be mistaken." [12]

The relation of history to belief or faith was a major theme in the thought of Martin Luther. One student of his work has summarized it in terms exactly appropriate to our present context:

> The attitudes of faith and unbelief are entirely different. The unbeliever views all things a priori. He wants to see things beforehand, face to face as it were. He wants to read the truth directly from events. The believer draws no conclusions while events are still in process. He does not know God in the moment of the event. Yet he does not become exasperated nor give way to unbelief. He waits, that he may understand afterwards. This is the a posteriori approach. Faith is satisfied to see God from behind as it were, without trying to behold his face. Unbelief desires to possess all things now.[13]

The Roman Catholic tradition, while it is more at home with speculative theology, also resists dogmatic integralism. That this was true even in St. Thomas Aquinas is noted by Josef Pieper. In our day, doctrinal integralism within Catholicism has been opposed by Catholics precisely because it demolishes the historical openness and patience and the humility which commends the church to others. Cardinal Suhard, for instance, can defend Catholic dogma and a particular way of setting it forth (Thomism) and then immediately suggest that the dogma and the system have not exhausted thought about the revelation, quoting Lacordaire: "St. Thomas is a beacon and not a landmark."

[12] See Reinhold Niebuhr on "Having, and Not Having, the Truth" in *The Nature and Destiny of Man* (New York: Scribner, 1948), II, 213 ff.

[13] Lennart Pinomaa, *Faith Victorious*, trans. Walter J. Kukkonen (Philadelphia: Fortress, 1963), p. 40; but see the whole chapter, "The Meaning of History," pp. 35 ff.

To preserve life, Modernism sacrificed forms; to preserve forms, Integralism sacrifices life. . . . We must not confuse integrity of doctrine with the preservation of its passing forms of expression.[14]

David E. Roberts, who was constantly concerned with the integrity of the personality, saw integralism to be a threat to it and a barrier to Christian mobility in the secular world. Integralism provides an insecure person with a sense of superior righteousness.

Under such circumstances a person needs to find ways of making his faith impregnable against criticism coming from others or from skeptical inclinations within himself. . . .

Man's capacities for imagination and for logical thinking can be employed to construct a system which *excludes* evidence from the world outside and doubts from within. When such a system derives its cohesiveness from the need of an insecure person to hold himself together and to reassure himself that the universe meets his specifications, it is bound to be employed in "filtering" or "retouching" reality. . . .

For the most part the Churches have not yet learned that the best way to pass from defensive rationalizations to secure faith is to let doubts, inconsistencies, confusions and rebellions come out into the open instead of using various forms of spiritual coercion to keep them hidden or to drive them from awareness altogether.[15]

[14] Suhard, *The Church Today, Growth or Decline,* trans. James J. Corbett (Notre Dame, Ind.: Fides, 1948), pp. 63-67.

[15] *Psychotherapy and a Christian View of Man* (New York: Scribner, 1950), pp. 70 ff. I commend this book to those who wonder why a nonintegral or historically oriented belief is consistent with integrity and wholeness in man.

In the end the open vision, compatible both with the biblical injunctions against anxiety over the future and with the nature of biblical revelation, cannot be advertised as a guarantee that belief is automatically born. The Christian tradition proclaims that belief and faith are gifts of God, born of his initiative. Man is culpable only when he indulges in idolatry as it is implicit in the integral systems or when he is inattentive. This is well explained by John Oman:

> In the Gospels, therefore, hypocrisy is the only deadly sin, because it is the refusal to allow the deep things of life to touch us, and so the one sure way of escaping the impact of God's truth. . . .
>
> Unbelief, then, is a sin, not because we fail to force ourselves to believe or to suppress doubt and inquiry, but because, to some evil intent, we are insincere with God's witness to himself. . . .
>
> In the strict sense, we should not even try to believe; for we have no right to believe anything we can avoid believing, granting we have given it entire freedom to convince us. . . .
>
> There is only one right way of asking men to believe, which is to put before them what they ought to believe because it is true; and there is only one right way of persuading, which is to present what is true in such a way that nothing will prevent it from being seen except the desire to abide in darkness; and there is only one further way of helping them, which is to point out what they are cherishing that is opposed to faith. When all this has been done, it is still necessary to recognise that faith is God's gift, not our handiwork, of His manifestation of the truth by life, not of our demonstration by argument or of our impressing by eloquence; . . .
>
> Because . . . as Professor A. B. Davidson put it, "perhaps mankind is one large Pharisee," unbelief is the most universal and deep-seated corruption in the human heart. Not be-

cause faith could be a moral effort, to be directly purposed and carried through, is unbelief culpable, but because the truth would always carry conviction, did we not use our privileges to pamper our self-esteem and create for ourselves a mail of proof of self-delusion to ward off its appeal, till we may end, where there can be at least no human hope of recovery, in loving darkness rather than light.[16]

Christians who are alert to the power of the secular realm as God's creation are, as Oman ably indicates, hesitant to apply a different standard to the outsider than to the insider of the believing community. Condemnation of nihilism, atheism, pantheism, secularism—is without effect unless identical standards are applied to the idolatries and inattentiveness which exist within the syncretistic and sacral forms of unbelief. Indeed, from the time of the apostles, through the Fathers and teachers and Reformers, down to the present, reflective Christians have concurred that precisely in the believing community the diagnosis of the varieties of unbelief is most urgent. It is here that it must be pursued with greatest intensity and surgical clarity. For in that community, where culpability is asserted, the temptations to idolatry and inattentiveness are strongest.

We have come full circle, then, back to the kinds of unbelief which were most paralytic: anomie and accidie, normlessness and apathy. Pierre Teilhard de Chardin and François Mauriac have shown us the ultimate dangers which integralism of doctrine, morality, or tactic brings to Christian faith's openness. In Teilhard's words:

The greatest danger which humanity may fear is not some exterior catastrophe, famine or plague . . . but rather that spiritual malady (the most terrible, since it is the most

16 *Grace and Personality* (New York: Association Press, 1961), pp. 121-124.

directly human of all the scourges) which is the loss of
one's love of life.

Without it, comments Yves de Montcheuil, there can be only
apathy and mediocrity.

It is a great illusion to believe that this love of life will
really exist in the religious life if it is prevented from existing on the level of the natural activities. From this we must
conclude that anything which deteriorates the man also
harms the Christian.

If this vision of the love of life applies only to one side of
man's nature and neglects the tragic sense of life, we can turn
to Mauriac to illustrate the virtues of openness in the auto-
biography of the man of tragic vision:

My own quest, my own confrontation with the Christ of
the Gospel, with the invisible and omnipresent Christ who
puts His trust in His loved ones, was inspired by a passion
which, though it may not have been totally pure, took its
strength from the weakness of my faith. I desired to prove
to myself that the Jesus of Emmaus is always there, in the
heart of this dark world, and that He dwells with us in this
stifling twilight.[17]

[17] Teilhard is quoted along with comment by Yves de Montcheuil, S.J.,
in A. Robert Caponigri (ed.), *Modern Catholic Thinkers* (New York:
Harper & Row, 1960), p. 99. Mauriac, *The Son of Man*, trans. Bernard
Murchland (New York: World, 1958), p. 76.

REFERENCE NOTE ON OPENNESS, HISTORY, AND FAITH

Readers who wish to carry the study of history and faith beyond
the legitimate scope of this chapter may pursue the following instances of a voluminous literature on the subject:

1. On Old Testament History and Faith:

Sheldon H. Blank, *Prophetic Faith in Isaiah* (New York: Harper & Row, 1958), a Jewish interpretation of the meanings of faith as "the faith that means doing" and "the faith that means believing."

Martin Buber, *Moses: The Revelation and the Covenant* (New York: Harper & Row, 1958). "He is the history God, which He is, only when He is not localized in Nature; and precisely because He makes use of everything potentially visible in Nature, every kind of natural existence, for His manifestation" (p. 127). In this spirit Jews and Christians should not be dismayed by desacralization of nature in the modern scientific world.

Millar Burrows, *What Mean These Stones?* (New York: Meridian, 1957), Chap. 1, on "Revelation and History," pp. 1 ff., with an excellent discussion on the misuses of archaeology to establish a base for certitude in faith.

Abraham J. Heschel, *The Prophets* (New York: Harper & Row, 1962), Chap. 9, "History," pp. 159 ff., discusses ambiguities and problems in Israel's view of history. "History is where God is defied, where justice suffers defeat. God's purpose is neither clearly apparent nor translatable into rational categories of order and design" (p. 168).

Edmond Jacob, *Theology of the Old Testament,* trans. Arthur W. Heathcote and Philip J. Allcock (New York: Harper & Row, 1958), Part 2, Chap. 4, "God the Lord of History."

Ludwig Köhler, *Old Testament Theology,* trans. A. S. Todd (Philadelphia: Westminster, 1957). Chap. 4, "The Scope (the History) of God's Activity," pp. 59 ff.

R. A. F. MacKenzie, S.J., *Faith and History in the Old Testament* (Minneapolis: University of Minnesota Press, 1963).

James Muilenburg, *The Way of Israel* (New York: Harper & Row, 1961). "The way of Israel is historical. It is historical to a maximum degree because its history belongs to God. History is God's gift to Israel and to the world" (p. 44).

H. H. Rowley, *The Faith of Israel* (Philadelphia: Westminster, 1957), Chap. 1, "Revelation and Its Media," pp. 23 ff.

2. *New Testament Background of History and Faith:*

The debate over history and myth, initiated by Rudolf Bultmann, has preoccupied this field; the literature on *Geschichte* and *Historie* is enormous. Many of the issues are focused in a book whose title at first seems to have little to do with this subject: James M. Robinson and John B. Cobb, Jr., *The Later Heidegger and Theology* (New York: Harper & Row, 1963).

The bibliography on what has come to be called "A New Quest of the Historical Jesus" is included (to 1959) in James M. Robinson's book of that title. (London: S.C.M. Press, 1959). Many have seen in this "quest" a basis for reopening the question of history.

Oscar Cullmann, *Christ and Time,* trans. Floyd V. Filson (Philadelphia: Westminster, 1950).

F. C. Grant, *Ancient Judaism and the New Testament* (New York: Macmillan, 1959). Chap. 9, "The Church's Heritage from Judaism," includes appeals for critical exegesis and an historical sense, to disrupt institutionalism and religion as well as integral dogmatism.

Ian Henderson, *Myth in the New Testament* (London: S.C.M. Press, 1952). See Chap. 3, "The Historical Element in Christianity."

3. *Systematic Theology:*

Hermann Diem, *Dogmatics,* trans. Harold Knight (Philadelphia: Westminster, 1959). Diem surveys the systematic scene after Bultmann's views became predominant.

A theologian who also works from an existential base but who uses "decision" as a base for stressing the importance for history in faith is Carl Michalson, *The Hinge of History* (New York: Scribner, 1959) and *The Rationality of Faith* (New York: Scribner, 1963). The reader who is interested in this subject will find in these two volumes a good introduction to the literature.

Schubert M. Ogden, "What Sense Does It Make to Say, 'God Acts in History'?" in *Journal of Religion, XLIII, No. 1* (January, 1963) is a radical statement by a systematic theologian who is informed alike by Heidegger's existentialism and Charles Hartshorne's process thought. Ogden is extremely Protestant in the way he disallows the seeing of signs in history.

4. Specifically on the Subject of Faith:

Emil Brunner, *Dogmatics,* trans. David Cairns (Philadelphia: Westminster, 1960), III, especially Chap. 11, "Faith and Unbelief," pp. 140 ff.

A position on faith as openness to history, which is very congenial to the viewpoint of this chapter, is systematically stated by Gerhard Ebeling, *The Nature of Faith,* trans. Ronald Gregor Smith (Philadelphia: Muhlenberg, 1961), and is implied throughout the essays in *Word and Faith* (Philadelphia: Fortress, 1960). See especially Chap. 15, "Faith and Unbelief in Conflict about Reality."

See also Friedrich Gogarten, *The Reality of Faith,* trans. Carl Michalson *et al* (Philadelphia: Fortress, 1959).

5. Integrating the Personality:

Gordon Allport, *The Individual and His Religion* (New York: Macmillan, 1960).

11

The Future of Belief and Unbelief

Christian believers make up a small minority of the population of the modern world. Each day they come into more and more contact with those who do not share their belief. We have suggested that when Christian belief is stated in integral terms or when it is housed in integral forms of institutions or religiousness it cannot well carry on creative interchange. Conversely, when secular forms of unbelief are made integral, they close themselves off from much real possibility of interaction with Christian belief and believers. The time has come for a summary statement of Christian tactics and approaches in such a time and situation.

Fundamental to this relation are two propositions:

1. "Belief and unbelief are much closer to one another than to pseudo-belief and pseudo-unbelief respectively."

2. "One finds people both inside and outside the Church who share substantially the same humanitarian aims; and they are ranged against ominous forces of repression, hatred, and regimentation that are at work in both the Church and the world." [1]

If these statements are true, Christians will not find it legitimate to lump together every "ism" they dislike and make of it some sort of doctrinaire secularism. To do so would be inaccurate, dishonest, and strategically unproductive. It provides seekers and questioners with a religion, a creed, a position, when they should actually be confronted with questions which would force them to subject their visions of life to systematic scrutiny. Even the negative tactic of showing that unbelief's house is divided has more merit than the homiletical simplifications.

[1] The first of these, the thesis of Swiss theologian Albert Rich, was cited by Eduard Schweizer in a lecture at Union Theological Seminary, Richmond, Va., in 1962; the second is from David E. Roberts, *Psychotherapy and a Christian View of Man* (New York: Scribner, 1950), p. 84.

Nor should Christians want to minimize the potency of other ideologies around them in order to make the institutional strength of Christianity look stronger than it is or to enhance a culture's self-image as being basically Christian. And Christians are just as unwise to exaggerate the other powers merely to frighten people into "crusades." Neither minimizing nor maximizing will do: Accuracy is the only approach that serves both church and world.

The three terms used throughout this book to describe the relations have been "conversion," "communication," and "conspiracy." By the third, conspiracy, is meant common action. No one can "go it alone." Christians who believe that God is active in the secular world, and who do not claim a monopoly of goodness, truth and beauty, will often find company among unbelievers. In such times alliances between integrists of belief and unbelief have usually been detrimental to both real secuIuarity and real Christianity. One thinks of the alliance between the atheism of Charles Maurras' self-professed integral nationalists in the *Action Française* movement and the Roman Catholic integralists; or between the radical political and the radical religious "Right" in the United States in the early 1960s.

Had the American Enlightenment been as ideological as was the French Revolutionary ideal, would creative alliances have been possible—as was the case between the Jeffersons and Madisons on the one hand, and dissenting (nonintegral) Christians, Baptists and Quakers, on the other? In each case there were common enemies to motivate strategic alliance. In the latter there was a greater area of shared ground without a loss of real conviction on the part of either in a process of syncretism. Examples could be multiplied indefinitely. In the American civil rights struggle an integral construct (if not a nihilistic and then pantheistic power) like the Black Muslims joins in unholy alliance with the equally integral American Nazi Party—black racism makes common cause with white

racism. It is the moderate Negro movement and its counterpart in the white community that finds it easiest to work in
concord. Each draws upon more than an ideology: they share
a consensus, a national experience, a practice, a hope. They
borrow from many sources: Greece and Rome and the Western humane tradition. Their alliance represents a real sharing
without a loss of identity or distinctiveness on those levels
where it must be asserted. The nature of the alliance between
two open groups and systems of belief is one in which anxiety
and self-defensiveness can be dispelled and men can work for
the common good.

Second, there must be communication as a parallel to conspiracy or "breathing together." Communication does not occur between two who share *no* beliefs, and integral ideologists claim to share nothing with others. Those who are open
to possibilities will want to speak and hear. This does not
mean that there are no ultimate commitments ("He that is
not with me is against me"; "No man can serve two masters"),
but only that those who have an identity and a confession
and state their views candidly and humbly will also best hear.

The third basis, and one which will not interest the integral unbeliever, is conversion. Wherever Christians believe in
extending the believing community through legitimate means,
by monstrating God the Trinity and presenting Jesus Christ incarnate; wherever they expose themselves as witnesses to the
world, they are faced with the issue of the kind of system they
would present. Often an authoritarian and closed system is
said to be most effective in the modern world. People look for
escape from anxiety into fanaticisms, sects, cults, authoritarian patterns, systems which have all the answers. The Christian who is open to the Bible and the record and witness of
faith through the centuries must ask: Is this authentic faith
that is being presented? Should men escape from freedom into
a system that would enslave them? Can God reach them if they

are self-justified by joining a religion? Are not those who trans-
fer from one authoritarian community to another (for example, from integral Communism to some forms of Catholicism, and vice versa) often themselves crippled emotionally
and experientially? Should not Christian and unbeliever alike
work to keep people more free and mobile, more open, rather
than being committed to any of the authoritarianisms?

Erik Routley has suggested that each conversion is *sui gen-
eris;* it cannot be fully typed. But in general the most con-
spicuous common quality is the sense of freedom. At the same
time, the free Christian does seek a dogmatic theology, so that
he is not fugitive and negative. This theology, however, witnesses to the mystery of the Trinity and the history of the Incarnation, and therefore it is interrupted by event and possibility and does not become closed. From the Roman Catholic
side, A. Liégé, O.P., has seen the modern no-man's lands
of ideology to be wearying to the potential convert. "Every day
he is offered programs for life by political parties, sects, denominations, ideological reformers: and he is tired of them."
Liégé counsels that he be confronted not with new ideology
or trivializing institutions, but with witness and the simplicity
of church life.[2]

The Christian who is mindful of the types and varieties of
unbelief will minister in a different way than will the one who
lumps all together or who minimizes or maximizes the real
situation of unbelief in the world. The questions of the godless
man, says John Courtney Murray, S.J., "are put to the people
of God; and their answer must be practical, programmatic,

---

[2] Erik Routley, *Conversion* (Philadelphia: Muhlenberg, 1955), Chap. 2,
"Archetypes," pp. 18 ff., and Chap. 11, "Conversion, the Church, and
Evangelism," pp. 120 ff. See also A. D. Nock, *Conversion* (New York: Oxford University Press, 1962), on Christianity in the Greco-Roman world
and A. Liégé, O.P., *What Is Christian Life?* (New York: Hawthorn, 1961),
pp. 71 ff.

expressed as post-modern atheism expresses itself—*in a total attitude and style of life.*" [3]

The question must be asked of unbelief in the Christian orbit: Has institutionalism or religion really embodied attitudes and styles of life or are they integral ideologies serving as façades for a secular way of existence? That is, a man may really belong to the world and its ways of thinking exploitatively. Then he joins a Christian institution or adopts a style of piety or a philosophy and need not call into question all the substrata of his life. But a total attitude and style of life calls him into daily reconnaissance of his inner life in the light of the witness to faith.

To minister in the world of unbelief does not mean that all Christians must become virtuosos in the art of detecting varieties of unbelief or dilettantes at forming typologies; they need not take a pathological or morbid interest in the psychology of unbelief. Out of a primal apprehension of faith and an inquisitiveness about the real world which confronts them can grow a healthy interest in all kinds of people, an empathy with them. They will, of course, find themselves tearing off masks from themselves as they do from others. They will face their own inner lives with openness, with criticism. They will find it necessary to confront their own churchly secularism in a new way and to work toward expressing their faith simply and economically. They may have to make room for the communion of saints and a division of labor. That is, they may need new tolerance for preachers, apologists, people on the boundaries of Christianity, artists and others who seek unconventional ways of relating to the secular. Several modes of expression will then be open to them.

The first is called "apology," a subject beyond the scope of this pre-apologetic book. The apologist is coming into his own again in the church. In the earlier Barthian period the apolo-

[3] "The Structure of the Problem of God," *Theological Studies,* XXIII, No. 1 (March, 1962), 25. (Italics added.)

gist had to run for cover; now more are coming to agree with
W. Norman Pittenger that it is hard enough to be a Christian;
should thought forms be adopted which exaggerate the intellectual difficulties? John Baillie, for instance, chastened by
Barthian mistrust of natural theology, consistently attempted
to carry on an understanding of the secular world and bring a
Christian witness to it.[4]

One must be careful not to use obsolete models in discussing
informed Christian defense or apology today. If apology ever
meant "proving the existence of God"—as it certainly did not
when St. Thomas offered his "proofs"—then it cannot mean
this today. Apologists know that proof is convincing only
when people are already predisposed to believe. They cannot
produce God or make him apparent and they are also learning
not to indulge in verbal sleight-of-hand tactics. People cannot well be cajoled or deluded into believing. The tests a
secular world presents are too many for such a faith to stand up
after the sleight-of-hand artist has left the scene. Instead, most
apologists are doing on philosophical grounds what we are attempting on historical grounds. They ask that the undecided
who are really receptive keep things open and unresolved, not
close themselves off to all kinds of evidence but one.

"Faith is a tender plant in comparison with sense percep-
tion," said John Baillie. The apologist must ask his listener
to keep feeding both the traces of faith and the varieties of
experience, so that he may be open to the many delicate modes
of apprehension.

The second approach may be called "preaching," though
the term is confusing. If by preaching is meant the dispensing
of authority from a pulpit to people culturally captive in a
pew at 11:00 A.M. on Sunday, expectation may be low. But

[4] John Baillie, *The Sense of the Presence of God* (New York: Scribner,
1962). Recently apology has moved from Baillie's defenses of a kind of
theism to the school of language analysts typified by Ian Ramsey, Frederick
Ferré, John Hutchison and others.

if preaching represents every form of involving one's own integrity as witness with what one has seen and heard *and* with a listener to whom one commends this witness, we are on different grounds. "Belief cannot argue with unbelief; it can only preach to it." [5] When this preaching takes on obsolete patterns, not nourished by the basic visions and apprehensions of people in today's world, it is not addressing unbelief at all.

Actually, the Christian and the agnostic have the same problem. This occasions the birth of preaching. The Christian does not preach or witness to integral unbelievers in the world and maybe not even in church. But the agnostic is one who does not know, because he has not seen God although he has seen evil. It is the same with the Christian. The preacher dare not be a poseur, exaggerating his own internal drama of doubt and faith. But if he has known no drama or if he obscures it, he will also not actually be preaching to the unbeliever who is open to hearing a real person.

The preacher is first of all involved in the reiteration of the event, a task he must undertake with discretion. He can point to the believing community as the only proof of faith: there it is, it is existent. It should not exist in the world. But it does. That is the problem for unbelief. Such preaching will answer questions in the mode they are asked. It will not provide answers to French grammar with examples from the back of an algebra book, suggests Carl Michalson. To use Kierkegaard's metaphor, it is the job of the circus manager, not the clown, to come and announce to the crowd that a tent is burning. It is the voice of a town crier, not a debater. It is the portrayal of Christianity not as an absolute—which would deny the cross— but as a witness to the fact that God has turned to man, that he is in a new situation before God. To use Philip Melanchthon's well-known phrase, preaching relates not to speculation about the mode of Incarnation, but with "enjoying Christ's benefits." It is based on listening, both to the healthy worldling and

5 Alasdair MacIntyre, quoted by Baillie, *ibid.*, p. 84.

to the inwardly secularized church people. It is a corollary of teaching a generation whose institutions and religion stifle curiosity about the ways of God. It represents a summons for belief as the voice best can.

The third major mode of approach, and vastly the most important first contact, is through action, through ethics. The modern world moves by images of what is seen and heard. Both secular unbelievers and religious unbelievers, from opposite motives, can yawn and lose curiosity in the presence of the Christian witness if the believing community shows no regard for the world as it is and if it does not move in the world in a way congruent with its profession.[6]

It is the ethical concern that is leading to a restudy of self-serving institutionalism and religious narcissism among Christians today. Karl Jaspers is no doubt correct when he says, "If the churches dared . . . to put themselves in jeopardy, the Word would be credible everywhere, every day, on the lips of priests and theologians." [7] He was citing a specific ethical instance, but we believe it can be generalized upon. To make the Word credible is not the same thing as saying that it will be believed. But a new situation for hearing presents itself. For this task the churches need to seek the grace of patience, perhaps having to be content with comparative formlessness for some generations.

While the churches revise their institutions and make their

[6] The Rauschenbusch Lectures are dedicated to the memory of a great Christian ethical thinker and are to be devoted to studies of the action of the Church vis-à-vis human problems. This book originated as a series of these lectures. When I proposed the topic of unbelief to the committee, there was no hesitation on its part, as there had been none on mine: We both agreed that "faith is made active in love" and that at the base of much Christian inaction or maldirection of action today is bad faith or unfaith and not mere apathy. I hope that this ethical interest in the world on its terms has shown on every page.

[7] The Future of Mankind, trans. E. B. Ashton (Chicago: University of Chicago Press, 1961), p. 259.

word credible, they dare not wait for fulfillment in a kind of false perfectionism. In the spirit of Luther's dictum that "God carves the rotten wood and rides the lame horse," they are free to work with history as they find it, not as they wish it could be remade.

One is tempted to speculate concerning the future of Christian belief and community in the world of unbelief. Many options are present.

1. It may prevail. This is logical but not a theological possibility. The promise that faith would prevail was never given; in fact, in history the disciples were warned not to expect prevalence over "the spirits," but only to rejoice that their names were written in the Book of Life. The historical improbabilities are so overpowering that this question may disappear as quickly as it is raised.

2. It may disappear. The only security that Christians have that it may not is one or two eschatological promises that the gates of death will not prevail against the church (which can be two or three people), and the biblical conviction that the word of the Lord abides forever. But Jesus' concerned question about whether he would find faith suggests that neither of these words about the end-time can provide a basis of a Christian program in the world.[8] It may be questioned whether the churches have really taken seriously the possibility that the believing community might virtually disappear.

3. It may survive as a nominal minority in the world. While the percentage of people called Christian dwindles in relation to world population each year, Christianity remains the largest of the world religions. In some parts of the world its institutions are strong. Within them the number of those who have a total Christian attitude and style of living cannot be reckoned. But to such people belongs, humanly speaking, the

8 Luke 18:8.

future of faith. They may see to the preservation of Christian institutions as nostalgic and aristocratic survivors, much as Greece survived in Rome. They may see to its expression in exile and mobility, as the Jews have done. They may be conscious of a divine mandate that calls them into as yet unconceived possibilities, for which there are no models.

4. There are no signs on the horizon which seem to reverse a trend toward increased secularization of ways of life accompanied by a mixed culture of resurgent world religions and the development of ideologies and *ersatz* faiths. There are no worldwide signs which point to the development of new "Christian cultures" after the models with which Christians worked for a millennium and a half. This means that Christianity will be working in secular or mixed cultures.

5. Apparently for some time secularization will take two forms. One is the attempt to live life apart from the living God to whom Christian faith witnesses. The other is a radical transformation of beliefs while there is a continuity of symbolism to disguise the change. Whether the latter trend is good or bad depends upon how Christians define their faith. There are few signs that those who promote Christian institutionalism or religion on an integral basis are aware of, or are ministering to, these critical changes. Those who are concerned are those who are heavily oriented toward biblical interpretation, historical thought, and contemporary analysis.

Étienne Borne's advice to Christians who refuse to escape from anxiety into bewilderment or paganism or to accept anxiety in a world of chance was that they "out-modern" the moderns. They may well participate in helping to kill the gods of nature and the ideologies of history. If they are motivated by faith they have the confidence that above the no-gods-land there will be the Living God, who in the cross of Jesus Christ experiences death—and resurrection.

"One could put it most sharply thus," writes Gerhard Ebeling: "Faith does not 'have' a future, it *is* the future. . . . It praises God as *the* future, and so transforms the face of this human future. . . . The meaning of the future has been revealed and expressed once for all by the Crucified One." [9]

[9] *The Nature of Faith*, trans. Ronald Gregor Smith (Philadelphia: Muhlenberg, 1961), pp. 175, 181.

Index

About
the Author

Martin E. Marty is associate professor of church history at the Divinity School of the University of Chicago and associate editor of *The Christian Century*. An ordained Lutheran pastor, he served twelve years in the parish ministry. Educated at Concordia Seminary, St. Louis (B.D.), Lutheran School of Theology, Chicago (S.T.M.) and the University of Chicago (Ph.D.), Dr. Marty has lectured widely and is well known for his radio and television appearances. He is also co-editor of *Church History* and a member of the editorial staff of *The Pulpit* and other journals.

Born in 1928 in West Point, Nebraska, Dr. Marty's published work from 1959 to 1964 is an extraordinary achievement. He has written eleven books, including *A Short History of Christianity*, *The New Shape of American Religion*, *The Infidel*, and *Second Chance for American Protestants*, and is co-author of four others, including *The Religious Press in America* and *Pen-ultimates*, both published by Holt, Rinehart and Winston. He has contributed chapters or articles to a dozen books as well as to the *Encyclopaedia Britannica* and other standard reference works, and has edited or co-edited seven books, including *The Place of Bonhoeffer* and *Religion and Social Conflict*.

As readers of this book may well appreciate, Dr. Marty enjoys a wide reputation not only for his prolific output but for sound scholarship and a strongly focused concern with relevant contemporary issues. Not surprisingly, he is represented in the select 1,780-volume White House Library. Other areas of his interest and competence are suggested by the fact that he was awarded honorary membership in both the American Society for Church Architecture and the Church Architectural Guild, and was active for several years as a liturgical artist and designer.